Stylistic Manipulation of the Reader in Contemporary Fiction

Advances in Stylistics

Series Editors:

Dan McIntyre, University of Huddersfield, UK and Louise Nuttall, University of Huddersfield, UK

Editorial Board:

Jean Boase-Beier, University of East Anglia, UK
Beatrix Busse, University of Heidelberg, Germany
Szilvia Csábi, Independent Scholar
Yaxiao Cui, University of Nottingham, UK
Manuel Jobert, Jean Moulin University, Lyon 3, France
Lorenzo Mastopierro, University of Nottingham, UK
Eric Rundquist, Pontifica Universidad Católica de Chile, Chile
Larry Stewart, College of Wooster, USA
Odette Vassallo, University of Malta, Malta
Peter Verdonk, University of Amsterdam (Emeritus), The Netherlands
Chantelle Warner, University of Arizona, USA

Titles in the series:

Chick Lit: The Stylistics of Cappuccino Fiction, Rocío Montoro
Corpus Stylistics in Principles and Practice, Yufang Ho
Crime Fiction Migration, Christiana Gregoriou
D. H. Lawrence and Narrative Viewpoint, Violeta Sotirova
The Discourse of Italian Cinema and Beyond, Roberta Piazza
I. A. Richards and the Rise of Cognitive Stylistics, David West
Mind Style and Cognitive Grammar, Louise Nuttall
Opposition in Discourse, Lesley Jeffries
Oppositions and Ideology in News Discourse, Matt Davies
Pedagogical Stylistics, Michael Burke, Szilvia Csábi, Lara Week and Judit Zerkowitz
Style in the Renaissance, Patricia Canning
Stylistics and Shakespeare's Language, Mireille Ravassat
Sylvia Plath and the Language of Affective States, Zsofia Demjen
Text World Theory and Keats' Poetry, Marcello Giovanelli
The Stylistics of Poetry, Peter Verdonk
World Building, Joanna Gavins and Ernestine Lahey
World Building in Spanish and English Spoken Narratives, Jane Lugea

Stylistic Manipulation of the Reader in Contemporary Fiction

Edited by Sandrine Sorlin

BLOOMSBURY ACADEMIC
LONDON • NEW YORK • OXFORD • NEW DELHI • SYDNEY

BLOOMSBURY ACADEMIC
Bloomsbury Publishing Plc
50 Bedford Square, London, WC1B 3DP, UK
1385 Broadway, New York, NY 10018, USA
29 Earlsfort Terrace, Dublin 2, Ireland

BLOOMSBURY, BLOOMSBURY ACADEMIC and the Diana logo are trademarks of Bloomsbury Publishing Plc

First published in Great Britain 2020
Paperback edition published 2021

Copyright © Sandrine Sorlin and Contributors, 2020

Sandrine Sorlin has asserted her right under the Copyright, Designs and Patents Act, 1988, to be identified as Editor of this work.

For legal purposes the Acknowledgements on p. ix constitute an extension of this copyright page.

All rights reserved. No part of this publication may be reproduced or transmitted in any form or by any means, electronic or mechanical, including photocopying, recording, or any information storage or retrieval system, without prior permission in writing from the publishers.

Bloomsbury Publishing Plc does not have any control over, or responsibility for, any third-party websites referred to or in this book. All internet addresses given in this book were correct at the time of going to press. The author and publisher regret any inconvenience caused if addresses have changed or sites have ceased to exist, but can accept no responsibility for any such changes.

A catalogue record for this book is available from the British Library.

A catalog record for this book is available from the Library of Congress.

ISBN: HB: 978-1-3500-6296-2
PB: 978-1-3502-6742-8
ePDF: 978-1-3500-6297-9
eBook: 978-1-3500-6298-6

Series: Advances in Stylistics

Typeset by Deanta Global Publishing Services, Chennai, India

To find out more about our authors and books visit www.bloomsbury.com and sign up for our newsletters.

Contents

List of Contributors	vi
Acknowledgements	ix
1 Introduction: Manipulation in fiction *Sandrine Sorlin*	1

Part I Manipulating positions, representations and viewpoints

2 Metalepsis, counterfactuality and the forked path in *The French Lieutenant's Woman* *Marina Lambrou*	31
3 Social deixis in literature *Andrea Macrae*	50
4 'The novel of the future': Author's manipulation in Henry Green's *Nothing* (1950) and *Doting* (1952) *Rocío Montoro*	70
5 Building a world from the day's remains: Showing, telling, re-presenting *Jeremy Scott*	92

Part II Readers' responses to stylistic manipulation

6 Manipulating inferences: Interpretative problems and their effects on readers *Billy Clark*	117
7 Surprise and story ending: Readers' responses to textual manipulation in a short story by J. D. Salinger *Laura Hidalgo-Downing*	146
8 Manipulating metaphors: Interactions between readers and 'Upon Opening the Chest Freezer' *Sara Whiteley*	172

Part III Genre-specific and multimodal manipulation

9 Manipulation in Agatha Christie's detective stories: Rhetorical control and cognitive misdirection in creating and solving crime puzzles *Catherine Emmott and Marc Alexander*	195
10 Untranslatable clues: Reader manipulation and the challenge of crime fiction translation *Christiana Gregoriou*	215
11 Multimodal manipulation of the reader in Abrams and Dorst's *S.* *Nina Nørgaard*	234
Index	251

Contributors

Marc Alexander is Professor of English Linguistics at the University of Glasgow and is Director of the Historical Thesaurus of English. His research primarily focuses on the study of words, meaning, and effect in English, including historical lexicology, Parliamentary discourse from 1803 to the present, and the stylistics of detective fiction.

Billy Clark is Professor of English Language and Linguistics at Northumbria University. His research and teaching interests cover a wide range of topics in linguistics and stylistics, including lexical and syntactic meaning, semantic change, phatic communication, prosodic meaning, multimodality, and pragmatic processes involved in reading, writing and evaluating texts. His publications include *Relevance Theory* (Cambridge University Press, 2013), *Relevance, Pragmatics and Interpretation*, co-edited with Kate Scott and Robyn Carston (Cambridge University Press, 2019) and *Pragmatics and Literature*, co-edited with Siobhan Chapman (John Benjamins, in press).

Catherine Emmott is Reader in English Language and Linguistics at the University of Glasgow. Her publications include *Narrative Comprehension: A Discourse Perspective* (Oxford University Press, 1997), *Mind, Brain and Narrative* (with Anthony J. Sanford, Cambridge University Press, 2012) and articles on cognitive stylistics, anaphora and rhetorical manipulation in detective fiction.

Christiana Gregoriou is Associate Professor in English language at the University of Leeds. She researches in (critical) stylistics and crime writing. Most notable are her three monographs: *Crime Fiction Migration: Crossing Languages, Cultures, Media* (Bloomsbury, 2017); *Language, Ideology and Identity in Serial Killer Narratives* (Routledge, 2011); and *Deviance in Contemporary Crime Fiction* (Palgrave, 2007).

Laura Hidalgo-Downing is Associate Professor at the Universidad Autónoma of Madrid. Her research interests include discourse analysis, metaphor and stylistics. She has co-edited the 'Special Issue on Metaphorical Creativity Across

Modes' (*Metaphor in the Social World*, 2013) and is co-author of *Persuading People: An Introduction to Rhetoric* (third edition, 2014).

Marina Lambrou is Associate Professor of English Language and Linguistics at Kingston University. Her research and publications are mainly on personal narratives including trauma narratives; narratology and disnarration; and literary, non-literary and media stylistics. Marina's publications include *Disnarration and the Unmentioned in Fact and Fiction* (Palgrave, 2019) and *Contemporary Stylistics* (co-edited with Peter Stockwell, Continuum, 2010). She is the current chair of the Poetics and Linguistics Association (PALA).

Andrea Macrae is Principal Lecturer at Oxford Brookes University. She is a stylistician, specializing in deixis and the language of charity fundraising communications. She has recently published *Discourse Deixis in Metafiction* (Routledge, 2019) and the co-edited collection *Pronouns in Literature: Positions and Perspectives in Language* (Palgrave, 2018).

Rocío Montoro is Senior Lecturer at the University of Granada. She co-authored *Key Terms in Stylistics* (with Nina Nørgaard and Beatrix Busse) and authored *Chick Lit: The Stylistics of Cappuccino Fiction*. She is Assistant Editor of *Language and Literature* and co-editor (with Paul Simpson) of the book series *Language, Style and Literature*.

Nina Nørgaard is Associate Professor of Applied Linguistics and Director of the Centre for Multimodal Communication at the University of Southern Denmark. Her research interests lie within the fields of stylistics, multimodality, multimodal stylistics, critical discourse analysis and the semiotics of typography. Her publications include *Key Terms in Stylistics* (2010; with B. Busse and R. Montoro) and *Multimodal Stylistics of the Novel: More than Words* (Routledge, 2019).

Jeremy Scott writes and researches at the border between language and literary studies. His current interests are in fictional technique, the relationship between narratives and identity, the language of improvised theatre, and stylistics-based approaches to creative writing and creativity in general. As well as his own fiction, he has published on narrative technique in contemporary British and Irish writing, representations of dialect in fiction, travel literature, creative writing and the stylistics of drama. He is the author of *Creative Writing and*

Stylistics (Macmillan, 2014) and *The Demotic Voice in Contemporary British Fiction* (Palgrave Macmillan, 2009).

Sandrine Sorlin is Professor of English Language and Linguistics specialized in stylistics and pragmatics at Paul Valery University in Montpellier, France. She is the author of a handbook of stylistics in French (2014), the co-editor of *The Pragmatics of Personal Pronouns* (John Benjamins, 2015) and *The Pragmatics of Irony and Banter* (John Benjamins, 2018). She authored *Language and Manipulation in* House of Cards (Palgrave, 2016). She is the current chair of the French association for the study of English stylistics, Editor of *Etudes de Stylistique Anglaise* and Assistant Editor of *Language and Literature*.

Sara Whiteley is Senior Lecturer in Language and Literature at the University of Sheffield. She specializes in cognitive discourse analysis and the cognitive stylistics of contemporary literary texts. She has co-authored *The Discourse of Reading Groups: Integrating Cognitive and Sociocultural Perspectives* (with David Peplow, Joan Swann and Paola Trimarco, Routledge, 2016) and co-edited *The Cambridge Handbook of Stylistics* (with Peter Stockwell, Cambridge University Press, 2014).

Acknowledgements

I would like to thank here all the contributors to this volume who accepted right away my invitation to bring their respective expertise to the notion of 'manipulation in fiction' during a workshop I organized in Aix-en-Provence in April 2017. It was a most pleasant and fruitful day of work among merry and experienced stylisticians. This study day was funded by the *Institut Universitaire de France*, which I wish to thank for making it financially possible to gather recognized experts around a common topic for, I hope, productive results. I extend my thanks to the editors of the series *Advances in Stylistics*, Dan McIntyre and Louise Nuttall, who accepted the project with interest and enthusiasm, and also to the reviewers of the book chapters for their time and precious insights, and more globally, to the Bloomsbury team which was so helpful during the whole publishing process (Becky Holland and Andrew Wardell especially).

The poem 'Do Not Go Gentle Into That Good Night' by Dylan Thomas (from *The Poems of Dylan Thomas*, copyright ©1952 by Dylan Thomas) is here reprinted by permission of New Directions Publishing Corp as well as by permission of The Trustees for the Copyrights of Dylan Thomas and the poem 'Upon Opening the Chest Freezer' (2010) by Simon Armitage is reproduced by permission of the author.

Introduction: Manipulation in fiction

Sandrine Sorlin

1. The two poles of manipulation

To speak of manipulation in fiction may seem counter intuitive for not only do we as readers consent to the lie fiction embodies (i.e. this is not reality) but we also take as a given the fact that fiction is not (normally) 'action-based'. Accordingly, it is not the intention in fiction to be the instigator of action in the reader, unless we are dealing with propagandist art. As Mills (2014: 137) underlines, 'One key difference between art and propaganda seems to be the degree to which the latter is focussed on getting someone else to act, to the exclusion of any other objective.' If fiction and art are powerful enough to sometimes trigger some action taken as a result of reading a book or watching a film (the crimes in the UK subsequent to the release of Stanley Kubrick's *A Clockwork Orange* (1971) come to mind, the link between the assaults and the fictional piece having been highlighted by the defence in court[1]), this is not the primary objective of authors or within the artists' hands to anticipate the potential perlocutionary effects of their work.

However, in speaking of manipulation of discourse in literature, I mean to show that although the aims are different, fiction can resort to strategies of manipulation through language that are comparable to discursive manipulation in other genres or even in 'real-life' interactions. I do not perceive fictional language as a specific discursive species that would embody some deviation from real, 'normal' language but rather as just one 'type of discourse' which is, like any other discourse, 'socially, culturally and historically situated and defined' (Semino and Culpeper 2011; Busse 2017: 199). Fiction construes reality relying on strategies of representation through linguistic means that are the same as in non-fictional genres. Pratt (1988: 22) advocated transcending useless dichotomies a long time ago by focusing instead on linguistic strategies of representation: 'There is much to be gained … from an analysis of linguistic representation which de-centers the question of truth versus falsehood, fiction versus nonfiction, literary genre versus non-literary genre, and focuses instead on generalised strategies of representation.' As Rancière (2017) more recently claims, what is at stake both in the avowed fictional nature of literature and 'unavowed fictions' of politics, social sciences or journalism, is a common attempt at constructing the perceptible and thinkable forms of a shared world.

'Strategy' as used by Pratt is indeed the term that could apply to all types of discourse and be particularly useful in my definition of manipulation as the *strategic* use of linguistic and pragmatic tools used by an author to intentionally produce certain effects on the reader and affect her in a certain way. In the wake of New Criticism and Barthes's 'Death of the Author' (1967/1984), this claim could be perceived as dangerously bordering on W. K. Wimsatt and Monroe Beardsley's 'intentional fallacy' (1954). But as will be shown below, making strategic choices to position the reader and affect her reactions to the text does not mean that the flesh-and-blood reader will respond to the effect as intended by the author. It seems better to think of the complex act of meaning-making as a combination between textual imposition (textual patterns do impose preferred and dispreferred interpretation) and readerly disposition (Stockwell 2013). Of course, there are bound to be 'many gaps between author's intentions and readers' conclusions about these intentions' (Phelan 2005: 48). Besides the author's intentions may be realized in a text in a way that s/he does not fully control. But all this does not mean that there is not some kind of authorial intention along with other factors that determine a text's meaning: James Phelan (2005: 47) shows that meaning arises from 'the feedback loop among authorial agency, textual phenomena, and reader response'. That these intentions are realized in the text indirectly or covertly and work on the reader with the latter being preferably unaware of their workings and origins is what deserves the term 'manipulation' in fiction. Manipulation has indeed close associations with covertness as Hart makes clear:

> Whilst many aspects of communication are covert without being manipulative, and whilst manipulation can still take place even when the audience is alerted to the manipulative nature of the utterance, without making explicit the precise nature of the manipulation, manipulation does intuitively at least seem to be dependent on covertness. (Hart 2013: 202)

This working 'underhandedly' is what has granted the term its negative connotation, which is due to its exclusive treatment in argumentative theories and philosophy of language as some form of *derailed* persuasion or *failed* communication. In ethical philosophical terms, it corresponds to a perversion of communication and cooperation between human beings perceived as entirely rational and reasonable. This distrust of language seen as capable of misleading rational thinking (*logos*) and abusing people's emotions (*pathos*) is of course as old as Plato himself holding in contempt the sophistic practices (see Guérin, Siouffi and Sorlin 2013). Transparent communication and irenic persuasion are based on a truth and morality bias that has also inspired more recent philosophies (Scanlon 1998; Gorin 2014; Habermas 1987; 2006). Likewise, pragma-dialecticians perceive manipulation as failing to abide by the right 'code of conduct' composed of ten rules for an efficient and reasonable cooperation (see van Eemeren and Grootendorst 2004: 190–6; van Eemeren 2010: 7–8) while discourse analysts construe manipulative discourse as the prerogative of dominant groups trying to control the others (Fairclough 1989; van Dijk 2006).

Counterbalancing this claim to truth that is also a claim to morality, Galasiński demonstrates the ubiquity of deception in our lives, contesting the Gricean maxim underlying his Cooperative Principle according to which to be cooperative one must be truthful (see Sorlin 2017a for a neo-Gricean pragmatic theory of manipulation):

> It seems, however, that everyday experience tells us that we are far from being universally and constantly truthful. We lie not to offend others; we lie to get away with being late for work or not meeting a deadline. The intuition that deception is something normal rather than abnormal in our lives and communicative practices is confirmed by numerous studies. (e.g., Barnes 1994; Nyberg 1993; Zagorin 1990; Galasiński 2000: 2–3)

In his book entitled *Hypocrisy: Don't Leave Home Without It*, Feinberg (2002) goes as far as saying that hypocrisy is inevitable in 'developed' societies, recalling an experiment proving his case that there is a hypocrite in all of us, only with different degrees of practice:

> Several years ago a sociologist at an American university proposed an experiment when the class was studying 'honesty'. He suggested that for one entire day the students be totally honest in all their relationships. After a half day of speaking nothing but the truth, a female student was reported by her roommate to the psychiatrist at the University Health Center. The roommate thought that the sociology student was having a nervous breakdown. Life without dissimulation is impossible in what we call civilized society. The question is not whether everyone is a hypocrite. Everyone is. The only variant is the degree of hypocrisy practiced by every person. (Feinberg 2002: 59)

Thus, truth/falsehood needs to be transcended – especially today in our post-truth times – and manipulative strategies need to be perceived in terms of degrees on a continuum formed by two poles, one that is 'benign' (what I would call entertaining deception) and another that is illegitimately used for 'exploitative deception' (Galasiński 7). What this book is interested in is the more joyous pole of (sought-for) fictional manipulation (that will be shown to be broader than the notion of deception that is very much restricted to truthfulness) whose perlocutionary function is *not* to have the addressee buy a product (as in advertising), vote for someone (in politics) or adopt certain beliefs, or worse, take up arms to defend themselves (propaganda), but rather to seduce, surprise, please or move the reader. Deceptive seductive manipulation would aim at dispossessing the victim of her own identity, thoughts and social ties to make her adhere to an ideological vision of an idealized world elsewhere that would make her take up arms to apply it (see Sorlin 2017b). As seen above, an in-between case of deceptive fictional manipulation would be instrumentalized fiction directing the addressee's emotions to the point of coercing her reactions. In (joyous) manipulation in fiction, the audiences are invited and sometimes required to engage in a particular way with fiction (emotionally and cognitively) as will be evinced in Section 3.

2. Literary communication: Different channels

Following Phelan, I regard a fictional work as a human communicative event: writing a fictional piece constitutes 'a rhetorical action in which an author addresses an audience for some purpose(s)' (Phelan 2011: 56) (see also Billy Clark this volume for a relevance-theoretic account of literature as an act of communication). There is thus a pragmatic dimension to this type of communication between an (actual/implied) *Author* (outside the text, situated in the historical moment of writing) and an actual reader (at the moment of reading), the first one being the general orchestrator relying on a series of variable *Resources* to influence the reading of and affect an (authorial and actual) *Audience* (such as occasion, paratexts, dialogue, style, voice, space, temporality, Free Indirect Speech, and narratee/narrative audience) – see Phelan's 2017 ARA three-column communicative model. For Phelan though, the actual/implied author does not entertain the same relationship as the authorial and actual audience:

> The implied author, in my view, is a streamlined version of the actual author, so there is always already continuity between the two agents. The actual audience, on the other hand, may be radically different from the authorial audience — as becomes obvious anytime we read a text from a different culture. (2011: 69)

Though the speech/thought presentation scale is part of the constructing agent's *Resource* in this communicative act, these valuable insights seem to be more narratologically rather than linguistically oriented. Who then, is better suited to the task of linking narratological considerations with a specific toolbox drawn from linguistics, cognitive poetics and pragmatic theories than the stylistician? The stylistician interested in the response of reading groups to texts especially can highlight the actual audience's reply to attempts at controlling the manipulation of their affects. In this volume for instance, Sara Whiteley focuses on the way the readers themselves manipulate the metaphors of a piece of poetry in reading groups' discussions, counter-manipulating so to speak the poet's intention. The contributors in this book all demonstrate how writers skilfully 'manipulate' – in the literal sense of 'handling' and 'modelling' – the linguistic material to steer interpretation and elicit specific emotions. The stylistician's role is precisely to give a rigorous, retrievable and replicable[2] analysis of the workings of the ways readings are invisibly influenced and emotions affected by literary communicative acts. Manipulation defined as the skilful use of linguistic and pragmatic techniques to achieve very specific effects usually works best when the strategies based on particular linguistic choices remain subtle and invisible. It is the stylistician's job to uncover how this subtle positioning of the reader works.

There is, in fact, as Phelan (2018: 113) highlights, a double consciousness that is activated when reading a piece of fiction, one that implies the reader 'projecting herself' into the position of an invisible observer within the storyworld, 'thus taking the character and events as real', and a second consciousness involving the authorial audience that brings about 'the awareness not only that the characters and events are invented but also that they have been invented for some reason'. The actual audience may be brought either to willingly suspend disbelief, on the one hand, as they are transported into the realm of fiction or, on the other hand, to perceive the layered constructedness of fiction (in telecinematic discourse, this would correspond to the difference Bubel (2008), after Clark (1996), makes between 'imagination' and 'evaluation'). But textual strategies can trigger mixed effects as well, appealing to both imagination and evaluation, like the typographical features in Abrams and Dorst's *S.* novel (2013) featuring some old-looking typefaces that Nina Nørgaard (this volume) shows work iconically to create verisimilitude but run the risk at the same time of drawing attention to the constructedness of the contemporary novel made to appear as an old book.

At the level of 'second consciousness' or appreciation, what is also at stake is the presentation of the (author's and) narrator's self: the author can choose between an overt or covert narrator that is either explicitly present or conspicuously absent (Rimmon-Kenan 2007: 97–100) in the 'author-narrator-audience channel' (Phelan 2011: 73) – this is the case in John Fowles's postmodern, multiple endings novel *The French Lieutenant's Woman* (2004 [1969]) in which the authorial and narratorial metalepses – examined here by Marina Lambrou – draw attention to the constructedness of the novel and its characters as invented creatures under the masterful control of the (implied) author. But the latter can choose another channel of transmission, bypassing so to speak the narrator, by adopting the 'author-character-audience channel' (Phelan 2011: 66). This is the choice made by Henry Green in his late writing for instance – as honoured here by Rocío Montoro – which is mainly made up of dialogue reflecting the author's claim that here lies the 'future of the novel'. Communication is indeed massively taken up by the characters, leaving it to the reader to grasp the characters' social relationships through a close attention to the linguistic and pragma-stylistic characteristics of their exchanges.

In this edited book, both the production and reception ends are taken into account in that it attends to the (actual) reader's point of view in reading groups (Whiteley), online comments (Clark) or through questionnaires to real readers (Hidalgo-Downing) but also to the author's point of view (Green's open verbalization about his literary practice; for instance, see Montoro, this volume). Production and reception are combined from a 'creative writing' perspective that focuses on the way to help would-be writers shape the linguistic material to create the most efficient effects and keep the reader on board. This implies some good negotiation and policing of what Jeremy Scott (this volume) calls a 'stylistic balance' especially in the 'problematic' homodiegetic narratives where the protagonist is part of the two channels mentioned above as both character and narrator at the same time and where the act of narration takes place simultaneously with the events being mediated. This subtle manipulation of stylistic balance would perhaps best be achieved when it reaches what Phelan (2011: 73) calls a 'synergy between the author-character-audience channel and the author-narrator-audience channel to communicate something greater than the sum of what's communicated in each channel'.

3. Guiding attention, influencing judgement

3.1. Constructing perspectives

How is the reader made to engage emotionally and cognitively with the narrative? Any psycho-sociological book dealing with the psychology of influence regards the necessity to attract 'attention' as the primary force in influence:

> For information to be persuasive, it is essential that it attract our attention. There are many ways of making it do this. Extreme images, unexpected twists, posing questions and humour are all common techniques, each applied in its own way and each triggering a different form of information processing. More than anything else, it is the way we process information that determines the success of any attempt at influence. (Van der Pligt and Vliek 2017: 13)

Attracting readers' attention has thus a linguistic and cognitive component. In fiction, attention is sustained, according to Sternberg (1978), by developing three key emotions: suspense, surprise and curiosity. These are generated on two axes: the axis of knowledge (incomplete knowledge as to the story development and outcome is likely to generate suspense by creating fear and hope) and the axis of predictability (that is concerned with the capacity to surprise the reader) (see Hogan 2014: 523). The crafty writer can thus play with these two axes to manipulate the reader's sense of progression and trigger a certain form of involvement in the plot. As Hidalgo-Downing shows in this volume, the surprising ending of Salinger's short story 'A Perfect Day for Bananafish' can retrospectively be made comprehensible by a close stylistic study of 'textual determinants' to use Toolan's phrase. Toolan (2009, 2016) indeed proposes eight 'verbal attractors'[3] that are likely to shape the reader's expectations while reading, thus creating specific reactions and projections. He gives the example of 'negation' as such an attracting device guiding reader's progression:

> Negated narrative sentences (*he could not find a real princess*; *she did not sleep a wink*) have long been acknowledged to be marked and attention-attracting. *Prima facie*, they are narratorially uncooperative, in telling what did not happen rather than what did happen. And we have all grown impatient, during ordinary talk, with the inept or unfocussed storyteller whose narrative is rendered shapeless and disjointed by irrelevant mentions of things that were not the case or did not happen. But – perhaps paradoxically – in the crafted telling of a skilled narrator or narrative these tellings of what did not happen are always found to be all the more important to plot progression. (Toolan 2016: 36)

This linguistic resource echoes narratological concepts of the disnarrated (Prince 1988) and the paranarratable (Warhol 2005) (see Lambrou this volume), but have also been analysed in other stylistic works that have highlighted the power of the device to steer the reader's curiosity and attract attention onto itself – see for instance, Simpson and Canning's analysis of Hemingway's paragraph-final negation such as 'In the dark it was like summer lightning, but the nights were cool and *there was not the feeling of a storm coming*' (2014: 294, my emphasis), as if responding to a positive counterpart version, shaping readers' sense of progression in a most peculiar way.

The way expectations of plot progression are shaped by specific linguistic resources (in harness, of course, with contextual factors) also relates to how the reader's presence within the text is shaped. Our emotional involvement depends on the textual capacity to immerse the reader within the storyworld. Using deictic shift theory (Duchan, Bruder, and Hewitt 1995), cognitive poetics (e.g. Stockwell 2002, 2009) and Text World Theory (Gavins 2007; Gavins and Lahey 2016) have shown how readers are drawn into the text-world through a subtle use of deixis, making them feel as if they were part of the world, adopting the cognitive perspective of some characters, processing the text from the perspective chosen. Shifts in deixis, triggering shifts in participation status for the reader, tend to alter the communication fictional channel and are bound to affect readers' response to it. This is what Andrea Macrae shows in this volume, highlighting the centrality of deixis in the construction of perspectives and the positioning of the readers.

The choice of perspective by the author from which the reader is to apprehend plot and characters also guides the reader's potential empathy[4] and sympathy[5]. Drawing from Sternberg (1978: 96–7), who speaks of the 'sequential manipulation of the reader's attitude and sympathies', Sklar (2013) for instance highlights how textual elements can control readers' reaction to texts and especially the amount of sympathy[6] constructed in favour of one character rather than another. He shows how the 'manipulation of distance' (49) through various narratological and stylistic means[7] can steer the reader's (dis)alignment with characters. Readers are thus 'manipulated' (Sklar speaks of 'persuasion') into observing, feeling and evaluating in a certain way.

What conditions readers' reactions, emotions and ethical judgements towards characters has much to do with stance and narratorial voice, on the one hand, and characterization on the other, as further explored in the next section.

3.2. Characterization and stance as resources

Let us begin with the influence of characterization following Jonathan Culpeper and Caroline Fernandez-Quintanilla's three dimensions that are essential in characterization: (1) The degree of 'narratorial control' (Are characters in the orbit of the narrator? Are they free to speak? Do we perceive the plot through their point of view or mindstyle? How are their thoughts and speeches reported? (these narratorial filters are essential in establishing closeness or distance between narrator and character)); (2) The presentation of self and other (how reliable are the characters in the way they present themselves and others, what image/ethos do they linguistically convey of themselves and how does this affect the reader?); (3) Explicitness or implicitness of the textual clues (the characters' traits can be explicitly provided or must be inferred from what they say, think or how they behave) (Culpeper and Fernandez-Quintanilla 2017: 93). These diverse strategies of characterization have an impact on how the reader is made to feel towards characters and/or give an ethical judgement of their behaviour/thoughts.

The second influential aspect is the stance taken by the narrator that can be more or less perceptible depending on whether the narrator is covert or overt (see above). Stance is indeed to be placed on Phelan's author-narrator-audience channel mentioned above. Here is how Daniela Landert (2017: 496) defines a stance in pragmatic terms: 'A stance expressed by the narrator is part of the communication between the fictional text and the reader' and 'evaluations and assessments of characters and events influence the reader's perception of the story'. Strategies of influence are at stake at the level of stance as well, especially when an overt narrator gives his/her opinion about how an event should be apprehended. Landert quotes one of Eliot's narrator's such intrusion marked by explicit stance markers in her direct address and rhetorical question to the reader:

> Instead of wondering at this result of misery in Mr Casaubon, I think it quite ordinary. Will not a tiny speck very close to our vision blot out the glory of the world, and leave only a margin by which we see the blot? (Eliot 1965 [1871–1872]: 456, *Middlemarch*, also quoted in Leech and Short 2007: 214)

Rhetorical questions have a specific influential nature that is often capitalized on in marketing. In *The Psychology of Influence* referred to in the previous section, the authors, Van der Pligt and Vliek, explain why. First, they put author and reader in an engaging communicative situation that is difficult to disregard, bringing readers to reflect on the question, creating a bond with the writer as the reader is brought to share his/her opinion:

> Several aspects of a *rhetorical question* make them useful in a persuasive context. First of all, rhetorical questions make us think because we have a strong innate tendency to answer the questions put to us. When we hear one, we instinctively start trying to formulate a response and so are forced to consider the topic it concerns (e.g., Swasy and Munch 1985). This in turn might make the receiver more receptive to other information about the subject.

In addition to the manipulation of the reader's innate tendency to engage (in a response), a rhetorical question also has another powerful effect:

> Second, according to Keiko Tanaka (1992, 1994) the power of rhetorical questions lies in the pleasure they deliver. Similarly, Hoeken (2005) compares rhetorical questions to cryptograms: solving one leads to a positive feeling. (van der Pligt and Vliek 2017: 47)

This pleasure of being part of the 'in-group' is similar in effect to the strategic use of irony where the narrator takes a stance in opposition to a character or a situation, positioning herself at a distance from her target, simultaneously generating a rapprochement with the reader (see Booth 1974; Stockwell 2002; Simpson 2003 for a study of triangular placement, Black 2006; Sorlin 2018a; Jobert and Sorlin 2018).

3.3. Cognitive control of the reading process

But the reader's mind can also be cognitively manipulated to a different extent. Toolan (2016) indicates that his textual determinants are easy to notice (they are salient) and to process (he speaks of 'low-cognitive effort process of recognition'). But sometimes, writers can try to impede the readers' cognitive efforts unawares. Pragma-cognitivists interested in manipulative strategies have shown how the receiver's interpretative faculties can be tampered with by the manipulator's restrictions of cognitive access to certain contextual assumptions. The manipulator cognitively controls interpretative effects (Maillat 2014: 74): manipulation indeed consists in misleading the reader's cognitive system by playing on its selection mechanisms, and thus constraining interpretation (Maillat and Oswald 2009). This is done by rendering some contextual assumptions more (or less) salient than others and more (or less) easily accessible by recipients. In a relevance-theoretic perspective (Sperber and Wilson 1995), the point is to have the addressee reach 'optimal relevance' 'before an extended context is constructed' that would expose some aspects of the information the manipulator tries to limit access to (Maillat and Oswald 2009: 368). Cognitive manipulation of the reader in fiction would thus consist in either foregrounding some information to the detriment of others or blocking access to certain contextual assumptions. The classical example given is that of the 'Moses illusion' that can be tested when asking the question 'How many animals of each kind did Moses take on the Ark?' Studies (Allott and Rubio Fernández 2002; Erickson and Mattson 1981) show that most readers will answer the question overlooking the lexical dissonance (Noah is the one embarking on the journey in the Ark and not Moses). What is suggested is that the 'Moses' information is 'shallow processed' by the recipients' cognitive systems. Not enough cognitive resources are allotted to its treatment, the addressees being cognitively focused on the task of answering the question that is asked of them. In relevance-theoretic terms, an ad hoc concept is constructed for 'Moses' that involves a pragmatic lexical adjustment by extension of the proper noun to the level of 'biblical figure' (see Maillat 2017, for instance).

One fictional example of writers' attempt at misleading readers could be Iain Bank's *Complicity* (1994), in which the author adopts very distinct styles for his dual 'I' and 'you' characters-narrators, giving (socio)linguistic cues to the reader to recognize who is who. But when the 'I' narrator seems to adopt the style of the 'you' narrator who is guilty of physical assaults, the reader is misled into thinking she is seeing the world through the 'you' protagonist-narrator's eyes. The writer seems to want the reader to map the misleading passage (seemingly written in the aggressor's mindstyle) onto the familiar scenario of a (future) crime scene (while it is, in fact, as we learn later, a lover's game with the 'I' narrator pretending to break into her lover's house and to rape her). This cognitive intentional misleading on the part of the author corresponds, in Sanford and Emmott's (2012) psycholinguistic framework, to the Rhetorical Focussing Principle, that is to say 'the idea that writers aim to focus attention on selective aspects of a text, causing some parts of the text to be processed more thoroughly than others' (Sanford and Emmott 2012: 101). The reader is led to process some aspects of the text and overlook certain anomalies in this impersonated style (like the use of the first-person pronoun for a start and other clues, see Sorlin 2015).

It is true that the crime novel as genre fiction is especially partial to cognitive misdirection. In this volume Emmott and Alexander reveal the tricks of the Queen of Crime, Agatha Christie, who does not always play fair with her readers, misdirecting their cognitive attention through rhetorical control of the information/evidence provided or misleading them into thinking a character is the culprit where s/he is not. Chapter 9 in this volume develops their previous description of plot-handling devices and techniques in crime novels (Emmott and Alexander 2010, 2014) used for 'burying an item' or 'burying its significance' in plot construction sometimes by placing it next to an unduly foregrounded item so that the reader's attention is brought to focus on the more prominent one. Here are a few of them that Emmott and Alexander present that will find an echo with other aspects highlighted in this whole introductory chapter:

- Use linguistic structures which have been shown empirically to reduce prominence (e.g. embed a mention of the item within a subordinate clause).
- Underspecify the item, describing it in a way that is sufficiently imprecise that it draws little attention to it or detracts from features of the item that are relevant to the plot. …
- Place information in positions where a reader is distracted or not yet interested. …
- Get the narrator or characters in the story to say that the item is uninteresting.
- Discredit the characters reporting certain information, thereby making them appear unreliable and giving less salience to the information they report. (Emmott and Alexander 2014: 332)

The manipulation of attention is at the core of detective fiction. Christiana Gregoriou (this volume) gives us a close illustration of some of these manipulative techniques within English and Greek contemporary crime fiction novels and across their translation into Greek and English respectively.

Readers can also be manipulated into aligning with ethically questionable characters. Burgess's first-person novel *A Clockwork Orange* (1962) does not entail a total condemnation of guilty Alex, which means that the reader's sympathies are stylistically and pragmatically controlled. Gregoriou (2011) shows that depending on the transitivity and agency choices made in crime narratives, the victim can be made to appear as deserving her plot, downplaying the killer's agentive role and responsibility in the aggression. What is true of crime fiction is also true of TV series featuring bad characters (Sorlin 2016). In the American political TV series *House of Cards* for instance, Francis Underwood is an expert at sowing moral disengagement cues for the reader to pick up, keeping her aligned with his aim and goal (Sorlin 2018b). Even repeated exposures to 'bad guy' series can have a manipulative effect that could be compared to the 'mere exposure effect' analysed as one of our cognitive biases according to which familiarity comes with repetition, as Bornstein and

Craver-Lemley (2004: 216) confirm: 'Without question, repeated exposure to a stimulus biases our attitude regarding that stimulus.' One becomes familiar with character roles and plot expectation in these 'bad guy' series. This is what Shafer and Raney (2012: 1031) point to when they claim (2012: 1031): 'Through repeated viewing of antihero stories, viewers can learn that plot pattern and develop corresponding cognitive structures that are activated when such stories are later viewed.' To link this cognitive aspect to what I said earlier, the way progression and suspense are built in the tale can overrule any moral scruples, as Simpson (2014b) shows in the study of Alfred Hitchcock's *Psycho* (1960). Giving a stylistic explanation to psychological research that is not always anchored in linguistic evidence as regards the creation of narrative 'urgency', Simpson shows that urgency overrides any good/bad character schema we usually draw on, manipulating the reader into following the plot beyond any ethical judgement.

3.4. Summing up

In previous works (Sorlin 2016, 2017a), I have situated manipulation on a continuum between persuasion on the left hand side and coercion as the other pole. The more we move to the right, the less freedom the addressee has in not adopting the speaker/writer's point of view and not doing as she is told. As seen above, fictional manipulation can be situated in between these two poles. I speak here of (joyous) manipulation going beyond simple persuasion towards hidden guiding of emotions, sympathies and attention with the hope the reader will respond to these (more or less visible) cues somehow. It is the stylistician's role to make these techniques visible, and to highlight the diverse degrees of manipulation from inviting (persuasion) to constraining (coercion) on the whole manipulative spectrum. I also correlate the manipulation continuum to (im)politeness theories. In the case of persuasive author-reader relationship for instance, a writer can be (over)polite with her reader (think of Henry Fielding taking his reader by the hand on the path of fiction, politely bringing him on his side to share his ethical stance, see Sorlin forthcoming). But on the impolite side of the continuum, the (implied) author might wish not to pay the reader any tribute and construe her presence as an inevitable encumbrance, in the manner of John Barth's famous address to the reader in his postmodern, metafictional work:

> The reader! You, dogged, uninsultable, print-oriented bastard, it's you I'm addressing, who else, from inside this monstrous fiction. You've read me this

far, then? Even this far? For what discreditable motive? How is it you don't go to a movie, watch TV, stare at a wall, play tennis with a friend, make amorous advances to the person who comes to your mind when I speak of amorous advances? Can nothing surfeit, saturate you, turn you off? Where's your shame? (1968: 127)

In between these pragmatic acts from flattering to threatening are more concealed manipulative strategies positioning readers, steering their perception and fostering their (affective) engagement with and immersion in the text-world, as exposed in the different chapters that follow.

4. Book content

This book is the first book-length treatment of the subject of manipulation through language in fiction, employing a wide array of methods and theoretical perspectives applied to contemporary texts belonging to diverse fictional genres (crime fiction, short stories, novels and poems). The range of approaches adopted in this volume include analysis theory-wise (relevance theory, cognitive poetics, social semiotics, 'classical' narratology, deixis and foregrounding) and methods-wise (reading group data, experimental data, corpus data, multimodal analysis and close stylistic analysis). This volume is composed of three parts. The first part focuses on the techniques of manipulation of perspectives and representations, starting with Marina Lambrou, who studies the forms and functions of unconventional literary techniques used by John Fowles in *The French Lieutenant's Woman* (1969) that plays with expectations of plot structure in its most postmodern offering of three potential endings. Lambrou analyses these endings in light of the concept of metalepsis (Genette 1980), underpinning the purpose of these intrusions that allow character, narrator and author to step in and out of the story- and discourse-world. Disrupting narrative hierarchy and ontological space boundaries, they also serve to give a voice to a specific social and political narratorial-authorial stance, thereby offering the readers food for thought and interpretation. Using Warhol's (2005, 2010, 2013) notions of 'narrative refusal' – that is, narratorial comment on what might have been but yet is not – and that of the 'paranarratable' (concerning events that would not take place given the conventions of the genre), the author evinces that metalepsis highlights both the author's 'omnipotent agency' (determining when and how the story comes to an end) and the fact that the characters have no existence outside of the author/narrator's imagination. If the first ending embodies disnarrated events (Prince 1988) that were first narrated then dismissed as part of the character's daydream, endings 2 and 3 embody Dannenberg's (2008) 'what if' scenarios creating counterfactual storytellings 'forking' plot trajectories as they evince contradictory pathways (Borges 2000 [1944]) in the novel's refusal of a conventional Victorian ending. Emphasizing the precise 'sliding doors' moment, Lambrou shows how the triple endings bring to the fore the dynamic construction of the storyworld. The first (false) ending can be said to constitute a red herring for the readers, the two others exist simultaneously, claiming to enact the male (Charles) or female (Sarah) character's freedom while being at all times under the yoke of a most manipulating author.

Andrea Macrae focuses on manipulation of the readers through what she calls 'social deixis' that leads them to conceptually follow 'speakers' paths of projection' as they try to make sense of the perspectives chosen by the different speakers involved in literary communication. (Social) deixis is indeed shown to be an essential aspect in the establishment of perspectives and the positioning of the addressee(s). Macrae reviews the literature on social deixis and also 'empathetic', 'subjective', 'relational' and 'relational social' deixis, categories which tend to overlap from one theorist to the next and/or differ in what is included and excluded. On the basis of this survey, Macrae simplifies the picture by bringing the scale of social deixis back to two useful subtypes: (1.) Attitudinal-experiential deixis (that would include use of demonstratives and determiners) and (2.) Socio-relational deixis (comprising terms of address and their related terms of reference), but adding a caveat that takes into account a variety of (intersecting) pragmatic factors such as (im)politeness factors, performative affirmation/disruption of speaker-addressee relationships, setting, activity type, all of which make social deixis 'less simply or purely deictic' than other deictic forms. The author then goes on to apply her new theoretical distillation to the study of the last stanza of Dylan Thomas's 'Do not go gentle into that good night' (1952), showing to what extent social deixis can contribute to offering insights into the poem. The analysis highlights the shift in participation status and discourse architecture at the end of Thomas's poem, where the apparent address to the reader shifts into a more specific personal address to 'my father', which may also potentially be a prayer to God. Macrae brings to the fore how the attitudinal-experiential deixis and the socio-relational deixis foreground these different layers of communication, with multiple readings hovering simultaneously between them, thus positioning the reader 'as both in-group addressee and out-group bystander, sometimes simultaneously, sometimes ambiguously, sometimes ambivalently'.

Rocío Montoro focuses on the writer Henry Green's theoretical claims as regards what should be the perfect novel 'of the future', advocating a reduction of the descriptive parts to a minimum in favour of dialogue. Montoro offers a rigorous analysis of these claims, confirming the writer's conscious manipulation of the linguistic material, as the shift to dialogue reaches over 85 per cent in his last two novels *Nothing* (1950) and *Doting* (1952). The dialogue thus constructed is called 'oblique' by Green and relies on indirectness and implicatures. By writing dialogue in this way, Green purposefully steers the participation of the reader in making sense of how and why conversation fails to honour Paul Grice's maxims, which also results in readers becoming even more involved in the work of art. Analysing how often Grice's maxims are flouted and classifying them, Montoro is able to depict an accurate picture of the oblique nature of Greenian dialogue in its post-1950 stylistically and pragmatically manipulated version. Lastly, using a corpus pragmatics approach (Romero Trillo 2017), she pushes the analysis one step further by detailing the grammatical components of the shift, showing that in the dialogue sub-corpora, oblique dialogue proves to be more interactive in nature than it was in Green's previous novels, with a higher proportion of certain parts of speech (adverbs and interjections, mainly) that semantically lay stronger emphasis on the communicative and interpersonal aspects of the exchanges.

In a chapter entitled 'Building a world from the day's remains: Showing, telling, re-presenting', Jeremy Scott focuses on the necessary negotiation a writer must carry out in his/her handling of what is told (diegesis) and what is represented (mimesis). After acknowledging the difficulty of telling apart the two Greek terms in fiction, the author nevertheless offers a way to rigorously distinguish them by combining the discourse presentation scale that is studied in 'steam stylistics' (as well as elements of focalization, modality and syntactic choice, etc.) with the perspectives of cognitive poetics – and Text World Theory in particular – that helps understand 'how readers read'. He demonstrates how this mutual enrichment can in turn be fruitful to creative writing practice in its capacity to highlight the most successful 'narrative techniques' the writer can use as strategies to produce specific effects. In the problematic case of homodiegetic narratives where the character is also the narrator and narrating simultaneously with the unfolding of the action, Scott argues that the storyworld can become inauthentic to the point of alienating the reader. He gives several instances of what he calls the 'moment of arrest' where the conflicting demands of mimesis (mediating one's own voice) and diegesis (mediating the storyworld) tend to compete to get the reader's attention. One way out of the 'paradox' of homodiegetic narration is to establish what Scott calls, using the metaphor of the seesaw, 'stylistic balance' between the two functions. Empathic engagement and experiential immersion depend on the writer's ability to 'police' this balance. Lastly, the author shows why Kazuo Ishiguro's novel *The Remains of the Day* (1989) successfully achieves this balance through a subtle interweaving of past and present storyworlds.

Part II focuses more specifically on readers' responses to stylistic manipulation. It opens with Chapter 6 by Billy Clark exploring how readers' responses to texts are affected by the way writers manipulate inferences by making explicatures and implicatures more or less accessible to them. Comparing three different twenty-first-century novels, he considers to what extent the nature of the inferential processes that the novels encourage readers to carry out contributes to their reading experience. He compares Elif Batuman's *The Idiot* (2017) which is fairly easy to understand in its specific parts as well as to represent as a whole (while making 'worthwhile conclusions' that would justify the effort of reading the novel difficult to derive for some readers) with Rachel Cusk's *Outline* (2014) which is comparatively more difficult for the reader to represent as a whole as the text consists in unorganized narratives that recount what the different people the narrator happens to meet tell her, leading readers to draw possible implicatures that are weakened by the fact that they cannot relate them to a more cohesive narrative. The third novel under investigation in this chapter (Eimear McBride's *A Girl is a Half-formed Thing*) manipulates the inferring process to a higher degree as the novel makes 'local' representations difficult (it is very hard for the reader to determine who speaks/thinks and what is going on), thus also making it difficult to see utterances as parts of 'a whole packaged narrative form' from which conclusions can be drawn. Clark points out how effective this challenging novel is in its immersive attempt at bringing the reader to more 'realistically' share the narrator's 'stream of pre-conscious' that is hers at that stage (the narrator is not born yet when the novel opens). Drawing illustrations from readers' comments on goodreads.com, he exemplifies (1.) how reading experience can be explained by (relevance-theoretic) pragmatics through a focus on the inferential process (thus fruitfully complementing accounts of immersion in psychological-empirical work on narratives as well as work using Text World Theory) and (2.) how novels are construed as 'acts of communication' by readers who, as in real-life interactions, expect authors to provide sufficient effects for the efforts they put into reading their works.

Laura Hidalgo-Downing addresses the notion of manipulation at two levels, the use of rhetorical strategies by an author in order to misdirect readers and the use of questionnaires by an analyst in order to elicit readers' responses. The aim of the chapter is to explore the relation between textual features and readers' textual processing and emotional responses to the story ending of 'A Perfect Day for Bananafish' (1953) by J. D. Salinger. Adopting a reader-based approach which is rarely carried on in studies on story endings (focusing more on textual features in narrative sequences or on the notion of 'closure'), she analyses readers' responses to Salinger's narrative development and story ending in a two-stage experiment with thirty-six students in English Studies at the Universidad Autónoma of Madrid during the academic year 2017/18. The first stage consists in removing the ending from the text and have students anticipate it, the second is to provide them with the original ending and a questionnaire of open and closed questions to understand whether they find it unexpected, whether it makes sense in the story development and how to connect the ending and the title, among other questions. Based on research into the narrativity of short stories (Toolan 2009, 2013, 2016), this empirical testing is made to investigate the relation between textual clues as picked up by the students and specific interpretations, especially as narrators tend to manipulate information by withholding it in order to guide readers' expectations and emotions in terms of curiosity, suspense and surprise which are the 'three master forces of narrative' according to Abbott (2013). Although the results show that most students find the ending surprising due to the lack of information provided and the 'dispreferred' outcome in the suicide of the male protagonist, they did not consider it the less expected one when asked to search for narrative coherence and establish links between the metaphorical meaning of the title and the interpretation of the ending in the light of the whole story. This, Laura Hidalgo-Downing shows, is in line with recent research making a distinction between readers' and analysts' responses (Stockwell 2013), reflecting potentially different degrees of involvement in the literary text at different levels.

Sara Whiteley brings to the fore the multidirectionality of manipulation in the interaction between texts and readers: in her stylistic analysis of Simon Armitage's poem 'Upon Opening the Chest Freezer' (2010), she highlights its subtle blending of perspectives and registers as well as the various personal pronoun shifts that are likely to produce ambiguity and interpretative confusion. She then goes on to conduct a fine-grained analysis of the responses of two reading groups (one entirely male, one female) to the poem, showing the way the different shifts in narrative voices and perspectives lead to discussions in the groups as to the agency and level of blame of the protagonists involved (the woman leaving her husband, an artist, who has got used to freezing a winter snowball and putting it in their freezer in order to exhibit it and photograph it in the summer). The reading groups also explore the metaphors that the title and the poem invite to interpret between the freezer as a source of conflict and the couple's doomed relationship, creating an original combination of conceptual domains of the type THE RELATIONSHIP IS A CHEST FREEZER itself built, the author shows, upon more conventional conceptualization of 'a relationship as container' for instance. Whiteley demonstrates how both reading groups manipulate the poem's metaphors not so much as to reach an ultimate understanding of the poem, but as to explore its metaphorical possibilities and 'press' the text 'into service' (Long 2003) for the conversation it can generate. The women's group even produce some narrative extension or 'imaginative replotting' (Gerrig 1993) – a common feature of reading group discussions, as the participants, 'mind-modelling' the literary characters (Stockwell 2009), go beyond the textual piece by imagining themselves in those scenarios (Peplow et al. 2016). The women readers also 'press' the text for the sake of humour, thereby creating a playful interaction around potential further meanings. Whiteley thus demonstrates the multi-directional dimensions of manipulation: if the text positions readers into occupying certain places and aims at producing certain effects and understandings through specific linguistic means, the author shows how active reading group members are in offering their own 'manipulation' of the text for specific conversational and social purposes.

Part III focuses on a specific genre and its translation as well as typography in a multimodal novel. Chapter 9 takes us as far back as the early 1930s with five novels and a short story by the detective fiction writer Agatha Christie (with texts published until her death in 1976 and posthumously) as analysed here by Catherine Emmott and Marc Alexander, who demonstrate how highly manipulative the detective genre is. Though literary critics may be wary of the intentional fallacy, it is difficult not to admit that Christie has clearly every intention of manipulating the reader. The two authors bring to the fore the language-based and task-based devices used by the writer to control the readers (and avoid them solving the crime before the 'solution stage'), focusing on two essential aspects in detective stories: the evidence and the suspects. They show that the 'granularity' of the descriptions of evidence can be purposefully low through the use of general superordinates that will keep readers from identifying incongruities until the final phase where the 'evidential lever' is pulled. Cognitive indirection as regards the ways suspects are selected and listed is the second technique Emmott and Alexander focus on here, which also draws on the 'cognitive limitations' of the reader. One technique consists of rendering the real culprit 'invisible' by giving the readers other 'puzzle-solving tasks' that deter their attention from considering a specific character or characters, thus creating what Simons and Chabris (1999) call 'sustained inattentional blindness'. Christie may, for example, encourage readers to overlook the possibility that an apparent victim may actually be the murderer, or prompt them to exclude some characters as suspects if they are either highly trusted ('above' suspicion) or as 'beneath' suspicion as servants or workers or any such script-based characters can be. The cognitive misdirection might be accounted for by the tendency of readers to allocate roles to characters and to remain cognitively committed to these roles after allocation. Through under-specified description, inadequate clues and attentional misdirection, the Queen of Crime might sometimes be said not to 'play fair' with her reader.

Drawing on Emmott and Alexander's (2010, 2014) and Seago's (2014a, b) list of rhetorical techniques that are meant to misdirect or mislead readers into understanding 'whodunit' (or 'whodunito') and hidden clues about the story development in crime fiction, Christiana Gregoriou details such language-specific techniques as the withholding of information, the foregrounding of irrelevant clues, the burying of the relevance of certain facts by giving them out of their context or the suggestion of misleading associations, highlighting the paramount role of the stylistician in uncovering these linguistic markers. She emphasizes what could be seen as a paradox of crime fiction which is both a highly readable/enjoyable and un-re-readable genre, as the reader cannot be manipulated into 'misreading' the text twice. Having shown how clues are hidden in crime fiction to create surprise in the mis/reading game the author is playing, Gregoriou then evinces how these reader manipulation devices can turn out very challenging in translation. Taking two novels/translations as case studies, Lionel Shriver's *We Need to Talk About Kevin* (2003), translated into Greek by Gogo Arvaniti in 2010, and Petros Markaris's *Amyna Zonis* (*Zone Defence* 1998), translated into English by David Connolly in 2006, the author displays to what extent the translators live up to the challenge of keeping the reader in suspense and misleading her. She focuses on specific ambiguous polysemous lexical items triggering misleading schema–processing; on the use of repetition in the source text that is an apt strategy for misdirection, drawing attention to a character's childish innocence, for instance (while in fact she is a murderer); or on the use of gender-neutral items in a target language like English which has no gendered endings. Most often translations turn out to be less 'manipulative', given language constraints or translating choices, sometimes impeding the reader's cognitive engagement with the narrative in the same way as in the original text. Gregoriou points out that these challenges require 'crime fiction-specific creative skills' on the part of the translator to be taken up successfully.

Lastly, Nina Nørgaard focuses on how readers can be manipulated not just by verbal means but also by other multimodal strategies in her study of typography in J. J. Abrams and Dough Dorst's novel, *S.* (2013). She evinces how the writers' typographic choices (as well as choices of layout and design on the overall spatial page) contribute to the creation of verisimilitude (and meaning), manipulating the reader into believing she is reading an 'old library book' (the book entitled *Ship of Theseus* that is contained within the book *S.* that comes in a cassette). Characterizing typefaces in terms of weight, expansion, slope, curvature, connectivity, orientation, endings, regularity, colour and size (see Nørgaard 2019), she shows that the angular, bold and upright forms on the front cover of the old book are typographic features culturally associated with men (as used on the commercial packaging of protein power, for instance). Arguing that typefaces reveal meaning that can be described as indexical, iconic or symbolic and discursive import (van Leeuwen 2005b), the author construes the choice of the typeface Umbra on the inside title page as iconic meaning, displaying elusive letters that mirror the absent identity of the amnesic protagonist S. and/or the unknown (fictive) author of *Ship of Theseus*. Combining these aspects to the concepts of visual salience (i.e. what stands out from the text) and visual modality (the truthfulness of a representation), Nørgaard then reveals how the authors of *S.* manage to make the readers believe that they see 'what they would have seen if they had been there' (van Leeuwen 2005a), displaying high modality, in particular in the very salient handwritten notes in the book's margins registering the exchange between two characters, Jen and Eric, about the very book, all written in distinctive handwritings and colours. If this complex designing (for which the authors worked closely with the book designers and producers) positions the reader with the characters, bringing her to see what they see, Nørgaard wonders how effective this suspension of disbelief is and whether this high degree of truthfulness in the representation is not in fact counterbalanced by a defamiliarizing, low modality as this disruption of novel conventions is likely to draw the reader's attention to its fictionality.

This book will hopefully show why stylistics is instrumental in exposing the techniques used by authors to lead us towards certain interpretations and deliberately play with our expectations. It provides a precious set of tools to help uncover the strategies of pragmatic positioning and cognitive misdirection as highlighted from difficult angles, corpora and perspectives in the chapters that I invite the reader to now turn to.

Notes

1. See for instance "Clockwork Orange' link with boy's crime', *The Times*, 4 July 1973. The crime, assault and rape perpetuated brought about a withdrawal of the film in the UK (at Kubrick's request and until the artist's death).
2. See Simpson's (2014a: 3–4) three R's: *Rigour, Retrievability, Replicability* that should inform any stylistic analysis.
3. Among them: 'Finite dynamic verbs, a clause argument or transitivity participant (e.g. subject or object; Actor & Goal); first sentence of paragraphs, sentences containing fully lexical frequent keywords and clusters, characters' represented thoughts (esp. FIT and DT), direct speech question, negation, verbs of modality and of mental processing/full complement, etc' (see Toolan 2016: 35–6).
4. That could be defined as the capacity to feel what we think is the emotion felt by others (see Keen 2007).
5. For Sklar (2013: 56), empathy is a 'precursor' to sympathy as an emotional response, the latter involving a greater aesthetic distance (and some form of judgement).
6. Smith quoted in Toolan (2016: 39): the structure of sympathy is 'a process involving recognition of the character, alignment with the character and a degree of moral allegiance to the character'.
7. For Sklar these means are narrative progression, expositional disclosure, focalization, levels of discourse and narrative voice.

References

A Clockwork Orange (1971) Director: Stanley Kubrick. Actors: Malcolm McDowell, Patrick Magee, Michael Bates and Warren Clarke. Based on Burgess, A., *A Clockwork Orange*.

Abbott, H. P. (2013) 'Narrativity', Paragraph 16, in Hühn, P. et al. (eds) *The Living Handbook of Narratology*. Hamburg: Hamburg University. Available at: http://www.lhn.uni-hamburg.de/article/narrativity (accessed 2 July 2019).

Abrams, J. J. and Dorst, D. (2013) S. New York: Mulholland Books.

Allott, N. and Rubio Fernandez, P. (2002) 'This paper fills a much-needed gap', in Afuta, P., El Ghali, A., and Toussenel, F. (eds) *Actes de l'Atelier des doctorants en linguistique*, pp. 97–102. Paris: Université Paris 7.

Armitage, S. (2010) 'Upon opening the chest freezer', in Armitage, S. (ed.) *Seeing Stars*, p. 17. London: Faber and Faber.

Banks, I. (1994) *Complicity* [1993]. London: Abacus.

Barnes, J. (1994) *A Pack of Lies*. Cambridge: Cambridge University Press.

Barth, J. (1968) *Lost in the Funhouse*. New York City: Doubleday.

Barthes, R. (1984) 'La mort de l'auteur' (1967), in Barthes, R. (ed.) *Le Bruissement de la langue. Essais critiques IV*, pp. 63–9. Paris: Seuil, 1984.
Batuman, E. (2017) *The Idiot*. London: Jonathan Cape.
Black, E. (2006) *Pragmatic Stylistics*. Edinburgh: Edinburgh University Press.
Booth, W. (1974) *A Rhetoric of Irony*. Chicago, IL: Chicago University Press.
Borges, J. (2000 [1944]) 'The garden of forking paths', in *Collected Fictions*, trans. Andrew Hurley, pp. 119–28. London: Penguin.
Bornstein, R. F. and Craver-Lemley, C. (2004) 'Mere exposure effect', in Pohl, R. F. (ed.) *Cognitive Illusions: A Handbook on Fallacies and Biases in Thinking, Judgment and Memory*, pp. 215–34. New York: Psychology Press.
Bubel, C. M. (2008) 'Film audiences as overhearers', *Journal of Pragmatics* 40(1): 55–71.
Burgess, A. (1962) *A Clockwork Orange*. Portsmouth: William Heinemann.
Busse, B. (2017) 'Pragmatics of style in fiction', in Locher, M. A. and Jucker, A. H. (eds) *Pragmatics of Fiction*, pp. 197–231. Berlin/Boston: De Gruyter Mouton.
Clark, H. H. (1996) *Using Language*. Cambridge: Cambridge University Press.
Connolly, D. (2006) *Zone Defence*. London: Harvill Press.
Culpeper, J. and Fernandez-Quintanilla, C. (2017) 'Fictional characterisation', in Locker, M. A. and Jucker, A. H. (eds) *Pragmatics of Fiction*, pp. 93–128. Berlin/Boston: de Gruyter Mouton.
Cusk, R. (2014) *Outline*. London: Faber and Faber.
Dannenberg, H. P. (2008) *Coincidence and Counterfactuality: Plotting Time and Space in Narrative Fiction*. Lincoln, NE and London: University of Nebraska Press.
Duchan, J. F., Bruder, G. A. and Hewitt, L. E. (eds) (1995) *Deixis in Narrative: A Cognitive Science Perspective*. Hillsdale: Lawrence Erlbaum.
Eliot, G. (1965) *Middlemarch* [1871–72]. Harmondsworth: Penguin.
Emmott, C. and Alexander, M. (2010) 'Detective fiction, plot construction and reader manipulation: Cognitive-rhetorical misdirection in Agatha Christie's *Sparkling Cyanide*', in McIntyre, D. and Busse, B. (eds) *Language and Style: In Honour of Mick Short*, pp. 328–46. Houndmills: Palgrave Macmillan.
Emmott, C. and Alexander, M. (2014) 'Foregrounding, burying, and plot construction', in Stockwell, P. and Whiteley, S. (eds) *The Handbook of Stylistics*, pp. 329–43. Cambridge: Cambridge University Press.
Erickson, T. A. and Mattson, M. E. (1981) 'From words to meaning: A semantic illusion', *Journal of Verbal Learning and Verbal Behavior* 20: 540–52.
Fairclough, N. (1989) *Language and Power*. London: Longman.
Feinberg, L. (2002) *Hypocrisy: Don't Leave Home Without It*. Greeley: Pilgrims' Process.
Fowles, J. (2004) *The French Lieutenant's Woman* [1969]. London: Vintage.
Galasiński, D. (2000) *The Language of Deception: A Discourse Analytical Study*. Thousand Oaks, CA: Sage.
Gavins, J. (2007) *Text World Theory: An Introduction*. Edinburgh: Edinburgh University Press.

Gavins, J. and Lahey, E. (eds) (2016) *World Building: Discourse in the Mind*. London: Bloomsbury.

Genette, G. (1980 [1972]) *Narrative Discourse: An Essay in Method*. Ithaca: Cornell University Press.

Gerrig, R. J. (1993) *Experiencing Narrative Worlds*. Boulder, CO: Westview Press.

Gorin, M. (2014) 'Towards a theory of interpersonal manipulation', in Coons, C. and Weber, M. (eds) *Manipulation: Theory and Practice*, pp. 73–97. Oxford: Oxford University Press.

Green, H. (1950) *Nothing*. London: Harvill HarperCollins.

Green, H. (1952) *Doting*. London: Picador.

Gregoriou, C. (2011) *Language, Ideology, Identity in Serial Killer Narratives*. London, New York: Routledge.

Guérin, C., Siouffi, G. and Sorlin, S. (2013) *Le Rapport éthique au discours : histoire, pratiques, analyses [Ethics and Discourse in Historical Perspective: Practice & Theory]*. Bern: Peter Lang.

Habermas, J. (1987) *Théorie de l'agir communicationnel. Tome 2. Pour une critique de la raison fonctionnaliste*, trans. J.-L. Schegel. Paris: Fayard.

Habermas, J. (2006) *Idéalisations et communication: Agir communicationnel et usage de la raison* trans. C. Bouchindhomme. Paris: Fayard.

Hart, C. (2013) 'Argumentation meets adapted cognition: Manipulation in media discourse on immigration', *Journal of Pragmatics* 59: 200–9.

Hoeken, H. (2005) 'Overtuigende taal', *Tijdschrift voor Taalbeheersing* 27: 139–50.

Hogan, P. C. (2014) 'Stylistics, emotion and neuroscience', in Burke, M. (ed.) *The Routledge Handbook of Stylistics*, pp. 516–30. London: Routledge.

Ishiguro, K. (1989) *The Remains of the Day*. London: Faber and Faber.

Jobert, M. and Sorlin, S. (eds) (2018) *The Pragmatics of Irony and Banter* [Linguistic Approaches to Literature 30]. Amsterdam: John Benjamins.

Landert, D. (2017) 'Stance in fiction', in Locker, M. A. and Jucker, A. H. (eds) *Pragmatics of Fiction*, pp. 489–514. Berlin/Boston: de Gruyter Mouton.

Leech, G. and Short, M. (2007) *Style in Fiction: A Linguistic Introduction to English Fictional Prose*. 2nd edition. Harlow, UK: Pearson Longman.

Long, E. (2003) *Book Clubs: Women and the Uses of Reading in Everyday Life*. Chicago: Chicago University Press.

Maillat, D. (2014) 'Manipulation et cognition: un modèle pragmatique', in Herman, T. and Oswald, S. (eds) *Rhétorique et cognition/Rhetoric and Cognition. Perspectives théoriques et stratégies persuasives/Theoretical Perspectives and Persuasive Strategies*, pp. 69–88. Bern: Peter Lang.

Maillat, D. (2017) 'Les manipulations du discours de séduction: éclairage pragmatique', *E-rea* [En ligne] 15(1). Available at: http://journals.openedition.org/erea/5970; DOI: 10.4000/erea.5970.

Maillat, D. and Oswald, S. (2009) 'Defining manipulative discourse: The pragmatics of cognitive illusions', *International Review of Pragmatics* I: 348–70.

Markaris, P. (2010 [1998]) *Amyna Zonis (Άμυνα Ζώνης, Zone Defence)*. Athens: Gabrielides Publishing.

Mills, C. (2014) 'Manipulation as an aesthetic flaw', in Coons, C. and Weber, M. (eds) *Manipulation: Theory and Practice*, pp. 135–50. Oxford: Oxford University Press.

Nørgaard, N. (2019) *Multimodal Stylistics of the Novel: More than Words*. London and New York: Routledge.

Nyberg, D. (1993) *The Varnished Truth: Truth Telling and Deceiving in Ordinary Life*. Chicago: University of Chicago Press.

Peplow, D., Swann, J., Trimarco, P., and Whiteley, S. (2016) *The Discourse of Reading Groups: Cognitive and Sociocultural Approaches*. London: Routledge.

Phelan, J. (2005) *Living to Tell About It*. Ithaca and London: Cornell University Press.

Phelan, J. (2011) 'Rhetoric, ethics, and narrative communication: Or, from story and discourse to authors, resources, and audiences', *Soundings* 94(1/2): 55–75.

Phelan, J. (2017) *Somebody Telling Somebody Else: A Rhetorical Poetics of Narrative*. The Ohio State University Press.

Phelan, J. (2018) 'Fictionality, audiences, and character: A rhetorical alternative to Catherine Gallagher's "Rise of Fictionality"', *Poetics Today* 39(1): 113–29.

Pratt, M. L. (1988) 'Speech presentation, the novel and the press', in van Peer, W. (ed.) *The Taming of the Text: Explorations in Language, Literature, and Culture*, pp. 61–81. London: Routledge.

Prince, G. (1988) 'The disnarrated', *Style* 22(1): 1–8.

Psycho (1960) Director: Alfred Hitchcock. Screenplay by Joseph Stefano.

Rancière, J. (2017) *Les Bords de la fiction*. Paris: Seuil.

Rimmon-Kenan, S. (2007) 'Narration: Levels and voices', in Rimmon-Kenan, S., *Narrative Fiction: Contemporary Poetics*, pp. 97–106. London: Routledge.

Romero Trillo, J. (2017) 'Corpus pragmatics', *Corpus Pragmatics* 1(1): 1–2.

Salinger, J. D. (1953) 'A perfect day for bananafish', in *Nine Stories*. Boston: Little, Brown and Company.

Sanford, A. J. and Emmott, C. (2012) *Mind, Brain and Narrative*. Cambridge: Cambridge University Press.

Scanlon, T. (1998) *What We Owe to Each Other*. Cambridge, MA: Belknap.

Seago, K. (2014a) 'Red herrings and other misdirection in translation', in Cadera, S. and Pintarić, A. P. (eds) *The Voices of Suspense and their Translation in Thrillers*, pp. 207–20. Amsterdam: Rodopi.

Seago, K. (2014b) 'Introduction and overview: Crime (fiction) in translation', *Journal of Specialised Translation* (special issue, July). Available at: http://www.jostrans.org/issue22/issue22_toc.php (accessed 8 August 2018).

Semino, E. and Culpeper, J. (2011) 'Stylistics', in Östman, J.-O. and Verschueren, J. (eds) *Pragmatics in Practice*, pp. 295–305. Amsterdam: John Benjamins.

Shafer, D. M. and Raney, A. A. (2012) 'Exploring how we enjoy antihero narratives', *Journal of Communication* 62: 1028–46.

Shriver, L. (2003) *We Need to Talk About Kevin*. London: Serpent's Tail.

Simons, D. J. and Chabris, C. F. (1999) 'Gorillas in our midst: Sustained inattentional blindness for dynamic events', *Perception* 28: 1059–74.

Simpson, P. (2003) *On the Discourse of Satire* [Linguistic Approaches to Literature 2]. Amsterdam: John Benjamins.

Simpson, P. (2014a) *Stylistics: A Resource Book for Students*. 2nd edition. London: Routledge.

Simpson, P. (2014b) 'Just what is narrative *urgency*', *Language and Literature* 23(1): 3–22.

Simpson, P. and Canning, P. (2014) 'Action and event', in Stockwell, P. and Whiteley, S. (eds) *The Cambridge Handbook of Stylistics*, pp. 281–99. Cambridge: Cambridge University Press.

Sklar, H. (2013) *The Art of Sympathy in Fiction: Forms of Ethical and Emotional Persuasion*. Amsterdam/Philadelphia: John Benjamins.

Sorlin, S. (2015) 'Person deixis and impersonation in Iain Banks's *Complicity*', *Language and Literature* 24(1): 40–53.

Sorlin, S. (2016) *Language and Manipulation in* House of Cards*: A Pragma-Stylistic Perspective*. Basingstoke: Palgrave Macmillan.

Sorlin, S. (2017a) 'The pragmatics of manipulation: Exploiting im/politeness theories', *Journal of Pragmatics* 121: 132–46.

Sorlin, S. (2017b) 'Vers une théorisation du discours séducteur', in Sorlin, S. (ed.) 'La Séduction du discours / On Seductive Discourse', *E-rea. Revue électronique d'études sur le monde anglophone* 15(1). Available at: http://journals.openedition.org/erea/5884

Sorlin, S. (2018a) 'The rolling stones promoting Monty Python: The power of irony and banter', in Jobert, M. and Sorlin, S. (eds) *The Pragmatics of Irony and Banter*, pp. 196–214. Amsterdam: John Benjamins.

Sorlin, S. (2018b) 'Strategies of involvement and moral detachment in *House of Cards*', *Literary Semantics*, 1–21. DOI: https://doi.org/10.1515/jls-2018-0002

Sorlin, S. (forthcoming) 'The author-reader channel from the nascent novel to digital fiction: Confronting Fielding's *Joseph Andrews* (1742) and Burne's "24 Hours with Someone you know" (1996)', *Narrative*.

Sperber, D. and Wilson, D. (1995) *Relevance: Communication & Cognition*. 2nd edition. Oxford: Blackwell.

Sternberg, M. (1978) *Expositional Modes and Temporal Ordering in Fiction*. Baltimore: Johns Hopkins University Press.

Stockwell, P. (2002) *Cognitive Poetics: An Introduction*. London: Routledge.

Stockwell, P. (2009) *Texture. A Cognitive Aesthetics of Reading*. Edinburgh: Edinburgh University Press.

Stockwell, P. (2013) 'The positioned reader', *Language and Literature* 22(3): 263–77.

Swasy, J. L. and Munch, J. M. (1985) 'Examining the target of receiver elaborations: Rhetorical question effects on source processing and persuasion', *Journal of Consumer Research* 11: 877–86.

Tanaka, K. (1992) 'The pun in advertising: A pragmatic approach', *Lingua* 87: 91–102.

Tanaka, K. (1994) *Advertising Language: A Pragmatic Approach to Advertisements in Britain and Japan*. London: Routledge.
Thomas, D. (1952) *In Country Sleep and Other Poems*. New York: James Laughlin.
Toolan, M. (2009) *Narrative Progression in the Short Story: A Corpus Stylistic Approach*. Amsterdam: John Benjamins.
Toolan, M. (2013) 'Coherence', Paragraph 24, in Hühn, P. et al. (ed.) *The Living Handbook of Narratology*. Hamburg: Hamburg University. Available at: http://www.lhn.uni-hamburg.de/article/coherence (accessed 16 February 2018).
Toolan, M. (2016) *Making Sense of Narrative Text: Situation, Repetition, and Picturing in the Reading of Short Stories*. New York and London: Routledge.
Van der Pligt, J. and Vliek, M. (2017) *The Psychology of Influence: Theory, Research and Practice*. London and New York: Routledge.
van Dijk, T. A. (2006) 'Discourse and manipulation', *Discourse & Society* 17(3): 359–83.
van Eemeren, F. H. (2010) *Strategic Maneuvering in Argumentative Discourse*. Amsterdam: John Benjamins Publishing.
van Eemeren, F. H. and Grootendorst, R. (2004) *A Systematic Theory of Argumentation: The Pragma-Dialectical Approach*. Cambridge: Cambridge University Press.
van Leeuwen, T. (2005a) *Introducing Social Semiotics*. London and New York: Routledge.
van Leeuwen, T. (2005b) 'Typographic meaning', *Visual Communication* 4(2): 137–43.
Warhol, R. R. (2005) 'Neonarrative; or, how to render the unnarratable in realist fiction and contemporary film', in Phelan, J. and Rabinowitz, P. (eds) *A Companion to Narrative Theory*, pp. 220–31. Oxford: Blackwell.
Warhol, R. (2010) '"What might have been is not what is": Dickens's narrative refusals', *Dickens's Studies Annual* 41: 45–60.
Warhol, R. (2013) 'It is of little use for me to tell you: George Eliot's narrative refusals', in Anderson, A. and Shaw, H. E. (eds) *The Blackwell Companion to George Eliot*, pp. 46–61. West Sussex: Wiley-Blackwell.
Wimsatt, W. K. and Beardsley, Monroe C. (1954) *The Verbal Icon*. Lexington: The University Press of Kentucky.
Zagorin, P. (1990) *Ways of Lying*. Cambridge, MA: Harvard University Press.

Part I

Manipulating positions, representations and viewpoints

2

Metalepsis, counterfactuality and the forked path in *The French Lieutenant's Woman*

Marina Lambrou

1. Introduction: Manipulating the reader

Readers of literary fiction are likely to have expectations of plot progression and how characters develop in the narrative based on their knowledge of story schemata formed from previous readings of different literary genres. Schematic knowledge provides a framework for story structure and content and can lead to influencing readers' interpretation of that text (Bartlett 1932; Rumelhart 1975; Mandler and Johnson 1977). In other words, a prior knowledge of literary fiction can generate levels of anticipation – of specific outcomes, for example – as a result of readers encountering similar works of fiction (Emmott and Alexander 2014). Readers of romantic Victorian fiction, such as works by the Brontës and Eliot, are likely to expect plots that engage with themes associated with the genre that are centred around the relationship between the male and female protagonists. The protagonists first have to overcome certain obstacles which prevent them from being together but ultimately their story ends with a happy union. As well as prior knowledge of the plot and structure, expectations are also likely to be formed in part from knowledge of the period of publication and an understanding of what could and could not be published according to literary conventions of the time (see Warhol 2005 on the paranarratable).

Fictional texts, however, do not always follow conventions, particularly those categorized as postmodernist literature, which are guaranteed to break literary norms and disrupt a readers' pre-existing story schemata. Some of the narrative strategies that can be used to creatively digress from expectations include counterfactual storytelling (Dannenberg 2008) that creates forked pathways, disnarration (Prince 1988) and the transgressive uses of narration and author metalepsis (Genette 1980 [1972]) for metafictive, self-reflexivity. It could be argued that using these devices to tell a story deliberately manipulates readers by creating a clash between expectation and the text's realization that leads to a need for schema refreshment so readers can realign their expectations to be able to comprehend similar texts in the future (Cook 1990).

In this chapter, the discussion explores the use of unconventional literary techniques to understand their form and function and, importantly, the effects they create and how this could manipulate readers. The earlier points on schema knowledge are raised to make the point that readers require an understanding of default narrative structures and plot patterns to recognize deviations in the narrative triggered by a range of strategies. The novel *The French Lieutenant's Woman* is presented as the work of fiction for analysis as it uses several literary techniques that play with expectations of plot structure and endings. A discussion of the literary devices that dominate the text is given following a synopsis of *The French Lieutenant's Woman*.

2. Synopsis: *The French Lieutenant's Woman*

The French Lieutenant's Woman is a novel by John Fowles and was first published in 1969. (The edition referred to in this chapter was published in 2004 by *Vintage*.) It is rightfully described as postmodern because of the narrative techniques that deviate from convention such as the use of metalepsis (which is defined and discussed further in the chapter). It is also described as a historical romance because of its setting in the past, beginning in the year 1867, and written in the style of a nineteenth-century Victorian romantic novel. As critics also describe the novel as engaging with issues of female empowerment, readers' expectations of prototypical Victorian characters in a plot associated with this literary genre may be primed at the outset to anticipate something different.

The story is set in Lyme Regis, England, and concerns the mysterious Sarah Woodruff, an impoverished young woman, formerly a governess who is ruined by an affair with a French sea captain. (It is not until much later in the novel that readers learn that the affair is not consummated.) Sarah is often seen waiting for her lover, the French sea captain to return, staring out towards the sea standing at the end of the harbour wall, known as the Cobb, a stone jetty that is built out into the sea. Sarah is isolated and is thought by locals to be mad and is also known as Tragedy because of her history. Charles Smithson, a wealthy gentleman, is visiting his wealthy fiancé Ernestina in Lyme Regis and encounters Sarah on the Cobb one day. Charles becomes obsessed by Sarah and her unconventional situation and wants to save her, but he loses his sense of propriety and they eventually embrace. The consequence of their liaison is a humiliating and public breaking off of Charles and Ernestina's engagement. Charles and Sarah begin a sexual relationship, but Charles discovers that Sarah is in fact a virgin and that her relationship with the French lieutenant is based on a lie. He realizes he has been manipulated by her. Charles loses his expected inheritance and flees to Europe, following miscommunication with a letter that Sarah never receives. Sarah flees to London carrying Charles's baby. Charles and Sarah meet some years later in London.

Most unusually for a Victorian romantic novel, the book ends unconventionally for the protagonists, who are given a hypothetical plot structure with two different endings (endings 1 and 2) that is heightened through different modes of narration which address the reader directly. An alternative ending for the main characters is offered earlier in the story (ending 1), which challenges the reader into believing that each presents the true outcome. The three endings for Charles, Sarah and Ernestina are:

> *Ending 1.* Charles and Ernestina marry though it is not a particularly happy marriage but conforms to expectations of the literary genre. Sarah is forgotten;
>
> *Ending 2.* Charles and Sarah meet some years later in London where Sarah is living and Charles is told of their child. There is some hope that the relationship may rekindle;
>
> *Ending 3.* Same events as in *Ending 2* up to the point of Charles and Sarah meeting some years later in London. However, the final meeting between them does not go well as Sarah wants her independence and does not want to be with Charles. Charles leaves feeling angry at having been manipulated and is unaware of his child.

(Readers familiar with the 1981 film directed by Karel Reisz starring Meryl Streep and Jeremy Irons as Sarah and Charles should note that the film is not a faithful adaptation of the novel and that only two endings are offered.)

The three endings in *The French Lieutenant's Woman* are unconventional for a Victorian romantic novel both in terms of narrative structure and the outcomes of the key protagonists, especially as the true outcome is left inconclusive. Arguably, however, they are acceptable within the unconfined possibilities of a postmodernist text. As Mandal (2017: 278) citing Derrida explains, 'Inconclusiveness is one of the hallmarks of postmodernism and indeterminacy marks postmodern subjectivity.' Indeterminacy invites interpretation as readers can decide the outcome they prefer. A closer look at the three endings against the narrative techniques of metalepsis, counterfactual storytelling and the forked path of the chapter's title is discussed in the following sections.

3. Narrators, narration and author intention

To understand how a story unfolds in a fictional work it is important to understand who tells the story or what Stanzel (1984 [1979]) describes as the 'narrative situation', which refers to the different types of narration. Stanzel (1984 [1979]) identifies a first-person narrative situation and authorial narrative situation similar to Genette's (1980 [1972]) description of the homodiegetic narrator who is a character in the storyworld (the diegesis) or a heterodiegetic narrator who is outside the storyworld as a third person or omniscient narrator. Omniscient narrators address readers outside the story as extradiegetic narrators (as opposed to intradiegetic narrators who exist in the story) and have an overview of the story events and characters' thoughts and feelings and can provide details that no single characters are able to see and tell. Moreover, the heterodiegetic narrator is relatively reliable (when compared to the homodiegetic, first-person narrator) and usually tells the story in a neutral voice reporting events. However, heterodiegetic narrators may also take a stance on events in the story as readers familiar with the narratorial style of Charles Dickens will recognize. Take, for example, the opening paragraph of Dickens's (1848: 1) *Dombey and Son*:

> Dombey sat in the corner of the darkened room in the great arm-chair by the bedside, and Son lay tucked up warm in a little basket bedstead, carefully disposed on a low settee immediately in front of the fire and close to it, as if his constitution were analogous to that of a muffin, and it was essential to toast him brown while he was very new.

The irony expressed in this description of the toasted baby is thought to be Dickens's opinion who is author-narrator. Dickens was known to be a great commentator on the abuses and social injustices of the time including those against children. A more blatant example of a narrator who intrudes into the story can be found in George Eliot's *Middlemarch* (1871–2) where the stylistic marker of a hyphen signals a narrative pause to allow for the insertion of a rhetorical question:

> One morning, some weeks after her arrival at Lowick, Dorothea – but why always Dorothea? Was her point of view the only possible one with regard to this marriage? I protest against all our interest, all our effort at understanding being given to the young skins that look blooming in spite of trouble; for these

too will get faded, and will know the older and more eating griefs which we are helping to neglect. (1871, Book. 3, Chap. 29)

The sudden change in the narration is dramatic. Eliot's narrator in *Middlemarch* is dramatized as an author constructing the text who stops to speak directly to readers about Dorothea Brooke and her marriage to the Rev. Edward Casaubon. What begins as a heterodiegetic narration, where the narrator is outside the storyworld, shifts to another level of the same type of heterodiegetic narration but one where the narrator breaks away from the storyworld back into the readers' world or discourse-world to comment on these characters and their situation. To explain, when an authorial narrator intrudes into the story to enact a deliberate transgression between narrative levels, it is called 'metalepsis', defined as 'any intrusion by the extradiegetic narrator or narratee into the diegetic universe (or by diegetic characters into a metadiegetic universe, etc.), or the inverse' with the aim of producing an effect that is 'comical or fantastic' (Genette 1980 [1972]: 234–5), as in the Dickens example above. However, Levin (2016: 292) states that a character moving between the storyworld into the discourse-world, or author's world or vice versa

> is no longer primarily used to produce humor but rather to test the convention of the author's omnipotent agency on the one hand and, on the other, the author's more recently suggested dissolution.

Moreover, metalepsis 'dramatizes the problematization of the boundary between fiction and reality endemic to the postmodern condition' because metalepsis disrupts the 'narrative hierarchy' to 'reinforce or to undermine the ontological status of fictional subjects or selves' (Malina 2002: 2).

It is worth pointing out that the term 'discourse-world' is a concept that emerges from Text World Theory (Werth 1999; Gavins 2007). Text World Theory provides an analytical framework to explain how readers conceptualize fictional texts by applying their knowledge of the real world, that is, the *discourse world*, to the spaces inhabited by characters in the fictional, *text-world*, to help them understand not just the plot and characterization, but also the narrators and author, which all influence interpretation of the text.

Genette (1988 [1983]: 88) identifies a further level of metalepsis within the diegesis called *author metalepsis*, which is defined as a

> deliberate transgression of the threshold of embedding ... when an author (or his reader) introduces himself into the fictive action of the narrative or when a character in that fiction intrudes into the extradiegetic existence of the author or reader.

Author metalepsis as a figure is exemplified in the following excerpt from Chapter 55 of *The French Lieutenant's Woman* where the narrator becomes a character and enters the extradiegetic existence of the storyworld at several points. The first encounter is during a train journey from Exeter to London (as Charles goes searching for Sarah), when a figure appears on the train and sits in the same coach as Charles. The unnamed character, with 'a massively bearded face' and 'a man of 40 or so' (Fowles 2004: 387) openly stares at Charles. Readers are told that he is disapproving of Charles 'as if he knew very well what man this was' (388) before the narration moves from (third-person) heterodiegetic narration to author-narrator to address readers directly through author metalepsis with 'You may one day come under a similar gaze' (389). The figure asks readers

> Now could I use you?
> Now what could I do with you?

and then compares his omniscient status to that of an 'omnipotent God' because 'there is only one profession that gives that particular look' (389). The startling shift in narratorial levels and the realization that the unnamed character is the author-narrator is unsettling. He goes on to address readers in the first person I-narration to inform them:

> Now the question I am asking as I stare at Charles … what the devil am I going to do with you? (389)

Readers are reminded that this is a work of fiction that is being constructed at the point of its telling and that the fate of its characters is at the mercy of the author-narrator. (There is an assumption that the narrator is John Fowles, who was born in 1926 and would have been about forty-three years of age at the time *The French Lieutenant's Woman* was first published. Fowles also sported a massive beard, just like the unnamed character with 'a massively bearded face' and described as 'a man of 40 or so' (Fowles 2004: 387). For this reason the narrator in my chapter is referred to as 'he'.)

As the discussion of Chapter 55 has shown, the narrative technique of metalepsis allows figures to step in and out of their own work. By pausing the story to insert an opinion that is not related to the plot, this transgression functions to undermine the separation of the diegetic universe and extradiegetic levels of narration. Fludernik (2003: 383) however, disagrees that metalepsis foregrounds 'the metafictional and transgressive (nonrealistic) properties of such an imaginative stepping into the story world' but instead claims that it is illusionary and functions to expose 'the narratee's (as well as the reader's) imaginative immersion into the story'. Yet, *The French Lieutenant's Woman* offers numerous examples of the metafictive and omniscient role of the author-narrator, as in the excerpt below where he offers an opinion on his characters when he evaluates their looks:

> Of the three young women who pass through these pages Mary was, in my opinion, by far the prettiest. (Fowles 2004: 77)

In her analysis of *The French Lieutenant's Woman* and Fowles' other works, Ferebe (2004: 377) describes the narrator's 'omniscient, omnipotent, objectifying mode of looking' by applying Mulvey's (1975) concept of *the male gaze* when describing the author's intrusion to comment on gendered roles.

4. The endings: Author metalepsis and manipulation

As outlined earlier, Fowles (2004) narrates three endings in *The French Lieutenant's Woman*, the first of which describes the marriage of Charles and Ernestina in Chapter 44. Readers, however, are then told the following:

> *And so the story ends.* What happened to Sarah, I do not know – whatever it was, she never troubled Charles again. ... Charles and Ernestina did not live happily ever after; but they lived together. (325)

Other than the fact that there are still over 100 pages left of the book until its end, there is no reason for readers not to accept this conventional union between Charles and Ernestina. The metafictive comment by the author-narrator on telling the story so far (italics above) and his comment on their less-than-happy marriage tells readers that all is not what it seems. The outcome goes against the expected happy union for romantic protagonists in the Victorian genre fiction is an example of what Warhol (2010: 46) describes as a *narrative refusal* defined as 'direct narratorial references to some of the specifics or what might have been and yet is not'. It is also an example of the *paranarratable* (Warhol 2005, 2013) which describes 'what would not (yet) be told because of literary convention'. The paranarratable refers to plot turns that would not be taken or would be thought improbable within the context of the genre and based on the literary conventions at the time of publication. So, for example, in Victorian fiction, female protagonists are expected to marry and where they do not marry it is usually because they die. Furthermore, in this first ending, the author-narrator states that Sarah was not present in Charles and Ernestina's lives because it would be improbable for a man of Charles's standing to continue to be associated with Sarah. In the following Chapter 45, readers are then told that this marriage did not take place, in a confusing plot turn:

> *Having brought this fiction to a thoroughly traditional ending* I had better explain that although all I have described in the last two chapters happened, it did not happen quite in the way you were led to believe ... the last few pages you have read are not what happened but what he spent the hours between London and Exeter imagining what might happen. (327)

This first ending is explained as a daydream imagined by Charles and dismissed by the author-narrator as he once again steps outside the diegesis through author metalepsis to emphasize the metafiction of the story and characters. By telling the story in this way, the author-narrator foregrounds the construction of events (italicized) by drawing attention to it and to his omnipotent role of determining when and how the story ends. Charles, Sarah and Ernestina are his creation and at his whim. The strategy of narrative refusal and the disnarrating of events that are narrated then dismissed as not having happened (Prince 1988 – see Section 5) reminds readers, who are immersed in the story and the truth of the text-world, that characters do not exist outside the author-narrator's imagination. It is a further example of the author-narrator demonstrating his power similar to that of God in Chapter 55, page 389 in the example given earlier in this chapter. If the marriage between Charles and Ernestina did not happen, which of the three endings is the true outcome?

Fowles deliberately plays with readers' expectations of the conventional Victorian novel form and the happy-ever-after ending through authorial and narratorial metalepses. By presenting multiple endings and exposing the metafictive devices that manipulate the text structure, readers are surprised and disoriented by these plot twists. Moreover, Fowles does not intentionally lie to his readers; instead, he invites readers to engage with the text and give them a choice to decide their preference on which of the final two endings is the most acceptable outcome – whether this is guided by an emotional response to the characters or a deeper understanding of consequences in the discourse-world applied to characters in the (idealized) storyworld of the Victorian fictional genre. Fiction is not real and yet Fowles obscures this fact by giving his main characters volition to enact their wishes and desires and make choices beyond the author's and narrator's control and contribute to the replotting of the story.

5. Counterfactuality, the forked path and disnarration

Another example of a transgressive narrative technique that intentionally manipulates the plot and, it could be argued, the readers, is counterfactual storytelling. Counterfactual storytelling gives rise to alternative and often unexpected plot scenarios and endings instead of following a single trajectory leading to the story's closure as the scenarios create 'alternative versions of past or present outcomes' (Roese and Olson 1995: 1). In her significant work on counterfactual paths that a plot can take, Dannenberg (2008) describes the options narrators make with their characters in terms of the hypothetical *what if* option. The *what if* options may arise when considering different situations and are plotted to create *counterfactual divergence* or the branching of time once the options are triggered (see Section 6). Dannenberg (2012: 125) also describes 'the spatialization of time … as part of the human cognitive dominant' which explains how time is conceptualized in terms of the *space* metaphor (see Turner 1987).

Text World Theory (Werth 1999), as mentioned earlier in the chapter, also provides a useful framework that helps understand the imagined first ending of Charles and Ernestina's marriage as Charles's daydream can be understood as a sub-world that is embedded within but departs from the diegesis of the text-world. Readers are taken into then brought out of the embedded sub-world level of Charles's daydream and into his text-world when the author-narrator dismisses this as counterfactual and not real.

6. The logic of narrative possibilities

The notion that a plot can present options or a 'network of possibilities' was first proposed by Bremond and Cancalon (1980: 388) to describe plot structure as being non-linear. Developed as a reaction to Propp's (1968 [1928]) linear and goal-oriented plot structure, Bremond and Cancalon suggest that characters may create an alternative pathway for themselves whenever there is a decision to make and by doing so, influence and change the direction of the plot. Bremond and Cancalon (1980: 387) claim that 'when the function which opens the sequence is proposed, the narrator always has the choice of having it followed by the act or of maintaining it in a state of virtuality'. In other words, the act can either be actualized and take place or not, and the event 'can follow or not follow its course up to the end which was foreseen'. In this way, a network of possibilities creating counterfactual divergence opens up, as represented in Figure 2.1.

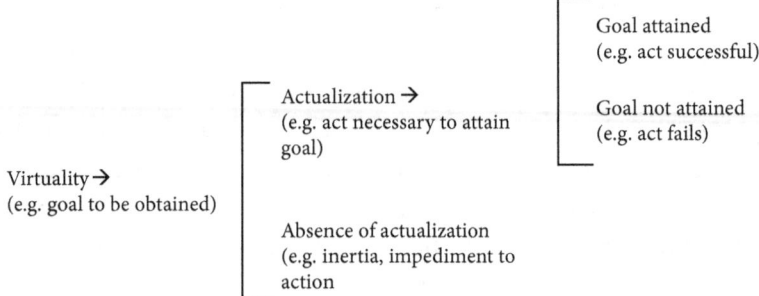

Figure 2.1 Bremond and Cancalon's (1980: 388) 'Network of plot possibilities'.

The imagined marriage between Charles and Ernestina in the first ending is the first example of a counterfactual scenario. Conversely, Riddle-Harding (2017: 124) argues that the imagined scenario, which is embedded as another story level in the narrative from the point of view of Charles, may not easily be characterized as counterfactual because

> a counterfactual associated with a character's point of view is counterfactual only from that character's perspective, and perhaps not from the perspective of the narrator or another character.

The author-narrator's role in creating this scenario through metafictive and self-reflexive narration can be considered an exception to this idea as it is he and not Charles who takes an *evaluative stance* on this counterfactual scenario. As has already been discussed, the author-narrator is responsible for determining and enabling Charles's thoughts and actions and this also results in more complex characterizations in that characters may seem more realistic because they are flawed.

The second ending in *The French Lieutenant's Woman* has Charles and Sarah meet some years later in a building where Sarah now lives and there is hope that their relationship may rekindle; while in the third ending, the author-narrator inserts himself into the storyworld as a figure/character standing outside the building where Sarah lives and will meet Charles (in events similar to the second ending). However, the author-narrator figure uses the magical device of turning back time by fifteen minutes to trigger an alternative path for these protagonists: Charles and Sarah meet in the same circumstances but it is a difficult meeting as Sarah does not want to reunite with Charles resulting in Charles awakening 'to the reality of the situation' (Chapter 61, 443). He walks out feeling bitter and angry. Time is turned back by the author-narrator character rewinding his wristwatch and this is the point that creates the counterfactual divergence, which is represented in Figure 2.2.

Counterfactual narratives create forking of plot trajectories as shown in both Figure 1 and Figure 2 where the virtualities of a narrative are presented through the coexistence of contradictory pathways (Baroni 2016) otherwise described as the *forked path*. The concept of a forked path was first proposed by the novelist Jorge Luis Borges (2000 [1944]) in his short story 'The Garden of Forking Paths'. The story sets out to resolve the mystery of the chaotic and senseless manuscripts written by one Ts'ui Pên that 'constructs a labyrinth' (p. 50). Initially thought to describe a physical labyrinth in the form of a garden, it is discovered that the labyrinth refers to the splitting of time and that the novel itself is the labyrinth. In other words, the claim is that all texts offer a *labyrinth* of plot options and multiple possibilities in that each time a character meets diverse alternatives and makes a decision, a forked path is created at the point of the decision, and this in turn generates parallel pathways. According to Borges (2000 [1944]: 51), 'In all fictional works, each time a man is confronted with several alternatives, he chooses one and eliminates the others.' Confusingly, in 'The Garden of Forking Paths', the creator of the manuscript, Ts'ui Pên chooses all pathways simultaneously so '*he creates*, in this way, diverse futures, diverse times which themselves also proliferate and fork'. In other words, none of the parallel pathways are counterfactual as they all exist as true.

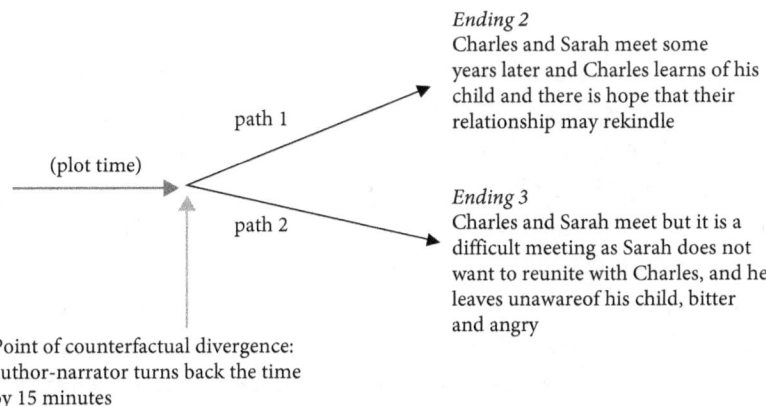

Figure 2.2 The point of counterfactual divergence leading to the two alternative endings in *The French Lieutenant's Woman*.

In the second and third ending in *The French Lieutenant's Woman*, it can be argued that the final ending is inconclusive (Baldick 2009) as neither is offered as true, suggesting that both endings exist as possibilities. How can this be? In a psychoanalytic discussion of *gender myths* in *The French Lieutenant's Woman*, Mandal (2017: 287) offers an explanation:

> It would be insufficient to say that the novel with its multiple endings is an experiment with the narrative form. There is something more in it, an impasse that resists any straightforward resolution to the story. With specific focus on the female protagonist, I claim that this impasse is Sarah Woodruff herself, the content of whose character produces multiple and contradictory effects and possibilities both for the narrative as well as for the male protagonist.

The complex character of Sarah is given as the reason for the complex plot structure rather than Fowles employing narrative devices to tell her story. I would argue that both cannot be separated as they are inextricably linked. *The French Lieutenant's Woman* is a mastery of plot structure and characterization that understands what Sarah would and would not do and how Charles would and would not react as their conscious and unconscious hopes, wishes and desires are real in their storyworld and all these factors come together to offer multiple plot possibilities and endings. If, however, readers decide to interpret or accept one of the multiple endings as true, then they, rather than the author-narrator, are disnarrating the less probable or hypothetical scenario as the very act of accepting one means the automatic elimination of the other. As explained by Prince (1992: 36) when one path is taken, the other is disnarrated as these are 'choices not made, the roads not taken, possibilities not actualized, goals not reached'.

It is worth noting that there is an expression to describe the experience of forked pathways and the precise moment the counterfactual divergence is created, namely a *sliding doors moment* after the 1998 film *Sliding Doors* (directed by Peter Howitt). In the film, the protagonist, Helen unknowingly has her life split into two parallel universes as a result of a two-second delay when catching the train. The film follows both trajectories (with one pathway showing Helen catching the train; and in the other, Helen missing the train). Both of Helen's stories have the same characters and relationships but each story leads to a very different outcome as Helen's fate, luck and misfortune are determined at the point of the plot divergence. For example, in the caught train scenario, she becomes empowered after discovering her partner being unfaithful and makes positive changes to her life, while in the other scenario where she misses the train and remains unaware of her boyfriend's cheating, she remains in a less than satisfying relationship and life. Dannenberg (2012: 122) claims that counterfactuality in films like *Sliding Doors* and the sci-fi drama *Donnie Darko* (made in 2001 and directed by Richard Kelly) whose 'narratives hinge on the speculation of how alternate worlds can be triggered by one key alteration in a sequence of events' offer a 'profitable plot motif'. I would also add the highly successful 2016 film *La La Land* to the list of films offering an alternative, counterfactual scenario imagined simultaneously by the protagonists Mia and Sebastian before being disnarrated. (See Lambrou 2018, 2019.)

7. The disnarrated: What does not happen

Where there is counterfactual storytelling generated by a forking path as described by Bremond and Cancalon (1980) and Borges (2000 [1944]) there is usually disnarration (Prince 1988). The very act of conjuring up two plot possibilities but only allowing one to progress means the automatic dismissal of the other, unless the plots exist simultaneously. The term 'disnarration' as a dimension in narrative fiction was first proposed by the narratologist Gerald Prince (1988: 2), from the French 'dénarré', to describe 'the events that do not happen but, nonetheless, are referred to (in a negative or hypothetical mode) by the narrative text'. Disnarrated events can be expressed by the narration, narrator or character and presents 'The elements in a narrative that explicitly consider and refer to what does not take place ("X didn't happen")' (Prince 2003: 22) and it expresses 'hopes, desires, imaginings and pondering, unreasonable expectations and incorrect beliefs' (Prince 1992: 34–5). One function of disnarration is that it foregrounds 'the dynamic construction of the storyworld, constitution of characters, plot development' while also 'radically undermining the suspension of disbelief' (McRae 2010: 128).

In *The French Lieutenant's Woman*, the first ending where Charles daydreams about his marriage to Ernestina is an example of events that are described and then dismissed as something that did not happen because in Chapter 45, readers are told that

> the last few pages you have read are *not what happened* but what he spent the hours between London and Exeter imagining *what might happen*. (327)

The revelation that the marriage is *not what happened* negates the fact that the event ever took place while imagining *what might happen*. The hypothetical scenario is imagined and signalled linguistically by the use of modality, that is 'the degree of assurance or commitment with which a speaker vouches for a proposition' (Fowler 1986: 57). Modality used in this context serves to convey the attitude and presence of the author-narrator as it is

> the means by which people express their degree of commitment to the truth of the propositions they utter, and their views on the desirability or otherwise of the states of affairs referred. (131)

The modal verb *might* expresses a hypothetical outcome in this case, a narrative refusal where 'direct narratorial references to some of the specifics or what might have been and yet is not' (Warhol 2010: 46). Narrative refusals expand Prince's (1988) work on the unnarratable and disnarration by offering further subcategories to account for these dimensions in fiction, such as paranarratable, described earlier in the chapter. The paranarratable or 'what wouldn't be told because of formal convention' which 'comprises that which transgresses a law of literary genre' (Warhol 2005: 226) would account for the final two inconclusive endings for Charles and Sarah as the literary genre and conventions of Victorian fiction would not favour plot outcomes where the male protagonist would consider a union with a progressive, anti-heroine like Sarah instead of the more conventional and socially equal Ernestina. In Chapter 55, Fowles comments on this point when discussing his endings as,

> the conventions of Victorian fiction allow ... no place for the open, the inconclusive ending; and I preached earlier of the freedom characters must be given. (389)

Why does Fowles give readers what Scruggs (1985) calls 'a red herring' to describe the first ending that ultimately works to confuse plot structure and the readers? One explanation is that while the novel is set in Victorian England, it is a postmodern text written in 1969 and therefore 'altered by the revisionist perspectives of the modern novel and modern criticism, as well as by the implications of the exploded, centrifugal universe of the modern world' (96). Fowles deliberately gives readers an anti-Victorian novel ending as Charles neither marries Ernestina nor Sarah. Mandal (2017) convincingly argues that the inconclusive ending is because it is Sarah who drives the plot rather than Fowles offering an experiment in fiction and narrative. Sarah is consistently described as a 'remarkable' woman throughout the novel (at least seven times) and, as Scruggs (1985: 102) points out, it is not because she fits the Victorian ideal but more because 'she fulfils it in a new way' and is given the progressive attitude and psychology of a modern woman (McHale 1987). Fowles creates a character in Sarah who appears autonomous and is wilful and as real as you and I in their story/text-world. This is also true of Charles, whose fateful meeting with Sarah could have been avoided, but early in the novel, in Chapter 13, the author-narrator comments on his inability to control his characters who must also have their 'freedom':

> It is only when our characters and events begin to disobey us that they begin to live. When Charles left Sarah on her cliff-edge, I ordered him to walk straight back to Lyme Regis. But he did not; he gratuitously turned and went down to the Dairy. (98)

The whole of Chapter 13 digresses from the novel and the author-narrator ponders through extradiegetic narration the role of the author and how his characters are not real yet have agency. It is a startling admission that breaks the illusion from fiction to address readers in the discourse-world with:

> This story I am telling is all imagination. These characters I create never existed outside my own mind. (97)

It is one of many examples in the novel of fiction about fiction where 'the supposedly absolute reality of the author becomes just another level of fiction' (McHale 1987: 197). Paradoxically, while Fowles (2004: 99) explains that his characters are fictional, he also asserts that they 'still exist' and have autonomy despite being subjected to the author-narrator's whim. Through author metalepsis, Fowles, as a figure inserted into the story carelessly, decides Charles and Sarah's destiny by flipping a coin. Interruptions in the plot and insertion of the author-narrator at various points in the diegesis function to show off the author's power as 'by breaking the frame around his world, the author foregrounds his own superior reality' (McHale 1987: 197). The act of 'frame-breaking' by novelists such as Fowles functions in that

> first they lull us into taking the 'picture' for 'reality,' strengthening our habitual tendencies, and then suddenly our attention is focused on the spectacles through which we are looking, and we are made to see that what we had taken for 'reality' was only the imposition of the frame. (Josipovici 1971: 297)

The author's reality is still the readers' fiction but by 'lulling' our attention and redirecting our focus, readers are engaged and entertained by the range of techniques Fowles uses to tell his story.

8. Conclusion

The French Lieutenant's Woman is a classic example of metafiction, or fiction about fiction, in a postmodernist novel. The novel self-consciously considers the fictionality of plot structure through the use of metalepsis including author metalepsis, as the author-narrator moves between levels of narration and transgresses the text's boundaries. Fowles (2004) as author-narrator presents readers with a challenging story structure that deviates from conventional patterns of storytelling to manipulate the plot and, consequently, the readers and their schematic expectations of a Victorian romantic novel in a strategy central to narrative refusals (Warhol 2005, 2010, 2013). The three counterfactual endings are as unexpected as they are unconventional, especially as the first is disnarrated as Charles's daydream, while the second and third endings may exist simultaneously as Charles and Sarah consider and enact their desires autonomously while under the direction of Fowles as author-narrator and character in the story. As stories conventionally have only one ending, readers are invited as part of the author's manipulation to engage with the plot and decide which of the final two counterfactual endings they prefer. In this process, readers actively engage with the disnarration of the other scenario at the moment of accepting one ending in favour of the other. The elimination of one path subsequently allows the other path to exist and provide a conclusive ending. Fowles's non-linear, counterfactual storytelling as a narrative dimension exemplifies Bremond and Cancalon's (1980: 388) concept of fictional stories offering a 'network of possibilities' and the reality of forked paths (Borges 2000 [1944]) as all texts offer a labyrinth of plot options. In *The French Lieutenant's Woman*, the unrealized possibilities are made explicit even if certain path options are not followed, drawing attention to the fictional status of the characters and the author's metafictive role in having created them. As Ryan (2005: 590) observes,

> Some events make better stories than others because they project a wider variety of forking paths on the narrative map. Even though the story can only follow one path, the understanding of these events involves a consideration of the 'virtual narratives' of the unrealised sequences that branch out of the event.

As Dannenberg (2008: 2) explains in her discussion of the function of counterfactual divergence triggered by the 'the bifurcation or branching of narrative paths', characters and plot are allowed to take alternative paths and characters are able to reflect and evaluate their situations. This is certain of Charles and Sarah as the final and third ending reflects their true selves and could not have resulted in a happy ending together. The subverted story schema of *The French Lieutenant's Woman* presents readers with a compelling, postmodern narrative with the additional outcome being that we as readers have all been manipulated.

References

Baldick, C. (2009) *Oxford Dictionary of Literary Terms*. Oxford: Oxford University Press.
Baroni, R. (2016) 'Virtualities of plot and dynamics of re-reading', in Baroni, R. and Revaz, F. (eds) *Narrative Sequence in Contemporary Narratologies*, pp. 87–103. Columbus: Ohio State University Press.
Bartlett, F. C. (1932) *Remembering*. New York: Cambridge University Press.
Borges, J. (2000 [1944]) 'The garden of forking paths', in *Collected Fictions*, trans. Andrew Hurley, pp. 119–28. London: Penguin.
Bremond, C. and Cancalon, E. D. (1980) 'The logic of narrative possibilities', *New Literary History* 11(3): 387–411.
Cook, G. (1990) *A Theory of Discourse Deviation: The Application of Schema Theory to the Analysis of Literary Discourse*. Unpublished PhD thesis. University of Leeds.
Dannenberg, H. P. (2008) *Coincidence and Counterfactuality: Plotting Time and Space in Narrative Fiction*. Lincoln, NE and London: University of Nebraska Press.
Dannenberg, H. (2012) 'Fleshing out the blend: The representation of counterfactuals in alternate history in print, film, and television narratives', in Schneider, R. and Hartner, M. (eds) *Blending and the Study of Narrative*, pp. 121–45. Berlin/Boston: De Gruyter.
Dickens, C. (1848) *Dombey and Son*. London: Bradbury and Evans.
Donnie Darko (2001) directed by Richard Kelly.
Eliot, G. (1871-2) *Middlemarch*. London: William Blackwood and Sons.
Emmott, C. and Alexander, M. (2014) 'Schemata', in Hühn, P., Meister, J. C., Pier, J., and Schmid, W. (eds) *Handbook of Narratology*. 2nd edition. pp. 756–64. Berlin: de Gruyter.
Ferrebe, A. (2004) 'The gaze of the magus: Sexual/scopic politics in the novels of John Fowles', *Journal of Narrative Theory* 34(2): 207–26.
Fludernik, M. (2003) 'Scene shift, metalepsis, and the metaleptic mode', *Style* 37(4): 382–400.
Fowler, R. (1986) *Linguistic Criticism*. Oxford: Oxford University Press.
Fowles, J. (2004) *The French Lieutenant's Woman*. London: Vintage.
Gavins, J. (2007) *Text World Theory: An Introduction*. Edinburgh: Edinburgh University Press.
Genette, G. (1980 [1972]) *Narrative Discourse: An Essay in Method*. Ithaca: Cornell University Press.

Genette, G. (1988 [1983]) *Narrative Discourse Revisited*. Ithaca: Cornell University Press.

Josipovici, G. (1971) *The World and the Book: A Study of Modern Fiction*. London: Macmillan.

La La Land (2016) directed by Damien Chazelle.

Lambrou, M. (2018) '"*La La Land*": Counterfactuality, disnarration and the forked (motorway) path', in Page, R., Busse, B., and Nørgaard, N. (eds) *Rethinking Language, Text and Context: Interdisciplinary Research in Stylistics in Honour of Michael Toolan*, pp. 29–42. London: Routledge.

Lambrou, M. (2019) *Disnarration and the Unmentioned in Fact and Fiction*. London: Palgrave.

Levin, Y. (2016) 'Metalepsis and the author figure in modernist and postmodernist fiction', *Twentieth-Century Literature* 62(3): 289–308.

Malina, D. (2002) *Breaking the Frame: Metalepsis and the Construction of the Subject*. Columbus, Ohio: The Ohio State University Press.

Mandal, M. (2017) '"Eyes a man could drown in": Phallic myth and femininity in John Fowles's *The French Lieutenant's Woman*', *Interdisciplinary Literary Studies* 19(3): 274–98.

Mandler, J. M. and Johnson, N. S. (1977) 'Remembrance of things parsed: Story structure and recall', *Cognitive Psychology* 9(1): 111–51.

McHale, B. (1987) *Postmodernist Fiction*. New York: Methuen.

McRae, A. (2010) 'Enhancing the critical apparatus for understanding metanarration: Discourse deixis refined', *Journal of Literary Semantics* 39(2): 119–42.

Mulvey, L. (1975) 'Visual pleasure and narrative cinema', *Screen* 16(3): 6–18.

Prince, G. (1988) 'The disnarrated', *Style* 22(1): 1–8.

Prince, G. (1992) *Narrative as Theme: Studies in French Fiction*. Lincoln, NE: University of Nebraska Press.

Prince, G. (2003) *Dictionary of Narratology*. Lincoln and London: University of Nebraska Press.

Propp, V. (1968 [1928]) *Morphology of the Folktale*. Austin: University of Texas Press.

Riddle-Harding, J. (2017) *Similes, Puns and Counterfactuals in Literary Narrative: Visible Figures*. London: Routledge.

Roese, N. J. and Olson, J. M. (1995) 'Counterfactual thinking: A critical overview', in Roese, N. J. and Olson, J. M. (eds) *What Might Have Been: The Social Psychology of Counterfactual Thinking*, pp. 1–56. Mahwah, NJ: Lawrence Erlbaum Associates.

Rumelhart, D. E. (1975) 'Notes on a schema for stories', in Bobrow, D. G. and Collins, A. (eds) *Representation and Understanding: Studies in Cognitive Science*, pp. 211–35. New York: Academic Press.

Ryan, M.-L. (2005) 'Tellability', in Herman, D., Jahn, M., and Ryan, M.-L. (eds) *Routledge Encyclopedia of Narrative Theory*, pp. 589–91. London: Routledge.

Scruggs, C. (1985) 'The two endings of "The French Lieutenant's Woman"', *Modern Fiction Studies* 31(1): 95–113.

Sliding Doors (1996) directed by Peter Howitt.
Stanzel, F. (1984 [1979]) *A Theory of Narrative*, trans. Charlotte Goedsche. Cambridge: Cambridge University Press.
The French Lieutenant's Woman (1981) directed by Karel Reisz.
Turner, M. (1987) *Death is the Mother of Beauty: Mind, Metaphor, Criticism*. Chicago: Chicago University Press.
Warhol, R. (2010) '"What might have been is not what is": Dickens's narrative refusals', *Dickens's Studies Annual* 41: 45–60.
Warhol, R. (2013) '"It is of little use for me to tell you": George Eliot's narrative refusals', in Anderson, A. and Shaw, H. E. (eds) *The Blackwell Companion to George Eliot*, pp. 46–61. West Sussex: Wiley-Blackwell.
Warhol, R. R. (2005) 'Neonarrative; or, how to render the unnarratable in realist fiction and contemporary film', in Phelan, J. and Rabinowitz, P. (eds) *A Companion to Narrative Theory*, pp. 220–31. Oxford: Blackwell.
Werth, P. (1999) *Text Worlds: Representing Conceptual Space in Discourse*. Harlow: Longman.

3

Social deixis in literature

Andrea Macrae

1. Introduction

This chapter explores manipulation of the reader through deictic positioning. It focuses in particular on the functioning of what is sometimes called 'empathetic', 'social' or 'relational' deixis (Lyons 1977; Levinson 1983; Stockwell 2002). Grishikova (2018: 201) notes that some deictic terms, such as 'this' and 'that', and 'here' and 'there', while often primarily having demonstrative or spatial meaning, may also signal 'empathy or sympathy, intimacy, intensive sensation, joint attention, familiarity, routine'. As Grishikova's list suggests, neither 'empathetic' nor 'social' really cover or clarify the range of meanings that words such as 'this' and 'that' can signal, and this is before we bring honorifics into the mix. 'Relational', on the other hand, is perhaps too encompassing: all deixis is relational in the sense of conveying a relationship. This chapter briefly explores some of the main theoretical issues within previous descriptions and discussions of social deixis. These issues include fuzzy definitions of, and varying stances on, some of the things often called upon as determiners of social deixis (e.g. 'social situation', 'social relationship'); perceived similarities with modality and evaluative language; and the pragmatic complexities of honorifics. On the basis of this exploration, the chapter offers some propositions about the functioning of social deixis, in general and in literature specifically, which might help to define and delimit it as a subcategory of deixis and enhance the analytical use value of that subcategory. The chapter then draws the discussion in, using these propositions to illustrate some of the social deictic functioning of aspects of Dylan Thomas's poem 'Do not go gentle into that good night', and in particular, the different dimensions of how this social deixis is functioning across the poem's discourse architecture.

2. A theoretical discussion of social deixis in literature

Deixis is language which points to its referent and in doing so encodes the particular perspective (the deictic centre) from which that reference is made (Bühler 2011). For example, within the sentence '*I'm going over there now to that stall*', each of the italicized word deictically encodes a relationship (spatial, temporal, etc.) between the speaker, the context in which that speaker is speaking (the 'context of utterance') and the stall to which the speaker is referring. Deictic words and phrases have a combined indexical and symbolic value (Burks 1948). They are indexical in that they tend to encode some characteristics of the referent (e.g. 'yesterday' can be used to refer to a 24-hour period, the end of that period preceding the instance of utterance by up to 24 hours). Their symbolic value is captured by Rauh (1978: 30, translated and cited in Herman 2002: 346–7) in the following: 'Their meaning cannot be described independently of their use, but is rather dependent on the situation of a speech event, the extralinguistic context of an utterance. The meaning of deictic expressions changes with the utterer of an utterance and with his or her position in space and time', hence the day one can refer to as 'yesterday' changes as each day passes. Deixis is an inherent property of some words (such as 'I' and 'you') but is more often a matter of usage (compare 'I'm leaving now', in which 'now' is referring to the immediate moment of utterance, with 'Now, what's going on here?', in which 'now' is more likely to be being used phatically to attract attention and take the conversational floor).

The primacy of context in deictic meaning is highlighted by Levinson (1983: 54) in his assertion that deixis 'concerns the ways in which languages encode ... features of the context of utterance ..., and thus also concerns ways in which the interpretation of utterances depends on the analysis of that context of utterance'. Context is also foregrounded in Fillmore's description of deixis as 'those formal properties of utterances which are determined by, and which are interpreted by knowing, certain aspects of the communication act in which the utterances in question have a role' (Fillmore 1971: 219). Deixis is fundamentally pragmatic in its context dependency, and indeed Levinson (1983: 58) explicitly describes the deictic centre as 'a set of pragmatic indices'.

Deixis in literature involves manipulation of the reader in the same way that deixis in face-to-face speech involves manipulation of the hearer: in order to comprehend the deictic language of the speaker, the hearer must conceptually project to the deictic centre around which that deictic language is oriented (Bühler 2011: 153; Duchan, Bruder and Hewitt 1995; Lyons 1977: 578–9). Often the speaker's language is oriented solely around her own deictic centre, and so this will be the initial locus to which the hearer will project, but sometimes a speaker herself might project to another deictic centre. One example of this is when a speaker tells a story which happened in the past, but shifts into the present tense part way through, for example, 'I got on the bus this morning, and I bump into a guy, and he says to me …'. Here the speaker is projecting into a past time version of herself and using the tense appropriate to that deictic centre, potentially to create a sense of immediacy. In the context of literary fiction and poetry, narrators and poetic personas, as de facto 'speakers', often project to the deictic centres of past or hypothetical versions of themselves, and also, more prevalently in fiction, to the deictic centres of characters (as is discussed in relation to Adamson 1995, below). Just as in face-to-face conversation hearers must follow speakers' paths of projection, in literary contexts readers must conceptually follow fictional speakers' paths of projection to make sense of and resolve the deictic cues (Macrae 2012). Deictic language therefore manipulates the reader in the sense that the act of processing deictic language entails that the reader conceptually re-positions her own deictic centre to the locus to which the deictic language is anchored. Deixis is in this way a fundamental part of the establishment of perspective: deictic language manipulates readers by leading them through paths of projection as part of their processing and conceptual construction of the perspectives of poetic personas, narrators and characters.

Discussions of deixis traditionally include five categories: person, spatial, temporal, social and discourse deixis. Person deixis includes personal, possessive, reflexive and demonstrative pronouns, along with the definite article. Spatial deixis includes spatial adverbs and verbs of motion. Demonstrative pronouns can also be used within spatial deixis to suggest relative proximity (e.g. 'that cup' is implicitly distal in contrast to 'this cup'). Temporal deixis includes tensed verbs, temporal adverbs and prepositions when combined with non-deictic temporal units of measurement (e.g. 'in two months'). Demonstratives are also used in temporal deixis (e.g. 'that day'). Temporal deictic expressions sometimes draw on spatial deixis, partly because time is often metaphorically conceptualized spatially (one can bring a meeting 'forward', look forward to 'the week ahead', etc., cf. Moore 2014).

Descriptions of person, spatial and temporal deixis are fairly consistent across accounts (e.g. Benveniste 1971; Jarvella and Klein 1982; Lyons 1977; Rauh 1983). Discourse deixis is more contentious (on which see Macrae 2019), particularly with regards to its relationship to anaphora. Social deixis, however, is arguably more contentious still, in that accounts of it vary to the extent of naming and conceptualizing the category in different ways. While Brown and Levinson (1978), Fillmore (1975), Levinson (1983), Lyons (1968) and Rauh (1978) are happy with the term 'social deixis', Adamson (1995), Lyons (1977) and Semino (1997) discuss 'empathetic deixis', Lakoff (1974) talks about 'emotional deixis', Green (1995) describes 'subjective' deixis and Stockwell (2000, 2002) prefers the term 'relational deixis'. There is substantial overlap between these theorists' descriptions, as we will see later – enough to be able to consider these accounts as describing broadly the same category of deixis, which this chapter will call 'social deixis' for now – but there are significant discrepancies too. There is therefore at present no clear agreement on what comprises this category of deixis, and what this kind of deixis is used to communicate.

The last stanza of Dylan Thomas's well-known villanelle, 'Do not go gentle into that good night'[1] (1952), is rich in deixis, all of which is italicized in the following:

And *you*, *my father*, *there* on *the* sad height,
Curse, bless, *me now* with *your* fierce tears, *I* pray.
Do not *go* gentle *into that* good night.
Rage, rage against *the* dying of *the* light.

Some of the different accounts of deixis listed above would include only a few of the italicized words as social deixis, while others would include all of them and more (e.g. sad, fierce and good). The stanza offers a good example, then, through which to explore and test out what social deixis may be, and what effects it contributes to within the reader's dynamic processing of the text, and the deictic manipulation of the reader's positioning and perspective through that processing.

One complicating factor in considering social deixis in literature, specifically, is what Short (1996: 260) refers to as literature's 'discourse architecture', in that literature often involves multiple speaker-addressee relationships. For example, novels stereotypically involve character-to-character communication, narrator-to-narratee communication and (overarching) author-to-reader communication. In the last stanza of 'Do not go gentle into that good night', we have a poetic persona addressing his father (and the pair may or may not be autobiographical representations of Dylan Thomas and his father), and additionally, overarchingly, Dylan Thomas addressing his many prospective readers. As we shall see, though, the speaker-addressee relations are potentially more complicated.

The significance of discourse architecture becomes apparent when one starts to look at definitions of social deixis. Fillmore (1975: 76) describes social deixis as 'that aspect of sentences which reflect or establish or are determined by certain realities of the social situation in which the speech act occurs'. For Huang, 'social deixis' (2007: 163), which he also calls 'relational social deixis' (2007: 164) is concerned with the relative social status of, and 'social relationship between', a speaker and addressee or third person (or entity) referred to (2007: 163). For Levinson (1979: 206), social deixis is 'those aspects of language structure that are anchored to the social identities of participants (including bystanders) in the speech event, or to relations between them, or to relations between them and other referents'. These theorists thus refer to 'social situation', 'social relationship' and 'social identities'. But what do these terms mean in practice, and how many different social relationships, for example, may be 'in play' at any one time? If we start to look closely at the kinds of language each of these theorists focuses upon in their descriptions of social (empathetic/ subjective etc.) deixis, we can infer what kinds of relationships and identities each perceives to be involved.

Several discussions of this kind of deixis start with (and indeed solely focus on) the use of the demonstratives 'this', 'that', 'these' and 'those' (and sometimes additionally 'the' and 'a'). As mentioned, demonstratives are used for person, spatial and temporal deixis, but, as Semino (1997: 34) discusses, they can also be used to convey 'psychological or emotional distance, in which case they reflect the speaker's attitude towards entities or people'. Semino follows Lyons (1977) and Levinson (1983) in calling this 'empathetic deixis', and offers the contrasting examples 'I would be really pleased to meet *this* new friend of yours' and 'I don't want *that* new friend of yours to come anywhere near this house!' (1997: 34, emphasis in the original). Semino writes 'The difference between *this* and *that* is not to do with physical distance but with the speaker's attitude to the addressee's new friend', the first example expressing the speaker's 'wish to have a close relationship with the friend', whereas in the second example 'the relationship is constructed as more distant' (1997: 34). Semino's 'empathetic deixis' therefore focuses on demonstratives as markers of attitude.

Lakoff (1974), though, points out that while 'this' and 'that' *can* function to express attitude (under the heading of 'emotional deixis', in her account), the picture is complex, in that there are many other possible functions, and in that the intended effects are not always discernible from the potentially unintended. Lakoff argues that 'that' can be used to 'establish emotional solidarity' between the speaker and addressee, and gives the example 'That Henry Kissinger sure knows his way around Hollywood' (1974: 352), whereby 'that' may primarily be an attention-drawing determiner and only secondarily a distancer regarding

'Henry Kissinger', while at the same time, suggesting the speaker anticipates the hearer will have a similar attitude to Kissinger (worthy of discussion, distanced, etc.). She also compares 'How's your throat?', 'How's the throat?' and 'How's that throat?' (1974: 352), and finds that 'both *the* and *that* seem colloquial' and also that they can function to convey less distance between the speaker and the hearer's problem (a bad throat) than the second-person possessive pronoun might. She suggests that 'the' perhaps has this effect in that it communicates that the speaker has thought about this issue before and therefore it is of concern to the speaker, 'since *the* is used of information the speaker assumes to have been previously known' (1974: 352, emphasis in the original). 'This', on the other hand, can replace 'a', as in the example 'There was this tradition in Ancient Greece that the Trojans were descended from Dardanus' (1974: 248) or 'I was driving home and this guy came out of nowhere' (author's own example). 'This' replaces 'a' here not just to signal that the information being discussed is not necessarily 'new' in the discourse (which Lakoff notes is one of its discourse deictic functions), but also to 'give greater vividness' to the utterance and to 'involve the addressee in it more fully' (1974: 349). Demonstratives and determiners do not necessarily fall simply along psychologically and metaphorically proximal versus distal lines. Arguably, what (and perhaps all) one can say is that these words 'indicate that (the speaker assumes that) the discourse participants share some knowledge or emotion about the referent of the demonstrative ... [which] is grounds for experiencing solidarity' in the sense of like-mindedness, empathy, etc. (Wolter 2006: 84, cf. Potts and Shwartz 2010). What this work usefully foregrounds, therefore, is that deixis of this kind can express the speaker's attitude to the referent and/or the speaker's beliefs about the hearer's attitude to the referent, and the two are not always clearly distinguishable.

Adamson (1995) uses the term 'empathetic deixis' differently, moving beyond demonstratives and determiners to explore focalization through a character where the person, spatial and temporal deixis slips to and from the loci of narrator-focalizer and character-focalizer. She describes this as a 'transference of subjectivity' and as 'empathetic subjectivity: a he/she is understood "as if" it were an I' (1995: 197). Adamson's discussion focuses on temporal deixis, specifically the predominance of phrases which combine use of the past tense (anchored to a narratorial deictic centre) and cotemporal deictic adverbials (anchored to a character's deictic centre) as a useful criterion marking 'empathetic narrative' (1995: 195) (e.g. 'Agnes was worried now'). Adamson's version of 'empathetic deixis', in the context of literature at least, is therefore chiefly concerned with narratorial projection (bringing the reader's projection along too) to the spatio-temporal context of a character. Here 'empathy' is less a matter of attitude than of kinds of identification.

Like Adamson, Lyons finds 'empathetic deixis' to be chiefly about projection to another's deictic centre. He writes:

> It frequently happens that 'this' is selected rather than 'that', 'here' rather than 'there', and 'now' rather than 'then', when the speaker is personally involved with the entity, situation or place to which he is referring or is identifying himself with the attitude or viewpoint of the addressee. ... There is no doubt that the speaker's subjective involvement and his appeal to shared experience are relevant factors in the selection of those demonstratives and adverbs which, in their normal use, indicate proximity. At this point deixis merges with modality. (1977: 677)

While Adamson describes a mix of deictic language oriented around the speaker's deictic centre and deictic language oriented around another deictic centre, Lyons's version suggests a more comprehensive (e.g. also attitudinal) projection to that other deictic centre. Notably, too, he feels that this kind of deictic projection 'merges with modality'. Modality is prominent in Green's 'subjective deixis' as well, which he defines as 'those elements and terms which encode the subjective experience of the encoder primarily through epistemic and deontic modal verbs. Although all aspects in some way reflect or encode the subjective position of the speaker, the modals explicitly do so' (1995: 22). Modality is not conventionally described as deictic in its own right, but Green and Lyons are not the only two to draw it into deixis.

Stockwell's 'relational deixis' is one of the broader approaches to this category. He defines relational deixis as expressions which 'encode the social viewpoint of the narrator and characters (Levinson (1983: 89) calls this 'social' deixis; Green (1995: 22) terms it 'subjective' deixis) and adds that this' is most easily apparent in the forms of naming and address used by narrators for other characters, including nicknames' (2000: 39). Stockwell also includes modality in this summary. Two years later he expands on this account to describe relational deixis as

> expressions that encode the social viewpoint and relative situations of authors, narrators, characters, and readers, including modality and expression of point of view and focalisation; naming and address conventions; evaluative word choices. For example, the narrating author of Henry Fielding's *Tom Jones* is very polite to the reader in direct address, and adopts different stylistic tones of 'voice' in relation to the different characters of his novel. (2002: 46)

He includes within relational deixis 'proper names and address forms ("Colonel Mustard", "Your Excellency") [which] serve to mark out relational deictic centres, as do evaluative and judgemental adjectives and adverbials, which indicate a narrative or authorial voice – a sense of a socially situated person "speaking"'. Stockwell (2002: 54) finds that 'expressions of social politeness and markers of modality ("it seems to be", "it might be", "may" "will", "would have been" and so on) also encode the attitudes and social relations of deictic centres'. Finally, he explicitly includes shifts in or maintenance of 'point of view and a character's apparent mind-style' as part of relational deixis (2002: 54). This version of 'social deixis' is unusually wide: while others like Lyons (1977) and Green (1995) have included within this category markers of attitude and point of view beyond and apart from a metaphorical scale of social and emotional proximity or distance, the range of language involved in Stockwell's account is markedly rich.

Parts of Lyons's descriptions of deixis (1977) focus on terms of address, and so intersect with Stockwell's definition. Lyons (1977: 574–5) tries to separate 'deictic and social' roles, seemingly discounting the latter from deixis, and yet he includes status-marking terms of address within his discussion of person deixis. He writes 'The most obvious effect of social role, as a contextual variable, lies in its determination of terms of address: as when "Sir", "Doctor" or "My Lord" (in the courtroom) are used with vocative function in English. The speaker in using such expressions accepts, and shows that he accepts, his role vis-à-vis the addressee' (1977: 575). 'Social role', for Lyons (1977: 641), is, then, specifically related to status, about which he proposes that 'since the principle is unaffected by the number of degrees and dimensions of status that are lexicalised in a language-system, we will, for simplicity, admit just one dimension and two degrees: superior and inferior, lexicalised in the opposition "master" : "servant"'. Describing 'social deixis' Levinson (1979: 206) has a similar focus and includes 'honorifics, titles of address, second person pronominal alternates and associated verb agreements, and the like', and Herman (2002: 332) likewise lists within deixis 'honorific terms and participles that index interlocutors' social status (sir, Dr. Herman)'. A concern with honorifics (and, arguably, dishonorifics) of different kinds is therefore a key part of several accounts.

Huang, following Brown and Levinson (1978), also focuses on honorifics. As mentioned earlier, Huang (2007: 164) paraphrases 'social deixis' as 'relational social deixis', and finds it to be concerned with the relative social status of, and 'social relationship between', a speaker and addressee or third person or entity referred to (2007: 163). Though he does not define 'social relationship', his subsequent account of relational social deixis suggests he is primarily concerned with relative status and formality. Huang (2007: 166), like Brown and Levinson (1978), notes that in some languages 'social deixis can be accomplished by a wide range of linguistic devices, including personal pronouns, forms of address, affixes, clitics and particles, and the choice of vocabulary'. With Huang, then, we again have a (albeit differently) widening scope for what can function as social deixis.

Huang describes 'four axes of relational social deixis' (originally defined as the 'honorific axes' by Brown and Levinson 1978) through which 'relational information in social deixis can be represented'. These axes are 'between (i) speaker and referent (e.g., reference honorifics), (ii) speaker and addressee (e.g., addressee honorifics), (iii) speaker and bystander (e.g., bystander honorifics), and (iv) speaker and setting (e.g., levels of formality)' (2007: 164). The first three axes originally come from Comrie (1976), to which Brown and Levinson (1978) added the fourth (speaker and setting). Reference honorifics and addressee honorifics are honorifics of the kind listed by Lyons (1977), Stockwell (2000) and Herman (2002) above. While, as mentioned, Lyons (1977: 575) argues that in using addressee honorifics a speaker 'accepts, and shows that he accepts, his role vis-à-vis the addressee', addressee honorifics, similarly to 'this' and 'that', can in fact have various pragmatic functions. Huang (2007: 170) points out that certain modes of address such as 'mate' can be used 'to claim in-group solidarity', while Brown and Levinson show that respect-marking forms of address can be 'strategically used to soften face threatening acts', as could be the case in their example 'Excuse me, sir, but would you mind if I close the window?' (1978: 188). Honorifics and the like are therefore not only markers of status (or, more directly, markers of acknowledgement of status) but can have a range of pragmatic purposes. Relative social status and relative social proximity can be conceptualized as two scales, with coordinates along them, and with relations between those coordinates. However, even with respect to referent and addressee honorifics alone, those scales may be difficult to separate, the coordinates of speaker, addressee(s) and referent may all be in play in any one utterance, and multiple pragmatic functions may be involved.

The third and fourth axes, speaker and bystander, and speaker and setting, bring in the significance to social deixis of overhearers and of context (though maintaining a focus on honorifics). Huang describes bystander honorifics as 'forms … used by the speaker to signify respect to a bystander, including participants in the role of audience and non-participant overhearers'. He gives the example of 'mother-in-law' languages in Australian aboriginal languages (e.g. Dyirbal) whereby 'nearly all … vocabulary has to be replaced by "special 'avoidance' lexical items"' when speaking in the presence of, even if not directly addressing, one's mother-in-law (2007: 164). Likewise, the speaker and setting axis is marked by 'replacement vocabularies'. Brown and Levinson (1978: 186) explain their inclusion of this axis as founded in the belief that there is 'a socially deictic relation between speakers and situations – or, perhaps better, between social roles assumed by speaker and audience, as partially conditioned by setting and activity type'. As an example, they point out that 'in English, on formal occasions, one may use *dine* to replace *eat*, *residence* to replace *home*, and *bestow* to replace *give* (1978: 181, emphasis in the original). Adjusting vocabulary according to respect for or the needs of overhearers or context (including socio-political contexts, institutional contexts, etc.) could, by extension, include even speaking in a different language (e.g. English speakers speaking in French when in the French embassy in London).

This survey of theory of social deixis illustrates a range of thinking. Within the work discussed here, social deixis is conceptualized both narrowly and widely. It is conceived of more narrowly in two ways: in terms of 'empathetic' or 'emotional' use of demonstratives and articles or in terms of 'social' or 'relational' use of honorific address. It is conceived of more widely in two ways, too, both under subheadings of more 'social' or 'relational' uses: including modality and evaluative language or including replacement vocabularies. The wider accounts evoke three questions. First, what is the nature of the deictic centre, and the deictic relationships, in modality, evaluative language and replacement vocabularies? Secondly, given the scope of evaluative language and replacement vocabularies, what, then, can be excluded from deixis as a category of language? Thirdly, what range or remit of social deixis, within that which has been discussed, is useful or relevant for analysis of the workings of deixis in literature, specifically?

What happens if we scale the concept of deixis back, and argue that modality, evaluative language and replacement vocabularies are *not* socially deictic, or at least not in the same sense as demonstratives, articles and terms of address? This argument can be made on two counts: an identifiable or implicit deictic centre seems less apparent in or essential to the workings of modality, evaluative language and replacement vocabularies and modality, evaluative language and replacement vocabularies do not seem to construct a relationship between speaker and referent, and/or between speaker and addressee, in the same sense as person, spatial and temporal deixis.

This would leave us with a smaller set of terms within social deixis, the function of which could possibly then be usefully divided into two subtypes: (1) *attitudinal-experiential deixis* and (2) *socio-relational deixis*. Attitudinal-experiential deixis would include the use of the determiners 'this', 'that', 'these', 'those', and the articles 'the' and 'a' (and feasibly also 'one'). Socio-relational deixis would include the use of terms of address (e.g. 'your ladyship') and related terms of reference (e.g. 'her ladyship') and titular and pronominal markers of relative social status or social or familial relationships. Notably, determiners, articles and terms of address have all been included within the category of person deixis in some accounts (e.g. Lyons 1977), but it is arguably worth demarcating their social function to the extent of distinguishing a separate social deictic category.

If we accept the proposition that there are two subtypes of social deixis – attitudinal-experiential deixis, and socio-relational deixis, as outlined above – we still need a caveat. This caveat can be formulated as follows: *an aspect of the meaning of determiners and articles, terms of address (and related terms of reference), and (dis)honorifics, etc., is socially deictic, but that deictic aspect may be less easily retrievable and/or less significant than other aspects of their meaning in some contexts because of various intersecting pragmatic factors.* Drawing on the survey above, these factors include, among others,

1. (im)politeness and the increase or redress of face threatening acts (as in the example from Brown and Levinson 1978 mentioned earlier)
2. the performative affirmation of (or, potentially, disruption of) the speaker-addressee relationship, through the linguistic construction of in- or out-group positions and/or solidarity. This is achievable through terms of address such as honorifics and nicknames, and through motivated selection of determiners and articles (as per Lakoff 1974). This kind of socio-relational deixis would contribute to broader language use determining and constructing a community of practice (Eckert and McConnell-Ginet 1992), including use of acronyms, slang terms, dialect words, etc.
3. the relationship between the referent and the addressee(s), as in the case of formal introductions in which the speaker may know the referent well (e.g. on first name terms) but the addressee does not, and so a more formal naming strategy may be more appropriate
4. setting, in the case where places carry tacit or formal codes of linguistic conduct determining terms of references and address, such as courts, schools and religious institutions
5. activity type (e.g. a speaker introducing a friend as a keynote lecturer through formal reference honorifics despite personal familiarity with the friend; a bride during wedding vows addressing her partner with her partner's full name)

6. symbolic referential value, specifically predetermined honorary status which is absolute rather than relative to the context or speaker, etc. (e.g. 'Madame President') (Levinson 1979: 207)
7. the salience of the referent to the speaker and addressee, specifically where the choice of demonstrative or determiner used to draw an addressee's attention to a specific referent is motivated by the relative prior salience of that referent to the addressee and/or speaker (Wolter 2006: 26).

In any one situation, a speaker's choice of determiner, article and/or term of address or reference may be motivated by several of these (often intersecting) factors, and those factors and their relative influence may be indistinguishable in practice. Social deixis is therefore arguably in many cases less simply or purely deictic than the other forms.

Bearing the preceding discussion in mind, less us now turn to how the suggested subtypes of social deixis can function in literature. Social deixis contributes most directly to two aspects of literary manipulation and meaning. First, social deixis supports the construction of structures of focalization. That is, social deixis contributes to language which signals whose perspective the voice of the narrator in prose fiction, or the poetic persona in poetry, for example, is currently focalizing through, and the nature of that perspective (as per Adamson 1995; Stockwell 2002). This perspective construction manipulates the reader in cueing conceptual projection. Secondly, social deixis conveys familiarity, status or respect, and so reflects and constructs in-group and out-group relationships (as per Lakoff 1974; Lyons 1977). In the contexts of fiction and poetry, this second function is relevant to relationships between characters, narrators/poetic personas, authors and readers.

It is particularly in relation to this second function that discourse architecture becomes significant. Literary communication always involves 'bystanders' in the sense that readers, while being the direct addressee of the author, are often positioned as 'overhearers' of address between other literary participants. This has a bearing on language beyond the specifically 'honorific axis' between speaker and bystander proposed by Comrie (1976) and Brown and Levinson (1978). For example, the fictional addressees and the reader-addressees often have different knowledge with respect to what is 'given' and what is 'new' (Clark and Haviland 1977), and are 'in' and 'out' of different groups. The author's choices with respect to use of social deixis will be variably shaped by each of the different communicative relationships (i.e. speakers and addressees) involved in any one communicative act, and can strategically overtly or covertly evoke the reader's consciousness of these communicative relationships, manipulating the reader's felt position in relation to in- and out-group identities.

3. Analysing social deixis as a means of literary manipulation of the reader: An example

The last stanza of Dylan Thomas's villanelle 'Do not go gentle into that good night' is a helpful example through which to briefly explore these matters within a literary context, and in turn a focus on social deixis adds to analytic insights into the text, in part because of the ways in which the communicative acts involved are distributed across its interesting discourse architecture. The title of the poem is also its opening line. This line goes on to alternate with 'Rage, rage against the dying of the light' as a stanza-closing refrain throughout the five tercets and final quatrain of poem. In the first stanza, these two lines function as imperatives as if addressed to the reader and/or potentially as self-address on the part of the poetic persona. In the four subsequent stanzas, the refrain modifies 'wise men', 'good men', 'wild men' and lastly 'grave men', for example 'wise men … rage, rage against the dying of the light'. For much of the poem, then, the reader may feel positioned as the primary addressee, addressed by the poetic persona. In the final stanza, however, the discourse architecture changes, or, to be more precise, the discourse architecture is revealed to have been more complex than might thus far have been thought. As Westphal (1994: 113) notes, the whole poem turns on line 16, 'And you, my father, there on the sad height'. The second person pronoun 'you' is used for the first time in the poem, and is swiftly followed by 'my father', which both clarifies the referent of that 'you' and introduces the 'father' of the poetic persona as the person, who it now seems has been the primary addressee all along. The reader is demoted to the position of an overhearer, and the communicative act of the poem as a whole is latterly reconceptualized as not a generalized urging of will to life but a personal and desperate plea from a son to his perhaps dying father.

Edwards (2016: 75) finds that the four words 'And you, my father' 'usher us into an intimate space'. He notes that Thomas's structure is replicated in Elizabeth Bishop's villanelle 'One Art' which talks generally of losing things throughout the first five tercets, and then, in the first words of the closing stanza, shifts, with 'Even losing you'. For Edwards (2016: 76), that 'both poems turn to a direct address to a loved one, that everything else in the poem becomes a way to load emotion onto that one word "you" is … not accidental'. The discourse architecture of both villanelles is such that with the closing stanza what had been read as general address by a poetic persona to readers is retrospectively reconceived as direct address by a poetic persona to a character-addressee, with the reader positioned as a 'bystander'. In both poems, the most 'intimate' reading is a biographical reading. Several critics have offered such a reading of 'Do not go gentle into that good night' (e.g. Edwards 2016; Westphal 1994). In these readings, the author and poetic persona are in at least some senses aligned, and likewise the referent of 'you' and 'my father' is aligned with Thomas's father. The 'activity type' of the communication is therefore conceivably both 'literary poem' and 'familial grief-stricken plea'.

If the final stanza did now position the reader only and simply as a 'bystander', the sudden shift in the social deictic positioning of the reader, relative to the depicted relationship between the speaker and (primary) addressee, might potentially evoke a sense of intrusion, voyeurism and the like, along with one or more of an array of feelings of transient confusion, wrong-footing, displacement, relief, etc. However, the social deixis of Thomas's final stanza seems to explicitly foreground both layers of the communicative act – that is, the son-to-father communication (the real Thomas and his father, or otherwise) and the simultaneous poet-to-reader communication. Furthermore, precisely what is interesting about this social deixis in this stanza is that it is interpretable in several ways, and that these several ways are not distributed distinctly along any separable lines within those two communicative layers.

The socio-relational deixis of the first line, particularly, seems to uphold this tension between the layers. Throughout Thomas's poem the imperative refrains initially seem to urge the (general) reader to determinedly persevere with living, and in doing so imply that we all share the experience of facing death. Given the lack of any specific addressee to indicate otherwise thus far, the 'you' in the final stanza is logically initially interpretable as a continuation of this address to the reader (albeit, in its parallelism with 'wise men', 'grave men', etc., potentially implicating a male reader and excluding a female reader). The subsequent words 'my father', though, as mentioned earlier, specify the addressee and referent of 'you' as the father of the poetic persona, though the addressee of the words 'my father' is more ambiguous. That is, 'my father' may be a socio-relational term of reference, referring to the father, and addressed to the general reader as a kind of explanatory aside, or a socio-relational term of address to the father, overheard by the reader. Notably, as a formulation of address to the father, the use of 'my' is marked: when addressing one's father, the possessive pronoun 'my' is redundant. 'And you, father' would be more conventional. The use of 'my' seems to be more oriented towards the reader-as-addressee, and may be intended primarily to explain to the reader who the speaker means by 'you', rather than being intended as part of the address to the father. Within the 'activity type' of a literary poem, the formality of the socio-relational deictic term 'father', as an explanation of a relationship, is also arguably fitting and conventional. Within the 'activity type' of a personal plea to one's actual father, on the other hand, 'father' is, for some, less fitting, in that 'dad' or 'pa' might be more likely (and less marked). That said, though 'my father' is more easily rationalized as a term of reference as part of reader-oriented address, it can nonetheless be rationalized and meaningfully interpreted as part of the address to the father if perhaps read as an overt proclamation of their connection.

The attitudinal-experiential social deixis in the first, third and fourth lines of the stanza similarly hovers indeterminably between the layers of communicative acts. The father is addressed, and described to the reader, as 'there on the sad height'. He is thereby distanced metaphorically through the 'there' (which can function as a spatially distal deictic, in contrast to 'here'). In the example from Lakoff mentioned earlier, 'How's the throat?', the use of the definite article was interpreted as avoiding the effect of the speaker distancing herself from the problem and identifying it more wholly with the addressee, as would be implied by 'How's your throat?' In that example, it has the effect of distancing the addressee from the problem as much as it distances the speaker from the problem. Thomas's use of 'the' in 'the sad height' occurs in a more complex context, however, given the father-as-addressee and reader-as-addressee, and the recent distal 'there'. The use of 'the' here perhaps suggests a sense of a shared relationship to death (shared, that is, by the speaker and his father, and by the speaker and reader), in that death is known to us all and is inevitable for all of us. However, as discussed, 'the' can convey a shared sense of distance between the speaker and addressee on the one hand, and the referent (in this case the 'sad height') on the other, and the father is being located at this 'sad height'. It is perhaps easier, therefore, to infer that this relational construction of a shared distance from or relationship to death is primarily being constructed between the speaker and the reader-as-addressee, with the father at that distance. The spatial and social deixis of the phrase 'there at the sad height' therefore conceivably manipulates the reader into alignment with the position (the place and experience) of the speaker (the implicit 'I' of the 'you', and furthermore implicitly 'here' at a distance from 'the sad height' 'there').

We also have the attitudinal-experiential social deixis of the two refrains to consider, as this is what makes up the stanza's third and fourth lines. Up to now, these refrains have implicitly been addressed to a general reader. By reorienting them at this point according to a more specific speaker-addressee relationship, the relational qualities of the determiners and articles ('that' and 'the') shift, and the reader is repositioned in relation to the referents involved. The pull here is contrary to that of the first line of the closing stanza: while 'the' is arguably general, 'that' of 'that good night' gains more specificity than it has heretofore had, in that it may now refer to the father's good night (i.e. his death) in particular, rather than to death in general. The spatially deictic 'go' in 'go gentle into that good night' has previously constructed a directionality away from the speaker's deictic centre. That is, to go towards death is to go away from where he is speaking from: death is away and apart from the perspective from which the poem is voiced. In the new context of the son speaking to his father, this 'go' gains overtones of the father leaving the son. That is, it can metaphorically suggest a departure from a relationship – even abandonment. The two definite articles within 'the dying of the light', meanwhile, arguably have a more ambivalent position, in that they can be read as maintaining a generality, or, like 'that', as more specific than their prior occurrences within this refrain, given the new layer of the discourse architecture with the father as addressee.

The second line of the final stanza, 'Curse, bless, me now with your fierce tears I pray', provides support for an argument which runs counter to the thinking that this final stanza narrows the address of the poem inwards to an autobiographical core; or, to be more precise, it offers a different, but also potentially autobiographical reading. If, as the words 'I pray' suggest, this poem can be read as a prayer, with an imperative to 'curse' or 'bless', the activity type shifts once again, and an additional layer of communication is implied – between the speaker and God. This creates yet more social deictic ambiguity. Within this reading, the stanza is still interpretable as primarily addressed to the speaker's father and as a plea to resist age-induced death a little longer, but either referring to or simultaneously doubling up as a prayer, with God as an overhearing 'bystander'. However, a further, if perhaps more reaching reading is possible, in which God is the primary, or potentially parallel, addressee of this stanza, or of part of it. The religious themes and spiritual conflict present in some of the sonnets within Thomas's previous collection *Twenty-five Poems* (1936) suggest this interpretation is not necessarily radical. Consider also Kidder's claim regarding the collection in which 'Do not go gentle into that good night' was published: 'These poems come to terms with death through a form of worship: not propitiatory worship of Death as deity, but worship of a higher Deity by whose power all things, including death, are controlled' (1973: 187). Such a reading could, furthermore, raise questions about the meaningful significance of 'my father' and could offer new meaning to the words 'there on the sad height'. If 'my father' is considered as a possible address to God, 'Our Father' would be more conventional, in which the first-person plural implies a shared 'in-group' identity, and the capitalized 'Father' implies respect for status. By contrast, 'my father' is marked in its singular 'my'. This perhaps foregrounds a sense of a personal relationship with God, and/or a personal crisis, but at the same time, excludes the reader from that relationship. The lower case 'f' of father, meanwhile, turns the term from having a primarily honorific function to primarily acting as a relational determiner. Like 'my', this may be emphasizing a personal relationship and arguably a kind of proximity (echoing similar choices by his poetic forefather, Gerard Manley Hopkins, in his lower case 'him', referring to he who 'fathers-forth', at the close of 'Pied Beauty'). In this reading, 'my father' could be rationalized as an explanatory term of reference for the benefit of and oriented towards the reader-as-addressee or as overhearer, or as a term of address to God as primary addressee (or as an addressee parallel to the speaker's father and/or the reader). Overall, the religious reading adds more layers of complexity and furthers the multiplicity of the potential socio-pragmatic meanings of the stanza's social deixis and the related potential positioning of the reader with respect to speaker-addressee relations.

In *The Poetry of Dylan Thomas*, Olsen (1954: 8) argues that Thomas often 'analogizes the anatomy of man [sic] to the structure of the universe ... and sees the human microcosm as an image of the macrocosm, and conversely'. The discourse architecture of 'Do not go gentle into that good night' reflects this, in that it initially seems to propose a general will to life from the poetic persona to the reader-as-addressee in the face of the shared macrocosmic experience of the inevitability of death, and then shifts to a narrower microcosm of a personal, familial plea from the author or poetic persona to his father-as-addressee, but one in which the general address, and indeed the generality, remains overlaid. As has been argued, a yet further communicative layer is inferable, in the explicit prayer as an address to God. The complex socio-relational deixis in 'my father' and the attitudinal-experiential social deixis in the determiners and articles in the final stanza position the reader as both in-group addressee and out-group bystander, sometimes simultaneously, sometimes ambiguously and sometimes ambivalently, seemingly as a means of allowing the poem to maintain its multiple speaker-addressee relationships and the plural meanings available across them.

4. Conclusion

This chapter has attempted to offer a contribution to ongoing developments in accounts of social deixis in literature. It has surveyed different accounts of social deixis and has explored some of the intersections between social deixis and related pragmatic factors. The chapter has proposed a limited account of social deixis (with a caveat) and has distilled some of the previous work into two subtypes: attitudinal-experiential deixis and socio-relational deixis. In the light of these subtypes, it has also proposed two core functions of social deixis in literature, both of which are bound up with literature's discourse architecture. Finally, the chapter has applied this account of social deixis to the closing stanza of Dylan Thomas's 'Do not go gentle into that good night' in order to illustrate analysis using this approach, and to offer insights into how social deixis contributes to meaning at this poem's poignant climax, with an emphasis on the relationship between social deixis, discourse architecture and the positioning of the reader. The ideas presented here warrant further exploration and application to literary texts of different kinds and with different discourse architectures, but it is hoped that this account adds further nuance and analytical potential to theory of deixis in literature.

Note

1 'Do not go gentle into that good night' by Dylan Thomas, from *The Poems of Dylan Thomas*, copyright ©1952 by Dylan Thomas. Reprinted by permission of New Directions Publishing Corp. Reprinted also by permission of The Trustees for the Copyrights of Dylan Thomas.

References

Adamson, S. (1995) 'From empathetic deixis to empathetic narrative: Stylisation and (de-)subjectivisation as process of language change', in Stein, D. and Wright, S. (eds) *Subjectivity and Subjectivisation: Linguistic Perspectives*, pp. 195–224. Cambridge: Cambridge University Press.

Benveniste, E. (1971 [1966]) *Problems in General Linguistics*, trans. M. E. Meek. Coral Gables, FL: University of Miami Press.

Brown, P. and Levinson, S. C. (1978) 'Universals in language usage: Politeness phenomena', in Goody, E. (ed.) *Questions and Politeness: Strategies in Social Interaction*, pp. 56–310. Cambridge: Cambridge University Press.

Bühler, K. (2011) *Theory of Language: The Representational Function of Language*, trans. D. E. Goodwin. Amsterdam/Philadelphia: John Benjamins.

Burks, A. W. (1948) 'Icon, index and symbol', *Philosophy and Phenomeno-Logical Research* IX: 673–89.

Clark, H. H. and Haviland, S. E. (1977) 'Comprehension and the given-new contract', in Freedle, R. O. (ed.) *Discourse Processes: Advances in Research and Theory*, pp. 1–40. Norwood, NJ: Ablex Publishing Corporation.

Comrie, B. (1976) 'Linguistic politeness axes: Speaker-addressee, speaker-referent, speaker-bystander', *Pragmatics Microfiche* 1(7): A3. Department of Linguistics, University of Cambridge.

Duchan, J. F., Bruder, G. A., and Hewitt, L. E. (eds) (1995) *Deixis in Narrative: A Cognitive Scientific Perspective*. Hillsdale, NJ: Lawrence Erlbaum.

Eckert, P. and McConnell-Ginet, S. (1992) 'Think practically and look locally: Language and gender as community-based practice', *Annual Review of Anthropology* 21: 461–90.

Edwards, J. (2016) '"Do not go gentle into that good night": Dylan Thomas and the art of dying', *The Use of English* 67(3): 71–8.

Fillmore, C. (1971) 'Towards a theory of deixis', *Working Papers in Linguistics* 3(4): 219–41.

Fillmore, C. (1975) *Santa Cruz Lectures on Deixis*. Bloomington, IN: Indiana University Linguistics Club.

Green, K. (1995) 'Deixis: A revaluation of concepts and categories', in K. Green (ed.) *New Essays in Deixis: Discourse, Narrative, Literature*, pp. 11–25. Amsterdam: Rodopi.

Grishikova, M. (2018) 'Multi-teller and multi-voiced stories', in Gibbons, A. and Macrae, A. (eds) *Pronouns in Literature: Positions and Perspectives in Language*, pp. 193–216. London: Palgrave Macmillan.

Herman, D. (2002) *Story Logic: Problems and Possibilities of Narrative*. Lincoln, NE: University of Nebraska Press.

Huang, Y. (2007) 'Social deixis', in *Pragmatics*, pp. 163–71. Oxford: Oxford University Press.

Jarvella, R. and Klein, W. (eds) (1982) *Speech, Place and Action: Studies in Deixis and Related Topics*. Chichester: Wiley.

Kidder, R. M. (1973) *Dylan Thomas: The Country of the Spirit*. Princeton, NJ: Princeton University Press.

Lakoff, R. (1974) 'Remarks on this and that', in La Galy, M. W., Fox, R. A., and Bruck, A. (eds) *Papers for the Tenth Regional Meeting of the Chicago Linguistic Society*, pp. 345–56. Chicago, IL: Chicago Linguistic Society.

Levinson, Stephen C. (1979) 'Pragmatics and social deixis: Reclaiming the notion of conventional implicature', *Proceedings of the Fifth Annual Meeting of the Berkeley Linguistics Society*, pp. 206–23. Berkeley, CA: Berkeley Linguistics Society.

Levinson, Stephen C. (1983) *Pragmatics*. Cambridge: Cambridge University Press.

Lyons, J. (1968) *Introduction to Theoretical Linguistics*. Cambridge: Cambridge University Press.
Lyons, J. (1977) *Semantics, Vols. 1 and 2*. Cambridge: Cambridge University Press.
Macrae, A. (2012) 'Readerly deictic shifting to and through I and You: An updated hypothesis', in Kwiatkowska, A. (ed.) *Texts and Minds: Papers in Cognitive Poetics and Rhetoric*, pp. 41–56. Frankfurt am Main: Peter Lang.
Macrae, A. (2019) *Discourse Deixis in Metafiction: The Language of Metanarration, Metalepsis and Disnarration*. London: Routledge.
Moore, K. E. (2014) *The Spatial Language of Time: Metaphor, Metonymy and Frames of Reference*. Amsterdam: John Benjamins.
Olson, E. (1954) *The Poetry of Dylan Thomas*. Chicago, IL: University of Chicago Press.
Potts, C. and Schwarz, F. (2010) 'Affective "this"', *Linguistic Issues in Language Technology* 3(5): 1–30.
Rauh, G. (1978) *Linguistische Beschreibung deiktischer Kompexität in narrativen Texten*. Tübingen: Narr.
Rauh, G. (ed.) (1983) *Essays on Deixis*. Tübingen: Gunter Narr Verlag.
Semino, E. (1997) *Language and World Creation in Poems and Other Texts*. London: Longman.
Short, M. (1996) *Exploring the Language of Poems, Plays and Prose*. London: Longman.
Stockwell, P. (2000) *The Poetics of Science Fiction*. London: Routledge.
Stockwell, P. (2002) *Cognitive Poetics: An Introduction*. London: Routledge.
Thomas, D. (1936) *Twenty-five Poems*. London: J. M. Dent and Sons.
Thomas, D. (1952) *In Country Sleep and Other Poems*. New York: James Laughlin.
Westphal, J. (1994) 'Thomas's 'Do not go gentle into that good night'', *The Explicator* 52(2): 113–15.
Wolter, L. K. (2006) *That's That: The Semantics and Pragmatics of Demonstrative Noun Phrases*. Unpublished dissertation thesis. University of California, Santa Cruz.

4

'The novel of the future': Author's manipulation in Henry Green's *Nothing* (1950) and *Doting* (1952)

Rocío Montoro

1. Introduction

The *Oxford English Dictionary*[1] (*OED*) assigns four senses to the term 'manipulation': (1) a method of digging silver ore; (2) in chemistry, the action of handling apparatus in experiments; (3) dexterity; (4) exerting influence, in a skilful manner, over another person; the subtle or underhand way of controlling others. Chilton (2011: 176) explains that the term has evolved to refer mainly to the act of treating someone 'unfairly, by skilful means to one's advantage' and argues that those means obviously include *verbal* means. Manipulation has been amply investigated from a variety of perspectives including those of rhetoric, critical discourse analysis, philosophy or pragmatics and each discipline has highlighted specific nuances associated with their own theoretical principles. In this chapter, I define manipulation in a narrower, more ad hoc sense which, nonetheless, still retains some of the connotations mentioned above. As my title indicates, I am concerned with 'the novel of the future' as defined by Henry Green. Green (1950b [1993]) argued that not only should such a novel consist almost entirely of dialogue but also dialogue should be 'oblique', meaning that 'it will not be an exact record of the way people talk' (1950b [1993]: 137). In this chapter, I view manipulation as the way in which this author guides his readership insofar as he spells out the characteristics of what he sees as the perfect novel. Unlike what is the case with other writers, we can 'hear' Green's voice directly in the multiple interviews and non-fictional writing in which he discussed these matters. Thus, in what follows, I consider to what extent Green's manipulation, understood as the open verbalization of his stance on his own literary practice, materializes in his work. I focus mainly on the two novels written at the time or shortly after Green airs such specific claims, namely *Nothing* (1950c) and *Doting* (1952). I use a corpus-pragmatic methodology (Grice 1975; Romero Trillo 2017) which combines an analysis of the creation of implicature in the Gricean sense and an examination of statistically salient parts of speech and semantic categories (as typically implemented in corpus stylistics). Comparing *Nothing* (1950c) and *Doting* (1952) to two previous novels, *Party Going* (1939) and *Concluding* (1948), allows me to consider whether Green's claims are supported linguistically and stylistically and whether the claimed shift happens progressively or mainly unfolds in his final works.

2. Henry Green's theory of art: Author's manipulation

In a series of interviews in the 1950s, Henry Green articulated what he considered the basis of his theoretical position on both the nature of art and the novel. Green started off by characterizing the art coetaneous with the time of making these claims as 'non-representational':

> For the past several years painting has tended to avoid representation, that is to say, a direct exposition of the objects seen, and has tended to look below the surface. ... Thereby painters produce something which isn't, that is to say, the result is non-representational, and yet if and when the painting is successful, it has a life of its own. This is also true of a good novel. (Green 1950a: 21)

In further discussions concerning non-representation and the 'good novel', he also highlighted the crucial role of the reader:

> To read a story of importance the writer has to include the reader to make an act of conscious imagination. ... The main difficulty before the writer is to fire the reader's enthusiasm with what he is reading sufficiently, first to catch his attention, secondly, to make him read each work as if he were not asleep, and finally to create a work of art – that is, something living which isn't – between the author and reader in a work, which, while non-representational, will be convincing and alive. (Green 1950a: 23)

Ultimately, Green's understanding of art as non-representational translated into a concern with experimenting with language at various levels.[2] Elsewhere (Montoro 2018), I have discussed Green's experimentation in *Living* (1929) where he dispenses with the definite article. In this chapter, I focus on the technique which characterized his final two novels and which, he argued, should define the novel of the future:

> What I am trying to write now is a novel with an absolute minimum of descriptive passages in it, or even directions to the reader (that may be such as 'She said angrily', etc.) and yet narrative consisting almost entirely of dialogue. (Green 1950b [1993]: 140)

Green specifically locates this shift in time:

> Until *Nothing* and *Doting* I tried to establish the mood of any scene by a few but highly pointed descriptions. Since then I've tried to keep everything down to bare dialogue. (Green 1958 [1993]: 240)

Nothing (1950c) and *Doting* (1952) became the forums in which to forge the new dialogue technique; furthermore, it ensued that dialogue should equally follow the principle of non-representation:

> If, then, you and I are agreed that dialogue is the best way for the novelist to communicate with his readers, this will be non-representational, that is to say, it will not be an exact record of the way people talk. (Green 1950b [1993]: 137)

Thus, Green's non-representational dialogue is that in which the author does not pursue a faithful imitation of real-life conversation (in fact, fictional dialogue is hardly ever 'an exact' reproduction of any spoken variety of language). Green honed his non-representational premise as it applied to dialogue by describing it as 'oblique':

> The journalist's approach must be the most direct of which he is capable, and the novelist's approach must be oblique. … In other words, you learn more from the lies of someone who is speaking to you, if you can find these out, than you will from direct statements which generally only represent a portion of what the person you are speaking to believes. (Green 1950a: 23)

This description of dialogue as 'oblique' shares core aspects with the creation of conversational implicature defined by Grice (1975), as I address fully in Section 5.

All of the above portrays Green as an author keen to let his readers partake in what, according to him, is the essence of his writing. As discussed in the introduction, my definition of 'manipulation' is rather ad hoc since I am not addressing issues more prototypically associated with this notion such as that of control in the sense discussed by Sorlin: 'Manipulation can be seen as sharing one external border with persuasion and another with coercion' (Sorlin 2016: 18). Instead, I view author's manipulation as the way Green deftly guides readers with regard to his own position on literary craftsmanship, that is, manipulation as a kind of loose combination of senses 3 ('dexterity') and 4 ('exerting influence in a skilful manner',) of the OED above. In the remainder of this chapter, I analyse whether this 'steering' of the reader results in firmly abided-by protocols or whether Green's open declarations fail to materialize fully in his writing. Thus, *Nothing* (1950c) and *Doting* (1952) portray decadent, very often hypocritical societies dominated by appearances. The way characters interact shows that they often lie to one another, that they are never clear about their intentions and that they are led by pretensions and appearances. In *Party Going* (1939), a group of idle rich people who are on their way to the South of France is detained at a London station because of fog. These characters have a similar social status to those in *Nothing* (1950c) and *Doting* (1952), so, I am interested in seeing whether non-representational dialogue is useful to reflect the type of society these novels depict. *Concluding* (1948) was published just before Green claimed to depart from his previous stylistic techniques to embrace dialogue. The story is set somewhere in an old English estate (not specified) now turned school for girls. By including this novel in my comparisons, I intend to contrast to what extent Green really diverges from his pre-1950s work, whether such a rupture is merely a theoretical matter or whether, instead, there is a gradual progression in the incorporation of dialogue.

3. Data and methodology

This chapter has, thus, three main aims:

1) To measure to what extent dialogue is over-represented in his last novels: I first consider whether there is a clear shift as far as the textual space devoted to the dialogue technique when compared to the narrative sections. If dialogue is the tool of preference in the novel of the future, it follows that the ratio of dialogue versus narration should be resolved in favour of the former.
2) To consider how non-representational dialogue is linguistically realized: Besides ascertaining the extent to which dialogue is used, I examine whether instances of dialogue are 'oblique' in the sense defined by Green, that is, by means of characters' conversing without using 'direct statements'.

3) To investigate, in more detail, the functions and characteristics of dialogue as, besides choosing dialogue over narration, Green also argues that letting characters speak directly to each other diminishes the overbearing presence of narrators. In fact, as will be seen, oblique dialogue also helps with characterization and the creation of humour.

The varied nature of this chapter's objectives means that my enquiries are multi-methodological and combine quantitative and qualitative approaches. I work with four different corpora and some sub-corpora depending on the line of enquiry I follow in each case. Thus:

1) To address the first objective, I implemented a quantitative analysis of the novels for which I created four main corpora (one per novel) as well as the corresponding dialogue and narration sub-corpora. Each corpus was then separated into narration and dialogue sub-corpora. Yet, this was not a straightforward task as deciding what counts as dialogue depends on the aims of the analysis and the criteria applied. In fictional dialogue, narrators present characters' utterances by using Direct Speech (DS). As Leech and Short (2007: 255) explain, 'To report what someone has said one quotes the words used verbatim.' To date, theirs ([1981] 2007)[3] is still the most sophisticated and widely used model of speech (and thought) presentation. In their model, the DS category is identified not just by the verbatim reproduction of what the characters have said but also by the quotation marks enclosing the reported string of speech as well as by the introductory reporting clause of the kind 'she said'. The associated category of Free Direct Speech (FDS) is a slightly freer way of presenting verbatim talk distinguished from the former because either the quotation marks, the reporting clause or both are removed from the particular instance of speech. In subsequent reworkings of the model, Short (1988) argued that the DS/FDS distinction should not be maintained as the latter is just a subcategory of the former. Axelsson (2009) also looks at DS in fiction but she compares it to naturally occurring speech. Unlike Leech and Short, Axelsson (2009) confines her classification of DS to the reported material, leaving the reporting clause out. In my analysis, I include DS and FDS in the dialogue sub-corpora which means that the reporting clause is viewed as part of the dialogue, not the narrative sections. On the one hand, unlike Axelsson (2009), I am not comparing fictional dialogue to naturally occurring data; on the other, Green claimed that fictional writing should

not be 'an exact record of the way people talk' so the fictionality of the characters' exchanges must be acknowledged which I do by including the reporting clauses:

> 'But could you conceive of the wife?' Mrs Middleton cried …
> 'Oh wasn't she!' this child agreed …
> 'Pretty fair rot to my ideas' Arthur Middleton insisted. …
> 'Then you do already, is that it?' (*Doting* 1952: 3, 6)

The manual separation of dialogue and narrative sections presented some additional challenges, especially with regard to the reporting clause's co-text. For instance, some of the issues I encountered sometimes pertained to the subject of the reporting verb which was occasionally realized by a complex noun phrase (e.g. relative clause elaborating on the name of the character); on other occasions, the meaning of the reporting clause was elaborated by either coordination or subordination. I viewed cases such as that of the complex noun phrase as part of the reporting clause in DS, so those instances were placed in the dialogue sub-corpus. Stretches of coordinated or subordinated clauses were categorized as part of the narration sub-corpus, as in the following:

> 'Oh no' she said, then began to shake. (*Nothing* 1950c: 6)

The DS string, '"Oh no" she said', was classified as dialogue; the elaborating information in 'then began to shake' was moved to the narration section as it contains details which do not directly pertain to the speech act itself. This manual analysis proved that separating the dialogue from the narrative parts is by no means a clear-cut task. Furthermore, it soon became apparent that the criterion I decided on could not be taken as a hard-set rule as I encountered plenty of complex, hard to disambiguate cases. My rule of thumb was to include the reporting clauses as part of DS/FDS but to classify any over-elaboration that went beyond the mere description of the speech act itself as narration.

2) The second objective of this chapter is to investigate the nature of 'oblique dialogue'. Looking at communication which takes place, as Green puts it, 'below the surface' entails that 'you learn more from the lies of someone who is speaking to you, if you can find these out, than you will from direct statements' (Green 1950a: 23). This kind of indirect communication shares some basic premise with the notion of conversational implicature defined by Grice (1975). Analysing how often the Gricean maxims are flouted,

therefore, could shed light on how oblique Green's dialogue really is. I, thus, identify and classify all the instances of floutings in the dialogue sections of the four novels.

3) Finally, I implement a corpus-based approach. Using the software Wmatrix (Rayson 2009), I compare each novel to the BNC Written Imaginative sub-corpus to consider whether there are any statistically salient parts of speech or semantic categories that could potentially account for the way oblique dialogue is linguistically realized as well as point out its effect(s) in the novels. This analysis is complemented by the intertextual comparison of the two works in which oblique dialogue is supposedly in operation, *Nothing* (1950c) and *Doting* (1952), to those published before the shift towards dialogue took place, *Party Going* (1939) and *Concluding* (1948). Finally, I contextualize my results by comparing them to those obtained with regard to the Gricean maxims.

4. Dialogue versus narration ratio: Textual space

To measure the real extent of the shift towards a more dialogue-based style I first consider how much textual space is devoted to dialogue in relation to the narrative sections. Following the criteria described in Section 3, I divided each novel into DS/FDS and narration. The results are summarized in Table 4.1.

These figures correspond to the number of words in the dialogue and narration sub-corpora in each novel respectively. On the back of these results, it can be confirmed that Green embraced dialogue fully in his final novels as over 85 per cent of the text is devoted to conversations between characters. Furthermore, these figures also demonstrate a kind of progression to incorporate the technique; *Concluding* (1948), published immediately before *Nothing* (1950c) and *Doting* (1952), increases the number of passages in dialogue format with respect to *Party Going* (1939).

Table 4.1 Dialogue/narration ratio

Novels	Dialogue (%)	Narration (%)
Doting (1952)	87.39	12.60
Nothing (1950)	86.74	13.25
Concluding (1948)	56.46	43.53
Party Going (1939)	42.21	57.78

5. Gricean pragmatics: Oblique dialogue

But devoting more textual space to dialogue, on its own, is not synonymous with non-representation as Green defined the term. For dialogue to fulfil that criterion, characters should not address one another in a direct way:

> There should be no direct answers in dialogue. If the fictional characters A and B are talking together in narrative, A should ask a question on which B should ask another, although the natural fatigue of the reader over such inconclusiveness should be carefully watched for. (Green 1950a: 23)

For instance:

> 'If you'd only heard him on the phone! He sounded so low, poor dear.'
> 'Which is the only reason you felt you had to go?'
> 'Why else?' she asked.
> 'And the father then? What sort of a man is Mr Shone? Didn't he like you?'
> 'Oh, he's much older than you.' (*Doting* 1952: 200)

Two characters, Arthur Middleton and Annabel Paynton, take part in this conversation. Although the former is married, he feels attracted to the latter and is jealous of a friend of Annabel's she has gone to visit. In this exchange, questions are met with further questions so nothing (or little) is ever resolved. When Annabel Paynton eventually provides an answer, she merely refers to the age of her friend's father, Mr Shone, implying that she is unlikely to have been physically attracted to him and simultaneously flattering Mr Middleton. This example illustrates the roundabout ways in which characters communicate in *Nothing* (1950c) and *Doting* (1952) often flouting the Gricean maxims and creating conversational implicature.

In 'Logic and Conversation' (1975) Grice famously developed the cooperative principle which, he argued, underlies any kind of successful communication: 'Make your conversational contribution such as is required, at the stage at which it occurs, by the accepted purpose or direction of the talk exchange in which you are engaged' (Grice 1975: 45). Together with this general principle, he added four maxims to clarify how this principle works:

1) The Maxim of Quantity relates to the quantity of information to be provided … .
2) The Maxim of Quality: Try to make your contribution one that is true … .
3) The Maxim of Relation: Be relevant.
4) The Maxim of Manner: Be perspicuous.

(Grice 1975: 45–6)

These maxims, however, are not always observed which can be achieved in a variety of ways.[4] I am interested in one of those ways, namely flouting, which occurs when speakers 'blatantly fail to fulfil' (Grice 1975: 49) the maxims. When this happens 'the assumption ... is not that communication has broken down, but that the speaker has chosen an indirect way of achieving it' (Black 2006: 25). This indirect way of achieving communication gives rise to 'conversational implicatures' (Grice 1975: 49) which, according to Black (2006: 25), are very much 'rooted in the situation in which they occur, and must be interpreted taking the context into account'. The way meaningful conversation exchanges are constructed in *Nothing* (1950c) and *Doting* (1952) owes a lot to the way conversational implicature is created since the characters do not openly tell, but rather suggest, hint or insinuate to each other. Therefore, looking at the creation of implicature can shed light on the linguistic make-up of Green's oblique dialogue.

One caveat to bear in mind is the fact that the cooperative principle and conversational implicature were notions originally formulated to account for instances of naturally occurring data. However, plenty of research (Black 2006; Kukkonen 2013; Mao 1992; Semino 2014) has proven that both concepts are equally in operation irrespective of whether the discourse is fictional or not. Black (2006) argues that the cooperative principle and conversational implicature are not only pertinent to fictional discourse but there are also various levels at which they operate:

> One would expect that the Gricean maxims should have some relevance for the processing of literary discourse, on the innermost level of character-to-character interactions. It is perhaps more interesting to consider whether it is not also applicable to our processing of the whole text, in the interaction between narrator and reader, and the relationship between narrator and characters. ... Furthermore, arriving at meaning via the maxims involves effort, and so increases engagement with the text. (Black 2006: 27)

I concur with Black for two reasons. On the one hand, the most obvious level at which we can observe the cooperative principle and conversational implicature is that of character-to-character interactions because of the, albeit fictional, nonetheless still interpersonal, nature of that discourse. In fact, because I investigate oblique dialogue, the analysis that follows only pertains to the dialogue (i.e. containing DS/FDS) sub-corpora.[5] On the other, I support Black's contention that pragmatic principles apply to our processing of the whole text 'in the interaction between narrator and reader' and that 'arriving at meaning via the maxims involves effort, and so increases engagement with the text' (2006: 27). Such a tenet is reminiscent of that contended by Green when he explained that 'to read a story of importance the writer has to include the reader ... to fire the reader's enthusiasm' (Green 1950a: 23). In fact, it is by marrying the two that we can arrive more successfully at an understanding of oblique dialogue. Following Green, thus, oblique dialogue could be best viewed as that in which the character-to-character level at which the floutings most clearly work is extended to include the reader too. In Green's oblique dialogue, the reader is hardly ever left uninvited to infer implicatures. Moreover, readers are often privy to information which is not accessible to the characters so implicatures are most of the time three- rather than two-pronged processes: character-to-character-to-reader. I am not arguing, though, that this three-way process is exclusively applicable to Green's writing. Fictional dialogue is hardly ever 'an exact record' of the way people talk and reader engagement is necessary for the processing of all fictional texts; so, in that respect, Green's writing is no different from any other fictional discourse. However, not every author is so vocal with regard to his literary practices or to what active role readers are assumed to play; by virtue of his open declarations, Green appears to 'manipulate' his linguistic material not so much to persuade as to 'show dexterity', as in sense 3 of the OED.

Considering oblique dialogue through a pragmatics lens, therefore, allows the analyst to pay heed to the author's 'on-record' manipulation but also helps shed light on how that is specifically achieved. In order to assess exactly how the creation of implicature can give rise to oblique dialogue, I focus on the floutings of the maxims in the four novels, specifically in the dialogue sub-corpus of each novel. Because I do not consider the narration sub-corpora, I refrain from making claims with regard to the higher narrator-reader plane. Table 4.2 contains the number of floutings in the dialogue sub-corpora of each novel, ranked in decreasing order.

Table 4.2 Number of floutings

Novel	Number of floutings
Nothing (1950)	116
Doting (1952)	79
Concluding (1948)	61
Party Going (1939)	39

The indirectness of oblique dialogue via the flouting of maxims operates mainly in *Nothing* (1950c), followed by *Doting* (1952), with *Concluding* (1948), interestingly, very close to the latter. Earlier, I discuss that *Concluding* (1948), published just two years prior to Green's declarations with regard to the novel of the future, moves towards that Greenian ideal in the sense that dialogue (56.46 per cent) textually outweighs, if only slightly, narration (43.53 per cent). Tallying those results with the number of floutings in Table 4.2 suggests that Green's work progressively rather than abruptly shifts towards the 'new novel'. This is supported by the fact that *Party Going* (1939) is at odds with the other three novels in terms of both the dialogue versus narration ratio and the number of floutings. Caution must be exerted, though, because quantifying floutings as I do here does not have any statistical weight; for these percentages to be statistically significant, the analysis would have to be extended to include much larger corpora. My results simply highlight the fact that in the data analysed here, there is a clear progression towards a more indirect way of presenting communication, just as Green claimed there would be. In this respect, Green's manipulation, in the sense I define in this chapter, does materialize in his writing. Furthermore, as Black (2006) argues, arriving at meaning via the maxims 'requires effort' and 'increases the engagement with the text' so Green seems to have shifted the onus on to a reader who is expected to infer a variety of meanings originated by the increasing amount of indirectness.

The next step was to isolate and classify which maxims were flouted in each case as summarized in Table 4.3.

Table 4.3 Distribution of floutings

	Doting (1952)	*Nothing* (1950)	*Concluding* (1948)	*Party Going* (1939)
Quantity (%)	29.1	33.6	4.9	30.75
Quality (%)	36.7	28.43	42.57	56.37
Manner (%)	24.03	18.09	31.9	7.68
Relation (%)	10.12	19.81	19.62	5.12

Because of space constraints, I only discuss the two most frequently flouted maxims in *Nothing* (1950c) and *Doting* (1952), that is, the quantity and quality maxims, although it is clear that there are further issues to address in relation to the other two novels as well. Thus, failing to observe the quantity maxim frequently results in the creation of humour, a feature often highlighted as prototypically Greenian (Hentea 2010; Holmesland 1986; Taylor 1965).

Therefore, to create something living between a writer and a reader, it is the presentation of the theme which creates the communication between the two, and as dialogue in life consists largely of humour, to create life between writer and reader, humour should in future be the bridge. (Green 1950a: 24)

Humour serves a twofold purpose. First, it seems an effective device to ease characters' interactions and to facilitate communication between them. But humour is also useful to entice the reader to persevere with his reading: 'If you can make the reader laugh he is apt to get careless and go on reading' (Green 1958 [1993]: 240). Both objectives, then, combine to shape the novel of the future. The flouting of the quantity maxim is amply exploited to achieve this aim, as in the following example:

'So you're afraid he'll never start a family is that it?' …

'Ah these Southerners' the lady remarked as she sat herself at table again. 'The other day Isabella came to me for half a crown. The last occasion she asked for money was only the whole return fare to go back to Italy to vote in the elections. So I naturally wanted to know what for this time and what d'you suppose she said, why simply to buy a mouse. "Get a mouse?" I said after I'd looked the word up in the dictionary. "Because Roberto" that's our cat "is so lonely" she answered. I screamed. I just yelled, wouldn't you? I can't bear cruelty to animals John dear. But she's so persistent and in the end of course she got her own way! Naturally I kept out of the house for a few days after that and forbade sweet Penelope the kitchen or I said I'd simply never speak to the child again. And then I forgot. Isn't it dreadful the way one does? I went down there for something or other and Isabella showed me. They were both drinking milk out of the same saucer. Roberto and his mouse. John is it sorcery, spell-binding or something?' (*Nothing* 1950c: 62–3)

The above extract is part of a conversation between the widow Jane Weatherby and John Pomfret, two former lovers now reunited because their respective children are engaged to be married. Both are aware of their and their children's lack of means so they are attempting to sabotage the marriage at all costs; besides, Jane Weatherby's ulterior motive is regaining the amorous interests of her former lover, John. Mrs Weatherby's flouting of the quantity maxim by over-elaborating unnecessarily gives rise to humour when she tells Pomfret how she misunderstood her Italian maid. Her answers are often full of trivialities which, nonetheless, are grandiosely shrouded in some sort of (non-existent) importance. Furthermore, through the non-observance of the maxims, she succeeds in avoiding controversial questions, such as the one that initiates this exchange in which John Pomfret queries her about her son's future.[6] She often dodges questions so that people do not find out she is actually penniless.

Together with the maxim of quantity, the quality maxim is flouted most frequently which serves to characterize the society depicted in each novel as deceitful, dishonest and false. Characters state that which they believe to be false regardless of the consequences, such as, for instance, hurting one's own child (as in *Nothing* (1950c)) or being unfaithful (as in *Doting* (1952)):

> 'But you see', she said, her eyes very wide 'I smelled you, Arthur!'
> 'You smelt me? This is something new! And what d'you mean by that?'
> 'Why the powder she had on, or the scent she used, Arthur!'
> 'Now my dear, which? You know you've always prided yourself on your sense of smell. If this is right, what you're saying, you ought to be able to tell one from the other?'
> 'Don't try and dodge', she informed him in the same sad voice. 'I did, I tell you.'
> 'I can't make this out at all. What am I supposed to have done now?'
> 'You'd put your hand on her leg, Arthur, and I can't, I shan't, ever, get over it.'
> 'Look darling', he said, most reasonably. 'Will you believe me when I say I have absolutely no recollection of anything of the kind.' (*Doting* 1952: 225)

In the above, Diana Middleton is adamant that the incident she had witnessed is proof of her husband, Arthur Middleton, and Annabel Paynton's affair. The incident in question happened some time earlier and Diana Middleton had not let go of her suspicions. Annabel Paynton was having lunch with Arthur Middleton and spilt some coffee on her skirt; she removed it at which moment Diana caught them. Readers are well aware that, though it is true that Annabel had spilt the coffee, Arthur's intentions were to initiate an amorous encounter. By pretending not to remember the incident, Mr Middleton is being rather cagey and expects his wife to believe that it was a genuine mishap. The three-way manner in which oblique dialogue works means that readers know how the incident really took place. Arthur Middleton has his own interests at heart so being untruthful satisfies his selfish needs as with most characters in this novel.

The flouting of the quality maxim serves a second important purpose as it also works as a characterization device. In *Nothing* (1950c), for instance, we find a very interesting contrast between Jane Weatherby and her son, Philip. Family values are crucial for the latter so much so that his idealistic take on life prevents him from flouting the quality maxim even once:

> 'We should've got married first. There's what we ought to have told them, not that we were only engaged.'
> 'I know but it's so rude to the relations when people elope.' (*Nothing* 1950c: 100)

In a conversation with his fiancée, Mary Pomfret, Philip is ready to sacrifice what could have secured his future happiness as that would imply lying. To Miss Pomfret's suggestion that they run away, his only concern lies with how impolite those actions would be for the rest of the family so there is no possibility of Philip not honouring this maxim. As a contrast, his mother is scheming so her adherence to the quality maxim is minimal. In *Doting* (1952) virtually all the main characters flout this maxim substantially, with the exceptions of Peter Middleton (Arthur and Diana's young boy and a minor character) and Claire Belaine (a young, confident woman who openly discusses her relationships).

As stated above, there are many other issues that I do not address here because of space constraints; for instance, in *Party Going* (1939) the quantity and quality maxims also play a crucial role. The latter, in fact, scores higher in *Party Going* (1939) than in the other three novels. What differs from his later work is the amount of textual space devoted to such a technique.

6. Corpus pragmatics: Stylistic saliency

I conclude by looking at the 'novel of the future' from a corpus-based perspective. Corpus pragmatics aims to describe 'language use in real contexts through corpora' (Romero Trillo 2017: 1). Corpus stylistics also adheres to this principle whereby language use is considered in the light of purposely constructed corpora; however, corpus stylistics attains that aim irrespective of whether language is fictional or not. This section combines the methodological tenets and concerns of corpus pragmatics and the fictional data focus of corpus stylistics. Furthermore, the results of my analysis are considered alongside the conclusions arrived at via a Gricean pragmatics approach. I, therefore, add a further analytical dimension to my study.

I use Wmatrix (Rayson 2009), a piece of software that uses the Constituent Likelihood Automatic Word-Tagging System (CLAWS) tagger to tag corpora for parts of speech (POS) and semantic categories (SEMTAG) information. The target corpora (full novels, dialogue and narration sub-corpora) were compared to a reference corpus, Wmatrix's BNC Sampler Written Imaginative sub-corpus.[7] Wmatrix uses, among others, the log-likelihood test (Dunning 1993) which measures the likelihood of the results obtained being due to chance alone. The higher the log-likelihood value, the higher the statistical significance of the results, that is, the more likely it is that the results are not due to chance alone. Any result over the critical value of 3.84 (95th percentile; 5% level; $p < 0.05$;

critical value = 3.84) is statistically significant so any conclusion drawn on that basis is backed up by statistical evidence. I implemented a series of comparisons:

1) Each novel's full, dialogue and narration sub-corpora were compared to the BNC Written Imaginative sub-corpus for POS information, that is, I looked at the grammatical make-up of my data.
2) To focus exclusively on the dialogue sections, I created two additional sub-corpora, one inclusive of the dialogue sub-corpora of *Nothing* (1950c) and *Doting* (1952), henceforth the 'oblique dialogue' sub-corpus, and a second one containing the dialogue sub-corpora of *Concluding* (1948) and *Party Going* (1939), henceforth the 'pre-oblique dialogue' sub-corpus. I start by focusing on the POS information emerging from comparing the two.
3) The final analysis considered the semantic categories (SEMTAG) of the oblique dialogue sub-corpus in the light of the pre-oblique dialogue sub-corpus to, once more, compare post-1950s novels to Green's pre-1950s work.

In sum, I carried out a full analysis of the grammatical and semantic structure of my corpora which not only provided extra methodological rigour but also highlighted certain aspects not brought to the fore by a pragmatics analysis and which, nevertheless, still project features that further characterize Green's work. As was the case in Section 5, I only discuss some of the overused categories due to space constraints.

Table 4.4 contains (a selection of) the statistically significant overused grammatical categories in each corpus (99.99th percentile; 0.01% level; $p < 0.0001$; critical value = 15.13) when compared to the BNC Written Imaginative sub-corpus:

The advantage of comparing the full novel, on the one hand, and the dialogue/narrative sub-corpora, on the other, is that the actual grammatical characteristics of dialogue or narration can be assessed separately as well as in relation to the full novel. For instance, first- and second-person pronouns are key in the full novel *Nothing* (1950c). However, this is only the case because dialogue takes up most of the textual space (over 85 per cent), as proven in Section 4. In the *Nothing* narration sub-corpus, first- and second-person pronouns are not key any longer. Secondly, the overused POS categories of the four narration sub-corpora demonstrate that the four novels are very similar in this respect and that they use the prototypical markers associated with narration, namely past tense and third-person pronouns. An interesting overused category is that of the preceding noun of title as in 'Miss Liz Jennings, Mrs Weatherby, Mr Pomfret,

Table 4.4 All corpora compared to BNC Written Imaginative_overused POS (p < 0.0001; critical value = 15.13)

Novel	Full novel	Dialogue	Narration
Doting (1952)	Second-person pronouns interjections general adverbs degree adverbs general adjectives	First- and second-person pronouns interjections general adverbs degree adverbs adjectives third-person pronouns	past tense preceding noun of title (Mr, Professor) third-person pronouns
Nothing (1950)	First- and second-person pronouns third-person pronouns general adverbs interjection degree adverb general adjective	First- and second-person pronouns third-person pronouns past tense general adverbs interjections degree adverbs general adjective	past tense third-person pronouns preceding noun of title (Mr, Professor)
Concluding (1948)	Third-person pronouns past tense general adverbs	First-person plural pronoun second-person pronouns interjections adverbs	past tense third-person pronouns preceding noun of title (Mr, Professor)
Party Going (1939)	Third-person pronouns past tense adverbs	Second- and third-person pronouns past tense adverbs	Third-person pronouns past tense

Mr Abbot' which is key in Green's final three works. This POS functions as a social distance marker which eschews the familiarity of first names. The indirectness of oblique dialogue discussed in the previous section seems aided by the marked social distance projected by this POS too.

Various other issues arise by focusing on the dialogue sup-corpora. Third-person pronouns are key both in *Nothing* (1950c) and *Doting* (1950) as is past tense in the former too. The overuse of these markers could initially appear at odds with the interpersonal purpose of dialogue as these markers characterize narrative discourse. However, this over-representation simply reflects the fact that, in this chapter, DS and FDS realize fictional dialogue and, so, the reporting clauses of the former account for such a prototypically narratorial indicator. *Nothing* (1950c) and *Doting* (1952) also coincide in the overuse of adverbs ('well', 'so', 'please', 'naturally', 'indeed'), interjections ('oh', 'oh no', 'oh goodness', 'oh heavens'), and first- and second-person pronouns which, as I discuss below, reflects the interpersonal nature of these novels.

In order to investigate the transition to oblique dialogue in more detail, I compared the two sub-corpora created for this specific purpose: oblique dialogue versus pre-oblique dialogue. I first looked at the POS information and followed by considering the SEMTAG information. Figure 4.1 includes the overused POS tags.

Looking exclusively at the dialogue sub-corpora allowed me to see the grammatical components of the shift towards oblique dialogue in a more detailed way. Of all the categories over the critical value 15.13, three clusters merit attention:

1) Pronoun categories: PPIS1 (first-person singular subjective pronoun 'I'), PPY (second-person personal pronoun 'you'), PPIO1 (first-person singular objective personal pronoun 'me').
2) Present tense categories: VBM ('am'), VBZ ('is').
3) Adverbs and interjections: RR (general adverb), UH (interjections).

Based on these results, Green's oblique dialogue differs from his pre-1950s work by underscoring not simply indirectness, as Green had claimed, but also the interactive aspect of dialogue which is projected by, on the one hand, the immediacy attained by the present tense frame, and first- and second-person pronouns and, on the other, the situational involvement created by certain

Item	O1 (obl. dial)	%1	O2 (pre-obl. dial)	%2	LL
GE	165	0.17	0	0.00	+172.95
PPIS1	3559	3.64	1694	2.51	+163.13
VBM	321	0.33	40	0.06	+156.80
RR	4926	5.04	2612	3.88	+119.83
VM	2318	2.37	1234	1.83	+54.81
VBZ	1318	1.35	640	0.95	+54.63
XX	2265	2.32	1205	1.79	+53.81
PPY	3407	3.48	1919	2.85	+50.65
JJ	4897	5.01	2964	4.40	+31.24
PPIO1	761	0.78	374	0.56	+29.60
VHI	413	0.42	189	0.28	+22.69
NP1	2919	2.99	1752	2.60	+21.03
RG	1004	1.03	552	0.82	+18.48
VM21	17	0.02	0	0.00	+17.82
UH	1312	1.34	751	1.11	+16.65
JJ31	53	0.05	11	0.02	+16.55

Figure 4.1 Oblique dialogue (O1) compared to pre-oblique dialogue (O2)_overused POS categories ($p < 0.0001$; critical value = 15.13).

Hot boiling water she cried out. fetched the mirror out of her bag. look so tired and they went seemed to catch herself up." no no , worse , it's the other, so ill ! "She beamed on him."	Oh God, Oh God Oh heavens Oh goodness oh dear Oh dear	and to think Mrs she said, once she had Mrs Middleton listen to me" she if I go on like this I aren't I being ill-nat

Figure 4.2 UH (interjection) concordances.

adverbs and interjections. The general adverb (RR) and interjections (UH) categories include items often classified as pragmatic markers (Fraser 2006; Aijmer 2013): 'These expressions occur as part of a discourse segment but are not part of the propositional content of the message conveyed, and they do not contribute to the meaning of the proposition per se' (Fraser 2006: 189).[8] In this category we find items such as 'Well, just, so, surely, oh dear, oh God' (Figure 4.2).

Fraser (1996: 168) argues that pragmatic markers 'signal the speaker's potential communicative intentions'; Norrick (2009: 888–9) adds that interjections are actually complex and multifunctional units which mark much more than just emotional involvement so they can function as response tokens, backchannels, to signal contrast, elaboration, etc. Thus, the over-representation of some adverbs and interjections in his post-1950s novels, signalling the speaker's potential communicative intentions, functioning as response tokens, backchannels or other, hints at a more interactive kind of discourse than was found in Green's pre-oblique work. Added to the immediacy emerging from the overuse of present tense forms and first- and second-person pronouns seems to qualify oblique dialogue as more interactive than had been in the past. Finally, I compared the post-1950s corpus to the pre-1950s novels but focused on the semantic categories. The results of Figure 4.1 are further confirmed by the overuse of the Z4 category, the so-called discourse bin (Rayson 2009), which includes discourse markers and emphatic communication terms (Figure 4.3).

Some of the items included in the Z4 category are: 'oh, no, of course, all right, you know, I mean, after all, oh well.' Viewed from a semantic perspective, the oblique dialogue is equally characterized by an emphasis on the communicative and interpersonal aspect of the exchange. Incidentally, the semantic analysis also corroborates that character exchanges are often introduced by a narratorial voice in the form of speech acts verbs (category Q2.2) inclusive of items such as 'asked, replied, tell, demanded, protested' prototypically introducing reporting clauses.

Item	O1 (obl. dial)	%1	O2 (pre-obl. dial)	%2	LL	
Z4	2852	2.92	1600	2.38	+44.00	Discourse Bin
A13.6	248	0.25	77	0.11	+42.16	Deg: Diminishers
Z6	2558	2.62	1431	2.12	+40.50	Negative
A13.4	164	0.17	51	0.08	+27.79	Degree:Approximators
Q2.2	2337	2.39	1372	2.04	+22.40	Speech acts

Figure 4.3 Oblique dialogue (O1) compared to pre-oblique dialogue (O2)_overused SEMTAG categories (p < 0.0001; critical value = 15.13).

7. Conclusion

In this chapter, I have delved into the characteristics of Henry Green's writing with a view to ascertain to what extent this author succeeds in 'manipulating' his readers by having manifestly declared what his literary art is about. I have focused on the one technique he vehemently argued would give rise to the novel of the future, that is, dialogue. As Hentea (2014) argues:

> Dialogue is the foundational edifice of Green's novels. ... Dialogue is ... sloppy and inconsequential, rarely leading to a determined point. Unlike dialogue in realist novels, which with its rounded paragraphs, clearly struck semicolons and well-placed modifiers is often no different than monologue, Green's abounds in hesitations, deflecting comments and unanswered questions. (Hentea 2014: 71)

Literary appreciations such as this, though hermeneutic, lack exactness. In this chapter, I rigorously qualify previous interpretive assessments of Green's work by applying a combination of disciplines and methodologies that shed light on Green's technique and style. My analysis confirms that Green's oblique dialogue is in effect primarily in his last novels though certain aspects are already in operation in *Concluding* (1948). Green's ultimate act of manipulation, however, was his elusiveness[9] (Stokes 1959) for he was an author who, despite postulating on art and the novel, never pontificated; instead, he simply opined that 'narrative prose in future must be as diffuse and variously interpretable as life itself' (Green 1950a: 22).

Notes

1 http://www.oed.com
2 Critics such as Mellor (2011) or Hentea (2014) highlight the role that modernism played as a direct influence on his experimental interests.

3   The model has been amply revised especially by Semino and Short (2004) who include writing presentation and additional sub-categories.
4   Grice (1975: 49) originally proposed three ways in which speakers fail to observe the maxims, later extended to four: violation, opting out, a clash or a flouting. However, Thomas (1995: 72) argues that Grice was not consistent in his use of terminology; in fact, other researchers have subsequently identified a fifth category: suspending a maxim.
5   I did not isolate and categorize instances of floutings by exclusively looking at the dialogue sub-corpora as those stretches of language would be lacking a context. For the quantification and categorization of floutings, I considered the novels as a whole but ignored floutings found in the narrative sections.
6   The maxim of relation is flouted too as Mrs Weatherby provides not only an extremely long answer but her reply is also not pertinent to the question of her son's marriage.
7   The BNC Written Imaginative is part of the BNC Written Sampler and contains only fiction, primarily though not exclusively, literary prose. For more information, see the BNC User Reference Guide. Available at: http://www.natcorp.ox.ac.uk/docs/URG/BNCdes.html.
8   The nature and function of pragmatic markers have been broadly discussed. Aijmer and Simon-Vandenbergen (2011: 227) argue that these forms can include 'connectives, modal particles, pragmatic uses of modal adverbs, interjections, routines (*how are you*), feedback signals, vocatives, disjuncts (*frankly, fortunately*), pragmatic uses of conjunctions (*and, but*), approximators (hedges), reformulation markers'.
9   Green disliked being photographed and even posed with his back to the camera.

References

Aijmer, K. (2013) *Understanding Pragmatic Markers*. Edinburgh: Edinburgh University Press.
Aijmer, K. and Simon-Vandenbergen, A. M. (2011) 'Pragmatic markers', in Zienkowski, J., Östman, J. O. and Verschueren, J. (eds) *Discursive Pragmatics*,
    pp. 223–47. Amsterdam/Philadelphia: John Benjamins.
Axelsson, K. (2009) 'Research on fiction dialogue: Problems and possible solutions', in Jucker, A., Schreier, D. and Hundt, M. (eds) *Corpora: Pragmatics and Discourse*, pp. 189–202. Amsterdam: Rodopi.
Black, E. (2006) *Pragmatic Stylistics*. Edinburgh: Edinburgh University Press.
Chilton, P. (2011) 'Manipulation', in Zienkowski, J., Östman, J. O. and Verschueren, J. (eds) *Discursive Pragmatics*, pp. 176–89. Amsterdam/Philadelphia: John Benjamins.
Dunning, T. (1993) 'Accurate methods for the statistics of surprise and coincidence', *Computational Linguistics* 19(1): 61–74.

Fraser, B. (1996) 'Pragmatic markers', *Pragmatics* 6(2): 167–90.
Fraser, B. (2006) 'Towards a theory of discourse markers', in Fischer, K. (ed.) *Approaches to Discourse Particles*, pp. 189–204. Amsterdam: Elsevier.
Green, H. (1929) *Living*. London: Harvill HarperCollins.
Green, H. (1939) *Party Going*. London: Harvill HarperCollins.
Green, H. (1948) *Concluding*. London: Harvill HarperCollins.
Green, H. (1950a) 'The English novel of the future', *Contact*(1): 21–4.
Green, H. (1950b [1993]) 'A novelist to his readers I', in Yorke, M. (ed.) *Surviving*, pp. 136–42. London: Harvill HarperCollins.
Green, H. (1950c) *Nothing*. London: Harvill HarperCollins.
Green, H. (1952) *Doting*. London: Picador.
Green, H. (1958 [1993]) 'The art of fiction', in Yorke, M. (ed.) *Surviving*, pp. 234–50. London: Harvill HarperCollins.
Grice, H. P. (1975) 'Logic and conversation', in P. Cole and J. Morgan (eds) *Syntax and Semantics*, vol. 3, pp. 41–58. New York: Academic Press.
Hentea, M. (2010) 'Fictional doubles in Henry Green's *Back*', *The Revue of English Studies. New Series* 61(251): 614–26.
Hentea, M. (2014) *Henry Green at the Limits of Modernism*. Eastbourne: Sussex Academic Press.
Holmesland, O. (1986) *A Critical Introduction to Henry Green's Novels*. London: Macmillan.
Kukkonen, K. (2013) 'Flouting figures: Uncooperative narration in the fiction of Eliza Haywood', *Language and Literature* 22(3): 204–18.
Leech, G. and Short, M. (1981 [2007]) *Style in Fiction: A Linguistic Introduction to English Fictional Prose*. Harlow: Pearson Education Limited.
Mao, L. R. (1992) 'Fictional conversation and its pragmatic status', in Stein, D. (ed.) *Cooperating with Written Texts: The Pragmatics and Comprehension of Written Texts*, pp. 259–76. Berlin and New York: Mouton de Gruyter.
Mellor, L. (2011) *Reading the Ruins: Modernism, Bombsites and British Culture*. Cambridge: Cambridge University Press.
Montoro, R. (2018) 'The creative use of absences: A corpus stylistic approach to Henry Green's *Living* (1929)', *International Journal of Corpus Linguistics* 23(3): 279–310.
Norrick, N. R. (2009) 'Interjections as pragmatic markers', *Journal of Pragmatics* 41(5): 866–91.
Rayson, P. (2009) *Wmatrix: A Web-based Corpus Processing Environment*. Computing Department: Lancaster University. Available at: http://ucrel.lancs.ac.uk/wmatrix3.html (accessed 15 September 2017).
Romero Trillo, J. (2017) 'Corpus pragmatics', *Corpus Pragmatics* 1(1): 1–2.
Semino, E. (2014) 'Pragmatic failure, mind style and characterisation in fiction about autism', *Language and Literature* 23(2): 141–58.
Semino, E. and Short, M. (2004) *Corpus Stylistics: Speech, Writing and Thought Presentation in a Corpus of English Writing*. London and New York: Routledge.

Short, M. (1988) 'Speech presentation, the novel and the press', in van Peer, W. (ed.) *The Taming of the Text*, pp. 61–81. London: Routledge.

Sorlin, S. (2016) *Language and Manipulation in House of Cards: A Pragma-Stylistic Perspective*. London: Palgrave MacMillan.

Stokes, E. (1959) *The Novels of Henry Green*. London: The Hogarth Press.

Taylor, D. (1965) 'Catalytic rhetoric: Henry Green's theory of the modern novel', *Criticism* 7: 81–99.

Thomas, J. (1995) *Meaning in Interaction: An Introduction to Pragmatics*. Abingdon: Pearson Education Limited.

5

Building a world from the day's remains: Showing, telling, re-presenting

Jeremy Scott

1. Introduction

This chapter is the most recent outcome of a series of linked investigations into the mutually enriching relationship that exists between theoretical frameworks drawn from stylistic/narratology and creative writing practice – or what might be more specifically termed *narrative technique*. Accordingly, its interest is in the mechanics of narrative fiction and the methodological and technical choices that a writer makes in the crafting of a fictional text, the resulting expressive effects on the reader (in the terms of this volume, how specific narrative techniques achieve aesthetic *manipulation of the reader*), and the ways in which stylistic analysis can draw attention to and explain these facets of reading and writing. The focus here is *not* upon the pedagogy of creative writing as a taught subject, but rather an exploration of just one of the ways in which stylistics theory and creative practice 'at the coal face' can be in dialogue with another. It is an underlying principle of what follows that the practice of stylistics can directly inform and augment the practice of writing.

So far, research and discussion within this area has approached the topic from two distinct (but, it is hoped, ultimately complementary) approaches: first, from the vantage point of what Carter (2010) terms 'steam stylistics'. This perspective has explored how a critical taxonomy drawn from literary stylistics and its analysis of extant literary texts might augment practitioners' understanding of the effects of, for example, focalization and point of view, figurative language, the presentation of character-generated discourse (speech, thought and writing), modality/attitude and syntactic choice (e.g. transitivity, nominalization and attribution of agency). Examples of this work include Nash (1980), Pope (2005) and Scott (2013). The second strand, both responding to and directly informing the cognitive turn across the Humanities (Garrett 2016), embraces perspectives drawn from cognitive poetics (Stockwell 2002, 2009; Gavins and Steen 2003) exploring how a richer understanding of how readers actually read could inform creative practice. Facets of cognitive poetics under discussion in this connection include schema theory, empathy and engagement, the concept of fictional minds (e.g. Palmer 2004) and, in particular, Text World Theory (Werth 1999; Gavins 2007). Examples of this work are more recent and fewer in number, but include Dietz (2012), Freiman (2015), Scott (2016, 2018) and McLoughlin (2016).

This chapter draws upon two theoretical and descriptive models drawn from each of these approaches with a view to combining their insights. The first is rooted in rhetoric and based upon corpus stylistic analysis of twentieth-century fiction in English to produce what is, to all intents and purposes, a complete linguistic description of the various strategies writers use to present the discourse of characters (Semino and Short 2004; Short 2007). The second, Text World Theory, is rooted in cognitive poetics and based upon the TEXT IS A WORLD metaphor. Short and Semino's updated discourse presentation taxonomy will be combined with aspects of Text World Theory and Herman's (2009) cognitive conception of storyworlds to address a specific question of narrative methodology which arises in processes of first-person, homodiegetic (Genette 1983) narration, where the controlling entity of the fictional world is simultaneously a *narrator* and a *character* in that storyworld. Herman defines a storyworld as follows:

> [Storyworlds are] global mental representations enabling interpreters to frame inferences about the situations, characters and occurrences either explicitly mentioned in or implied by a narrative text or discourse. As such, storyworlds are mental models of the situations and events being recounted – of who did what to and with whom, when, where, why, and in what manner. Reciprocally, narrative artefacts (texts, films etc.) provide blueprints for the creation and modification of such mentally configured storyworlds. (Herman 2009: 72–3)

This chapter will usually default to the term *storyworld* in this sense (a mental model built in response to a narrative artefact) instead of text-world in order to capture the fact that the fictional worlds under discussion here are broader in scope than those typically discussed in Text World Theory analysis; where the latter aims to map a reader's conceptual world-building processes at the level of sentence and paragraph, the concern of this chapter is mainly with the larger-scale worlds that fictional texts build in their entirety. That said, terminology and concepts from Text World Theory will be deployed as and where relevant to identify and analyse exactly how and where and by what linguistic cues the switches between different worlds are achieved.

Of particular interest in this connection will be the intermeshing of the conflicting demands of *mimesis* in relation to *diegesis*, and how these twin demands are negotiated when the narrator is functioning as both *representer* (telling the story, setting the scene etc.) and *represented* (as the central protagonist of the storyworld). What will be termed the 'problem' of homodiegetic narration seems particularly acute when the narrative discourse is in the present tense, and the narrating voice appears to be 'floating' in an undefined context or conceptual space. The narrating entity must simultaneously represent what she or he is thinking, what she or he is doing and also what other characters are doing too (Phelan (2005: 117) discusses these distinctions in terms of 'narrator's focalisation and voice', defining 'focalization', in line with Prince (2001) and Chatman (1990), as perception by a character in the story). In short, the homodiegetic narrator must mediate her own voice (mimesis) while, at the same time, mediating the storyworld: its contents, the movements of characters within it, what they say and do and so on (diegesis). It will be suggested here that, at times, this need to combine the two processes can have a detrimental effect on the world-building functions of the narrative, sometimes to the point of alienating the reader. The challenge for the writer is to avoid that moment of arrest, the point where the storyworld, with its ambitions towards a kind of 'authenticity' that will facilitate the reader's experiential immersion within it (Ryan 1999: 112–4), becomes too incompatible with or estranged from the reader's understanding of the actual world. This moment of arrest can happen in the split discourse-world (Gavins 2007: 26)[1] of homodiegetic narration, through various kinds of linguistic compatibility, or within the storyworld itself, when the homodiegetic narrative voice is required to fluctuate, with equiponderance, from one side of the mimesis-diegesis cline to the other. The discourse presentation scale combined with aspects of Text World Theory can illustrate and indicate how and where the 'problem' arises, and also, crucially, point the way towards a possible solution. Addressing a question rooted in stylistics will point towards a revealing answer to one of fictional technique.

2. Key terms and concepts: Mimesis and diegesis, discourse presentation and stylistic balance

It is no easy matter to define *mimesis* and *diegesis* in a rigorous manner, and the history of the terms' usage is fraught with contradictions, re-interpretations and new applications. The words are, of course, classical in origin; semantic traces of the original meaning of *mimesis* can be found in modern English verbs such as *mimic, imitate* and *mime* – all denoting some process of representing reality that involves 'copying' or 'counterfeiting' (involving also the pejorative connotations that can be attached to these terms). For Plato, however, diegesis was the overarching category that denoted all of the poet's[2] processes of world-building; diegesis *entails* mimesis. Plato divided diegesis into three separate types:

1) *Haple diegesis*: 'plain' (or unmixed) diegesis in the voice of the poet.
2) *Diegesis dia mimeseos*: narrative through mimesis, that is, in the represented voices of characters.
3) *Diegesis di' amphoteron*: 'mixed' diegesis which combines these modes, as in Homeric epic.[3]

Thus, in Plato's exploration of the concept, all verbal art relies upon diegesis: the building of a world through language. Any instance of narration is, by its very nature, diegetic. For Aristotle, on the other hand, all art (and this includes verbal art) is mimetic in that it inevitably and intrinsically imitates reality to a greater or lesser extent (*Poetics*, 3.1448a19-24); he does not use the term 'diegesis' at all.[4]

In more recent literary and narratological criticism and theory (see Lodge 1990; Genette 1983; Rimmon-Kenan 1989; Chatman 1990), the terms have tended to be simplified and condensed as follows. *Diegesis* is used to refer to representation of action in the voice of a narrator; *mimesis* signals the representation of the imitated voices of characters. Mimesis 'represents', diegesis 'reports'. Mimesis 'embodies', diegesis 'narrates'. Mimesis 'transforms', diegesis 'indicates'. Mimesis knows only a continuous present, while diegesis looks back on a past. It could be argued, however, that Plato's approach was closest to the truth of the matter. *All* narrative discourse entails diegesis, as 'pure' mimesis in language is all but impossible. Even in the forms of direct discourse such as Free Direct Speech and Thought (FDS/T), textual representations of spoken (or 'thought') utterances can never be a perfect rendering of what exactly was said (or thought) and the manner in which it was spoken. Note too that mimesis always entails *representation* or *mediation*. In verbal art, this representation is enacted via the voice of a narrator. Rimmon-Kenan sums up this position as follows:

> No text of narrative fiction can show or imitate the action it conveys, since all texts are made of language, and language signifies without imitating. Language can only imitate language, which is why the representation of speech comes closest to pure mimesis, but even here ... there is a narrator who 'quotes' the

characters' speech, thus reducing the directness of 'showing'. All that a narrative can do is create an illusion, an effect, a semblance of mimesis, but it does so through diegesis. (Rimmon-Kenan 1989: 108)

It would be understandable, therefore, to arrive at the conclusion that the two terms are insufficiently distinguishable in any rigorous or principled sense to be of much utility in a discussion of narrative technique rooted in stylistics. This holds particularly true for novelistic discourse, which will often contain a plethora of character discourse presentation strategies and methods, and a continual blending of the two modes. However, this chapter will follow (and augment) the approach outlined in Scott (2013): that the terms *can* be made more rigorous by considering *linguistic* composition (or style) in addition to their aesthetic effect (the ways in which they manipulate the reader and inform the process of world building). This means taking into account the extent to which a particular piece of narrative is dominated by character discourse or, conversely, by the discourse of the narrator, and/or a blend of both discourses, with reference to the discourse presentation scale as originally theorized by Semino and Short (2004) and revised and updated in Short (2007).[5]

A cline of narratorial influence can be traced between Narration, at the bottom of the table, where diegesis and the narrator's discourse are dominant, through to FDS, Thought and Writing at the top, where the narrator's language is (or seems to be?) absent and the language of the represented character dominates (mimesis), with a mid-point occurring in Free Indirect Discourse (FID; encompassing writing, speech and thought), where the discourse of character and narrator blend. This can be represented diagrammatically (see Figure 5.1).

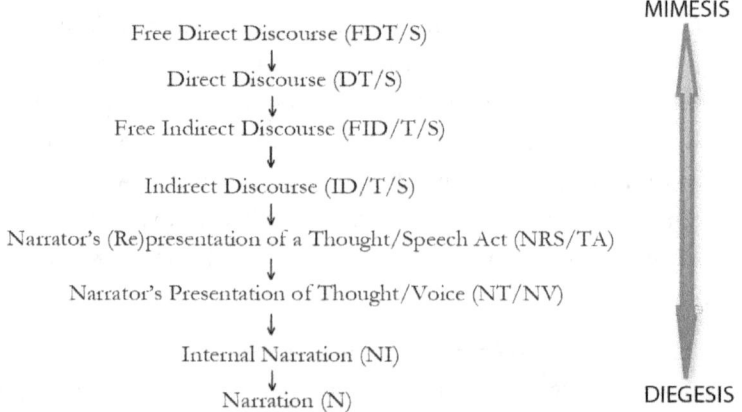

Figure 5.1 The cline between narrator and character discourse.

Table 5.1 Discourse Presentation Taxonomy [place call-out under table, please]

		Discourse Presentation			
Speech Presentation		**Writing Presentation**		**Thought Presentation**	
FDS	Free Direct Speech	FDW	Free Direct Writing	FDT	Free Direct Thought
DS	Direct Speech	DW	Direct Writing	DT	Direct Thought
FIS	Free Indirect Speech	FIW	Free Indirect Writing	FIT	Free Indirect Thought
IS	Indirect Speech	IW	Indirect Writing	IT	Indirect Thought
NRSA	Narrator's (Re)presentation of a Speech Act	NRWA	(Re)presentation of a Writing Act	NRTA	(Re)presentation of a Thought Act
NV	Narrator's presentation of Voice	NW	Narrator's presentation of Writing	NT	Narrator's presentation of Thought
				NI	Internal Narration
N	Narration	N	Narration	N	Narration

Until now, there has been no satisfactory analysis of how this taxonomy functions when applied to homodiegetic narrative situations of the kind to be discussed in this chapter: where the narrator is also a principal character in the storyworld, and where the action unfolds in the 'here and now' of the act of narration (a narrative device termed *simultaneity* in Scott 2009: 11). The 'problem' should be summarized again here for the sake of clarity. A first-person narrator may be both, as it were, 'thinking aloud' (at the moment of narration) and narrating diegetically (i.e. telling the story, narrating events that are happening simultaneously with the act of narration or narrating past events). Surely, though, it is desirable for stylistic analysis to be able to distinguish between the two effects. The term 'direct thought' implies *a priori* external discourse which is being represented by a fictional entity separate to the one that generated it. There must be an instance of external discourse to present; for example, the narrator might present the speech (or, less often, their interpretation of the thoughts) of another character. However, the homodiegetic character/narrator is certainly thinking (they are articulating their thoughts in the 'now' of the act of narration). In other words, they are representing their own thoughts, and no discourse presentation is taking place. These two different tendencies of homodiegetic narration (corresponding to the mimetic and diegetic aspects of narrative discourse as properly defined above) must work closely together to mediate the world of the fiction as effectively as possible, given the nature of the particular artistic project in hand. Concepts drawn from Text World Theory (and, more broadly, cognitive conceptions of storyworlds) can help to distinguish more rigorously between the two, and, perhaps, to pinpoint those moments of 'arrest' where particular ontological and epistemological frameworks are in danger of blending where they should be separate.

It will now be useful to provide some examples of this 'problem' of homodiegesis (a problem both of stylistic classification and of aesthetic effect on the reader) in action:[6]

> [1] Vic slides the jar carefully back into the box. [2] It's eleven twenty by Slattery's clock and it feels less churchy. [3] There's more punters coming in. [4] Someone puts on the music machine. [5] Going back some day, come what may, to Blue Bayou ... . [6] That's better, that's better. (Swift 1996: 12)

The above short excerpt from the opening of Graham Swift's *Last Orders* (1996) attempts to mediate three aspects of the storyworld (almost) simultaneously. First, there is the diegetic description of what is going on around the narrator (this takes up sentences 1–4). Second, the song that starts playing on the jukebox, 'Blue Bayou', is represented via a snatch of its lyrics (sentence 5). Third, the thoughts of the narrator (a character called Ray), in this case his reaction to the music as it spreads around the pub, are presented verbatim in sentence 6 ('That's better, that's better'). Were this an instance of heterodiegetic narration, with the narrator occupying a conceptual and ontological space *other* than that of the storyworld, then it would be a relatively straightforward matter to classify this sentence as Free Direct Thought, or FDT (Short 2007: 232): the precise thoughts of the character are presented unmediated, as far as this is possible, by any intrusion on the part of a narrator, who is a separate entity to the character. However, *Last Orders* is an instance of homodiegetic narration (the narrator is *of* the storyworld), and so, as discussed above, the application of Short and Semino's discourse presentation scale becomes problematic. The discourse is 'generated' by the same fictional entity that presents it, and thus, in the terms of this chapter, mimetic and diegetic processes occur conterminously.

This fact draws attention to the somewhat paradoxical nature of the narrative conventions which are in play here. The narrator, Ray, is also a character, and is attempting to present the storyworld for the benefit of the reader as it unfolds around him, simultaneously with the 'here and now' of the action. A blend of mimetic and diegetic functions can be identified, with sentences 1, 2, 3 and 4 corresponding broadly to the latter (setting the scene for the benefit of the reader in narratorial mode, despite their being classifiable also as character discourse) and sentences 5 and 6 to the former (his own thoughts and reactions to the scene). The character/narrator Ray's narrative voice seems to 'float' in undefined space: he is not *writing* in the fictional world of that novel, and neither is he speaking aloud. Also, he must represent the action of the world, construct it for the benefit of the reader, as well as represent his own thoughts and reactions to the events that take place within it. He is both actor and director in his own drama. The difficulty hinges on whether we treat homodiegetic narrators of this type first and foremost as *narrators* or as *characters* in the storyworld. They are both, of course as Phelan (2005: 114–7) argues, 'narrators can be focalizers') – but it would be useful from the perspective of both stylistic analysis and the principled discussion of creative practice to be able to distinguish as far as is possible between the roles and effects of the two agencies.

A similar narrative situation occurs in Niall Griffiths's demotic novel *Kelly + Victor* (2002):

> I pick the kettle up to test its weight, see if there's enough water in it for a brew. There isn't, so I work the lead out of its attachment, take the kettle over

> to the sink – which involves, in this tiny kitchen, no movement other than a 180-degree spin – turn the cold tap on, hold the spout under the flow an keep it there for a count of three. Spin back, reattach the lead, flick the two switches; the one on the wall socket an the one on the kettle itself. I bend an put me ear to the kettle to listen for the rumble, I like doin this, I don't know why. (Griffiths 2002: 123)

In this example, the discourse of the character-narrator is occupied chiefly with diegesis: the description of activity in the storyworld. In contrast to the excerpt from *Last Orders*, the fact that the narrator is describing *his own* actions and movements as they take place rather than his surroundings seems to foreground the essential artificiality of the convention even more starkly. These words do not (re)present (or mediate) his actual thoughts, and are thus diegetic. The final two clauses, however, ('I like doin this, I don't know why') are mimetic in orientation, and *do* present the character-narrator's own thoughts about and reactions to what he is doing. Again, however, it would still not be appropriate to label these two clauses as examples of FDT; the narrator's discourse is not being 'presented' as such, it occurs with and as part of the act of narration itself, in the 'here and now' of the storyworld. To emphasize this point, consider the excerpt if re-written as heterodiegetic narration:

> He spins back, reattaches the lead, flicks the two switches; the one on the wall socket and the one on the kettle itself. He bends an puts his ear to the kettle to listen for the rumble, he likes doin this, he doesn't know why.

The first sentence and the first clause of the second are Narration (N). The last two clauses can now with confidence be labelled as Narrator's Presentation of Thought (NT). More arguably, 'he likes doin this' could be classified as Internal Narration (NI) with 'he doesn't know why' as NT. The introduction of NI into the thought presentation scale has proved problematic to some extent. Short (2007: 235) defines it as 'the narration of internal states and events'; in other words, as more generalized statements that a narrator makes about characters' inner worlds, rather than about the external storyworld of the fiction. However, Toolan (2001: 142) has argued that these kinds of statements are simply acts of narration (in the terms of this chapter, purely diegetic), and should thus be considered as outside the thought presentation scale. I would suggest that the crucial difference between NI and NT or Narrator's Representation of a Thought Act (NRTA) is that instances of NI *do not relate to a specific instance of internally articulated discourse in the storyworld*. Rather, they present emotions, feelings, reactions and so on (such as 'he likes doin this'). Further, mental states and emotions are, of course, not always simply articulable as coherent thought which can be 'translated into', or represented by, discourse. Thus, this excerpt illustrates both a problem of stylistic classification and a methodological problem: the essential artifice inherent in a character-narrator describing his own actions simultaneously with the moment in which they happen in the storyworld. The conditions of what Leech and Short, in reference to thought presentation, call 'a necessary licence' (2007: 70) have been violated.

The following final example of 'the problem of homodiegesis' is taken from Patrick McCabe's 1992 novel *The Butcher Boy*:

> [1] Or maybe you didn't know you were a pig. Is that it? [2] Well, then, I'll have to teach you. [3] I'll make sure you won't forget again in a hurry. [4] You too Mrs Nugent! [5] Come on now! [6] Come on now come on now and none of your nonsense. [7] That was a good laugh, I said it just like the master in the school. [8] Right today we are going to do pigs. [9] I want you all to stick out your faces and scrunch up your noses just like snouts. [10] That's very good Philip. [11] I found a lipstick in one of the drawers and I wrote in big letters across the wallpaper PHILIP IS A PIG. [12] Now, I said, isn't that good? [13] Yes Francie said Philip. ... [14] Mrs Nugent, I said, astonished, that is absolutely wonderful! [15] Thank you Francie said Mrs Nugent. [16] So that was the pig school. ... [17] I told them I didn't want to catch them walking upright anymore and if I did they would be in very serious trouble. [18] Do you understand Philip? [19] Yes he said. [20] And you too Mrs Nugent. [21] It's your responsibility as a sow to see that Philip behaves as a good pig should. ... [22] I am a pig said Philip. [23] I am a sow said Mrs Nooge. (McCabe 1992: 60–1)

This extract contains a torrential blend of discourse presentation, yet still, crucially enveloped within an overarching homodiegetic narrative situation. The following examples appear to be classifiable as FDS: sentences 1–10, with the exception of the brief instance of Narration (N) at the end of sentence 7, 12–15 and 18–23. There is also an instance of Indirect Speech (IS): sentence 17. However, it is important to note that, in the storyworld, all of this action takes place in the character-narrator Francie Brady's imagination. It is a fantasy, and thus presentation, once again, of the narrator's *own thoughts*, not of anterior character-generated discourse occurring independently of the narrator. The lack of any speech marks bears out this observation. Once again, the discourse presentation scale is not applicable. In addition, the 'artificiality' (the foregrounding of an overly ostensible process of narration) of the approach taken in *Kelly + Victor* is avoided.

A final concept needs to be introduced that will be relevant to the ensuing discussion: *stylistic balance*. This is best envisioned as a (probably) Platonic (and thus) chimerical ideal where the mimetic and diegetic functions of narrative discourse as defined previously are working together harmoniously and effectively. In the examples discussed above, the two functions are, arguably, to a greater or lesser extent, at war with one another, with one function in the ascendance at one moment before switching abruptly to the other. In the terms of stylistics, and most obviously in the first two examples, less so in the third, there is a continual and at times disruptive fluctuation between what Phelan (2005: 115) calls 'telling' and 'representing'. Boulter (2007: 77) summarizes the notion as follows, with two sentences that could be read as a summary of the central contention of this chapter:

Stylistic balance does not call attention to itself. It calls attention to the fiction.

This is the key concept: the most appropriate or apposite style for any individual piece of imaginative writing should, as far as is possible, *call attention to the fiction*.[7] The concept is illustrated diagrammatically in Figure 5.2.

Greater emphasis on one side of the seesaw leads, inevitably, to a lessening of emphasis on the other. The canvas of a piece of imaginative writing is of a fixed size. It is the task of the writer to manipulate the balance between these two functions of narrative discourse in the most effective way possible. When this process is successful, the reader is engaged, empathetic, and experientially immersed (Toolan 2008: 106). When it fails, the reader is disinterested and alienated. This failure occurs when the homodiegetic narrator, by definition a character in his or her own fiction, unwittingly draws back the curtains at the side of the stage to reveal the author as puppeteer, crouching, no longer hidden.

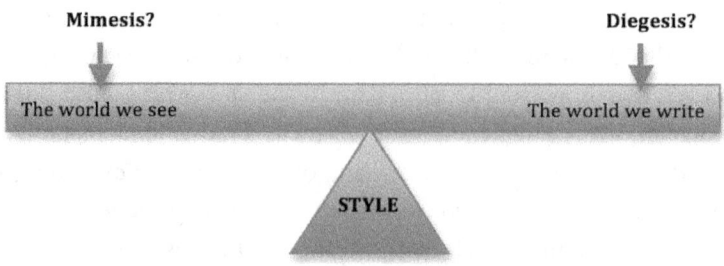

Figure 5.2 Stylistic Balance.

It will be useful now to summarize the discussion thus far. In *heterodiegetic* narrative situations:

- mimesis and diegesis can be seen as occurring on a cline of influence between narrator and character (with FID as a blend of both perspectives);
- the discourse of the narrator will merge with the discourse of the character at the mid-point of the scale;
- character discourse will be ascendant in FDS/T and narrator discourse will dominate in N;
- the narrator discourse is *representing* (chiefly through N), character discourses are *represented* (through various discourse presentation strategies);

In *homodiegetic* simultaneous narrative situations:

- the character-narrator represents and is represented in the 'now' of the storyworld; there is no *a priori* discourse to be presented (only that of other characters, principally through speech/voice); therefore, the taxonomy defined in Short (2007) does not apply to the narrator's discourse;
- the 'epistemic space' around the narrator and mediator of the storyworld is smaller, more confined, and less flexible;
- the canvas upon which the writer paints is of a fixed size: bearing in mind that the latter is accessed, of course, via the discourse of the former, there can be more emphasis on character, less on storyworld, or more on storyworld, less on character; the relationship between the two has been termed 'stylistic balance';
- this stylistic balance is delicately poised, and easily disturbed (the seesaw metaphor);
- sometimes, the character (mimetic) mode is dominant; at other times, the narrator (diegetic) mode is dominant;
- the same entity performs both functions, and sometimes this can be unwieldy, drawing unwitting attention to the narrative process and inhibiting engagement and immersion.

As a final example, the opposite ends of the seesaw can be seen moving up and down in turn in this further extract from *Last Orders*:

> [1] She looks again at the water. [2] 'You know how when he had a change of mind, the whole world had to change too.' [3] He said, 'we're going to be new people.' [4] She gives another little snort. [5] 'New people.'

[6] I look away across the garden because I don't want her to see the thought that might be showing in my face: [7] that it's a pretty poor starting-point, all said, for becoming new people, a bungalow in Margate. [8] It's not exactly the promised land.
[9] There's a nurse chomping a sandwich on a bench in the far corner. [10] Pigeons waddling. (Swift 1996: 15–6)

Sentences 1, 4, 6, 9 and 10 are Narration, pure diegesis ('the world we write'). Sentences 2, 3 and 5 are Direct Speech (the narrator presents the discourse of another character). Sentences 7 and 8 are the narrator's own thoughts, presented as they occur, and thus mimetic ('the world we see'); yet, they cannot be classified as Free Direct Thought since, once again, this is *not* an instance of a fictional entity presenting the *a priori* discourse of another. Note, in addition, the elision present in sentence 10, 'pigeons waddling', which attempts to mimic thought patterns in the manner characteristic of stream-of-consciousness techniques; syntactic or grammatical deviation of this type is virtually a defining feature of stream-of-consciousness writing (Scott 2013: 110). It must be remembered that these varying presentation types all occur within the overarching framework of a homodiegetic narration, and thus the narrative voice's status as a presentation of discourse is arguable. The narrator (Ray) is not representing another's discourse, but simply translating his 'thought' into words; that is, in a general sense, he is narrating. There is no discourse external to his own consciousness to represent. However, this narration attempts to carry out two functions simultaneously: on one hand, it mediates action in the world for the benefit of the reader (in Phelan's terms, it *tells*); on the other, it *represents* Ray's idiosyncratic perception of that world. Thus, the extract constitutes a continual toing and froing between the extremes of mimesis and diegesis; stylistic balance as defined above is not achieved.

A final, but significant, caveat: it is, of course, perfectly possible to argue that the foregrounded tension between mimetic and diegetic function in the above examples is unimportant. The reader of these types of homodiegetic narration is happy to accept, through a kind of acculturation to literary convention or the acquisition and activation of narrative schema (Mason 2014), that the narrative voice comes at him or her from an undefined space. A comparison might be made with silent film or opera, for example: the audience is content to 'suspend disbelief' when dialogue is presented via flashcards or when a character bursts into song. However, the central argument of this chapter is that discussion and analysis of these kinds of narrative situation lead the way towards important lessons for narrative technique and creative practice, as well as for the principled stylistic description of fictional discourse, and that there are other, perhaps more effective, ways of working with character narration that more successfully manipulate the reader.

3. *The Remains of the Day*

An example of a novel which, it will be argued, achieves stylistic balance is Kazuo Ishiguro's *Remains of the Day* (1989). The text negotiates the interplay of mimesis and diegesis in homodiegetic narration simultaneous with action in the storyworld very effectively and manages to avoid an 'upset' in the processes of building a fictional world through a narrative technique which makes use of analepsis, or flashback. The novel is narrated by Stevens, a butler to, first, an English Lord and owner of the stately home Darlington Hall and, second, to his successor, an American businessman. There are two principal storyworlds to be mediated by Stevens's narrative: one in the 'now' of the act of narration (the year 1956) and the other in the past, in the run up to the Second World War, and built through flashbacks instigated by the narrator. The primary storyworld, as with the previous examples, is located in the 'now' of the act of narration; hence, it is more mimetic in orientation, and associated with presentation of Stevens's train of thought. The various past storyworlds are cued up by temporal deictic shifts; hence, they can be construed as narrative in the conventional sense, and thus diegetic in orientation.

Of course, the situation is more complex than that and the novel as a whole has a very rich and varied texture. The past and present storyworlds intertwine and coexist, and detailed Text World Theory analysis of the novel (e.g. Whiteley 2011) can unpick and deconstruct this texture to useful effect, capturing world-switches at a minute level, often within the space of a single sentence. However, as already discussed, for the purposes of this more 'wide-angle' discussion of the novel's narrative technique it is sufficient to distinguish between two main storyworlds. One can be considered primary (July 1956 and the journey from Darlington Hall to the English West Country) inasmuch as it is the first world the reader is introduced to, and also that it unfolds in the here and now of the act of narration (simultaneity). This principal world is augmented by the series of past storyworlds (the run-up to the Second World War); this approach is justified through careful examination of the text, which shows that the world-shifts are indeed, primarily but not exclusively, temporal, constituting a simple tense shift, and the novel shows itself to switch between past and present worlds in a relatively simple, alternating pattern. The principal storyworld, then, occurs at the level of the discourse itself and involves stylistic specification of the 'now' of the act of narration, while the past worlds occur at the level of 'story' and are dependent upon areas of character-narrator knowledge.

The first extract to be analysed comes from the opening of the novel:

> [1] It seems increasingly likely that I really will undertake the expedition that has been preoccupying my imagination now for some days. An expedition, I should say, which [2] I will undertake alone, in the comfort of Mr Farraday's Ford; an expedition which, as I foresee it, will take me through much of the finest countryside of England to the West Country, and may keep me away from Darlington Hall for as much as five or six days. [3] The idea of such a journey came about, I should point out, from a most kind suggestion put to me by Mr Farraday himself one afternoon almost a fortnight ago, when I had been dusting the portraits in the library. In fact, as I recall, I was up on the step-ladder dusting the portrait of Viscount Wetherby when my employer had entered carrying a few volumes which he presumably wished returned to the shelves. On seeing my person, he took the opportunity [4] to inform me [5] that he had just that moment finalized plans to return to the United States for a period of five weeks between August and September. [6] Having made this announcement, my employer put his volumes down on a table, seated himself on the chaise-longue, and stretched out his legs.
>
> It was then, gazing up at me, [7] that he said, [8] 'You realize, Stevens, I don't expect you to be locked up here in this house all the time I'm away.' (Ishiguro 1989: 3)

Sentence 1 sets up the initial text-world, the primary storyworld of the novel, and its temporal and spatial position is dual in that it occupies the moment of narration, made clear by a heading at the opening of the text: 'July 1956, Darlington Hall' (note the deictic 'now' which aligns the time of narration with that date), but also the future. In sentence 2, the future tense becomes clearer, enacting a deictic world-switch, enactor-accessible, reflecting the narrator's perspective and inner thoughts about his plans for the journey. Here at the opening point of the novel, two worlds seem to coexist: a present and a future, preparing the reader for the continual time shifts that come later. Almost immediately, in sentence 3, another deictic world-switch takes place which introduces the first of a group of past text-worlds which, taken together, form the other of the two primary storyworlds of the novel. The initial storyworld of July 1956, while primary in that it contains the act of narration itself, is backgrounded to a great extent throughout the novel, and this is of course of thematic importance. The other, past, storyworld is cued up by a tense shift, and temporal deixis: 'The idea of such a journey came about, I should point out, from a most kind suggestion put to me by Mr Farraday himself one afternoon almost a fortnight ago.' The rest of the extract builds that second world in more detail, with another world-switch occurring with the Direct Speech (of Lord Darlington) at sentence 8.

Note also the many epistemic modal markers and indicators of uncertainty in the extract – *seems increasingly likely, should say, as I foresee it, I should point out, as I recall* – which indicate a very obvious *unreliability*. This foregrounded modality lends the opening of the novel a sense of being, in the terms of Text World Theory, an epistemic modal-world (this point will be returned to and expanded upon shortly). In any case, it is the world of July 1956 to which the reader is returned continually from the many flashbacks that occur throughout the rest of the novel, and Stevens is its enactor, both building it and indicating attitudes to it through modality.

When it comes to discourse presentation strategies, in the primary storyworld as introduced, briefly, at the opening of the extract (sentences 1 and 2), the discourse is oriented towards a *mimetic* function. It is a presentation of the thoughts of the narrator. Accordingly, Stevens is in this world functioning primarily as a *character* and thus it is acceptable to argue that the narrative discourse takes on the tone of presentation of thought (or direct thought) – even though there is no *a priori* discourse being presented.

Another extract from the primary storyworld will bear out this observation:

It would seem there is a whole dimension to the question 'what is a "great" butler?' I have hitherto not properly considered. It is, I must say, a rather unsettling experience to realize this about a matter so close to my heart, particularly one I have given much thought to over the years. But it strikes me I may have been a little hasty before in dismissing certain aspects of the Hayes Society's criteria for membership. I have no wish, let me make clear, to retract any of my ideas on 'dignity' and its crucial link with 'greatness'. But I have been thinking a little more about that other pronouncement made by the Hayes Society – namely the admission that it was a prerequisite for membership of the Society that 'the applicant be attached to a distinguished household'. My feeling remains, no less than before, that this represents a piece of unthinking snobbery on the part of the Society. However, it occurs to me that perhaps what one takes objection to is, specifically, the outmoded understanding of what a 'distinguished household' is, rather than to the general principle being expressed. Indeed, now that I think further on the matter, I believe it may well be true to say it is a prerequisite of greatness that one 'be attached to a distinguished household' – so long as one takes 'distinguished' here to have a meaning deeper than that understood by the Hayes Society. (Ishiguro 1989: 119)

This section reads as thought 'set down', ordered and crystalized in language; note the predominance of *mental* processes in terms of transitivity and relational function-advancing propositions: 'It strikes me that', 'I have been thinking', 'My feeling remains', 'I believe' and 'it occurs to me that'. Of course, there is an enormous amount that remains 'unsaid' in Stevens's discourse; the reader will be constantly 'looking beyond' the surface of the discourse itself to the unstated truths about Stevens's inner life: his loneliness, his unfulfilled love for Miss Kenton, the devotion to his job which masks a deeper absence in his world and so on. This impression of reticence, or understatement, is, again, abetted by the foregrounded modality in the extract ('would seem', 'may have been' etc.). It is possible to argue that an epistemic modal-world is cued up which is reader-accessible, but not enactor-accessible; indeed, this narrative situation could well provide a workable definition of narrative unreliability. Stevens seems unaware of (or deliberately ignores) his own feelings, so removed has he become from them; or, if he is aware of them, he denies them, or, to use a slightly threadbare psychoanalytical term, he represses them. Thus, a primary thematic concern of the novel, which, arguably, branches out into an exploration of Englishness and a notion of peculiarly English mindsets, is reprised narratologically. In any case, in the primary storyworld of July 1956, in the 'now' of the act of narration, Stevens is articulating his thoughts (thought is being presented, perhaps by being written down in journal form, although this is never made completely clear). Thus, he functions primarily as a *character* and the stylistic balance is oriented towards a mimetic mode.

The second extract to be analysed comes from one of the past storyworlds, cued up by a series of deictic world-switches. The narrative situation here is markedly different:

> [1] The study doors are those that face one as one comes down the great staircase. [2] There is outside the study today a glass cabinet displaying various of Mr Farraday's ornaments, but throughout Lord Darlington's days, there stood at that spot a bookshelf containing many volumes of encyclopedia, including a complete set of the Britannica. [3] It was a ploy of Lord Darlington's to stand at this shelf studying the spines of the encyclopedias as I came down the staircase, and sometimes, to increase the effect of an accidental meeting, he would actually pull out a volume and pretend to be engrossed as I completed my descent. [4] Then, as I passed him, he would say: 'Oh, Stevens, there was something I meant to say to you.' [5] And with that, he would wander back into his study, to all appearances still thoroughly engrossed in the volume held open in his hands. [6] It was invariably embarrassment at what he was about to impart which made

Lord Darlington adopt such an approach, and even once the study door was closed behind us, he would often stand by the window and make a show of consulting the encyclopedia throughout our conversation.

What I am now describing, incidentally, is one of many instances I could relate to you to underline Lord Darlington's essentially shy and modest nature. (Ishiguro 1989: 63)

The style here is characteristic of Narration, including one instance of Direct Speech in sentence 5. The tense in sentence 1 and in the first clause of sentence 2 is present, identifying the new world explicitly with the primary storyworld of the 'now' of narration. Stevens begins his flashback, or analepsis, by providing us with a point of connection between the two worlds – the way in which the study doors are still in the same place, but what is opposite them has changed – before enacting a world-switch in the second clause of sentence 2: a shift to past tense (characteristic of N), using 'would' to indicate repeated action. In this extract, and in other instances of the past storyworld, Stevens's primary function (or orientation) switches from that of character as in the previous two extracts to that of *narrator*. Indeed, he is enactor of the new text-world *and* narrator, and, accordingly, presents the discourse of another character. As already mentioned, there is an instance of Direct Speech in sentence 4 and in sentence 6 an instance of NRTA; the discourse presentation scale can be usefully applied. Uncharacteristically, the modal adverb 'invariably' lends the discourse an air of certainty so often lacking from Stevens's discourse elsewhere. Furthermore, in another linguistic feature characteristic of the narrative, diegetic orientation of novelistic discourse, the function-advancing propositions in the extract are dominated by *material* rather than mental processes: 'stood', 'came down', 'pull out', 'pretend' and so on. As in the opening of the novel, there is a strong sense of the two storyworlds, past and present, being concomitant; again, this narratological conceit highlights another central theme of the novel: the coexistence of past and present, and how we live and experience our lives both 'in' and 'out' of 'the now'.

4. Conclusions

This chapter has argued that homodiegetic narration which occurs simultaneously with the unfolding of the story's action is prone to certain methodological paradoxes, the most prominent of which is the 'upsetting' of a delicate stylistic balance due to the requirement for the narrator (often) to be both narrating and thinking (diegetically telling and mimetically representing) at the same time. If greater emphasis is placed on one side of the seesaw, then, inevitably, less will be placed on the other. Pushing down on one end of the plank causes the other end to rise up in the air as the two ends are, of course, interdependent.

In contrast to some of the examples discussed earlier in this chapter, Ishiguro's novel avoids the conflict between the twin demands of diegesis and mimesis characteristic of homodiegetic narration through a deft intermeshing of the two main storyworlds of the novel and the movement (or alternation) between them. The storyworld of July 1956, occurring simultaneously with the act of narration, is oriented towards *mimesis*. In this world, Stevens functions primarily as a *character*, and thus Short's (2007) discourse presentation taxonomy is only relevant inasmuch as the narrative discourse takes on the tone and texture of presentation of thought: Stevens's own thought. The storyworld built around the events leading up to the Second World War is oriented towards *diegesis*, and here Stevens functions primarily as a *narrator*; the discourse presentation scale applies in full, as would be the case if the narrator were heterodiegetic. Stylistic balance is achieved by virtue of the fact that the twin effects of diegesis and mimesis are working with one another rather than competing for the reader's attention. The moments of arrest which can occur when particular epistemological and ontological frameworks blend and/or become entangled are avoided here through deft separation of their functions and effects.

The insights provided by this analysis for stylistics-based discussions of creative practice and fictional technique will be summarized as follows. Applying Short's (2007) discourse presentation taxonomy to homodiegetic narration can be problematic because its status as narration or presentation of thought of some kind is often uncertain; it is often difficult to say with certainty whether homodiegetic narrators of this type function as narrators first and foremost, or as characters in the storyworld. Of course, the answer is that they are both; however, from the perspective of creative practice, it is useful to distinguish between the two functions (or orientations). A clear distinction could help the writer in several ways. First, better understanding of the importance of stylistic balance (foregrounding of 'story', or diegesis, versus foregrounding of 'character', or mimesis, and the interchange between the two) will allow the writer to make an informed practical decision about where on this cline her or his work should be positioned. For example, Lodge (1990: 44) has argued that the foregrounding of diegesis is a hallmark of postmodern fiction, describing it as '[characterised by a] revival of diegesis: not smoothly dovetailed with mimesis as in the classic realist text, and not subordinated to mimesis as in the modernist text, but foregrounded against mimesis'.

Second, careful consideration of stylistic balance can facilitate the acknowledgement of the epistemological framework within which a homodiegetic narrator operates. It allows the writer to become attuned to what knowledge about the storyworld the particular narrator has access to, and, indeed, what knowledge the *reader* will have access to which, as in the case of Stevens, the narrator himself might not. As mentioned previously, the existence of a reader-accessible epistemic modal-world which is *not* enactor-accessible could be advanced as a definition of narrative unreliability.

Third, in a similar vein, focusing on the particular function that a homodiegetic narrator is occupying at a particular point in the narrative can help with avoidance of what Graham Swift (quoted in Bernard 1997: 218) has described as 'the paradox of the invulnerable writer': the writer who 'insists on himself', meaning that a 'writerly' style or register (e.g. overtly poetic, descriptive, even verbose or mannered), can ride roughshod over an authentic presentation of a character's idiolect.[8] In this case, the register of the character/narrator is in conflict with the register of the author. The latter can at times obscure and deform the former (Scott 2009: 137–44), with the character-narrator having access to lexis, style and register which seem inappropriate or out of context.

There is also an argument to be made that this kind of narrative method is in fact essentially *realistic*, and thus less demanding of a reader's acquiescence to particular types of literary convention or narrative schema. Surely, this is indeed how we experience the world as we move through it, and how we mediate between the external and the internal. We are all narrators and writers of our own past at the same time as being characters in and interpreters of the here and now. We live our lives both in and through the day's remains.

Notes

1 In Text World Theory, the discourse-world surrounding a fictional text is 'split' because the enactor of the text-world and the reader of the text 'exist' in different spatial-temporal locations, as opposed to the situation that prevails in face-to-face communication where participants in the discourse occupy the same space.
2 For Plato, the word 'poet' designated the creator of the text and is used in that sense here; in modern terms, we might prefer 'author'.

3 Plato famously cites the opening of *The Iliad* as an example of *diegesis di' amphoteron*, which mixes the voices of the narrator and characters (*Republic*, 3.392c–3.398b).
4 It should be pointed out, however, that interpretations of the relevant sections of *Poetics* are complicated and problematized by textual corruption and possible mistranslation (Else 1957).
5 It is beyond the scope of this chapter to discuss and illustrate the discourse presentation scale in depth. In any case, it is hoped that many readers will be familiar with it already. For detailed discussion and examples, see Short 2007.
6 In Plato's terms, all three of the examples here would be categorized simply as *diegesis dia mimeseos* (through the represented voices of characters).
7 It is always possible, of course, to conceive of exceptions to this general statement. It is not advisable – nor desirable – to make completely hard and fast pronouncements about what constitutes 'good writing', although it is certainly possible to talk, as Toolan does, about 'excellence of technique' (1998: ix). However, in general terms, I would argue that unnecessary ebullience or effervescence of style (where not called for explicitly by the particular aesthetic goals of the piece of writing) can create an undesirable impediment to the reader's world-building processes, and thus to effective imaginative engagement with the storyworld.
8 This particular stylistic problem is termed 'The Morvern Paradox' (after Alan Warner's 1995 novel *Morvern Callar*) in Scott (2009). See this book for detailed discussion of the issue.

References

Bernard, C. (1997) 'An interview with Graham Swift', *Contemporary Literature* 38(2): 217–31.

Boulter, A. (2007) *Writing Fiction: Creative and Critical Approaches*. Basingstoke: Palgrave Macmillan.

Carter, R. (2010) 'Methodologies for stylistic analysis: Practices and pedagogies', in McIntyre, D. and Busse, B. (eds) *Language and Style*, pp. 55–70. Basingstoke: Palgrave Macmillan.

Chatman, S. (1990) *Coming to Terms: The Rhetoric of Narrative in Fiction and Film*. Ithaca, NY: Cornell University Press.

Dietz, L. (2012) 'Adaptive fiction: How can evolutionary and cognitive approaches to literature impact creative writing?' *New Writing: The International Journal for the Theory and Practice of Creative Writing* 9(2): 147–55.

Else, G. F. (1957) *Aristotle's 'Poetics': The Argument*. Cambridge, MA: Harvard University Press.

Freiman, M. (2015) 'The art of drafting and revision: Extended mind in creative writing', *New Writing: The International Journal for the Theory and Practice of Creative Writing* 12(1): 48–66.

Garrett, P. (ed.) (2016) *The Cognitive Humanities*. Basingstoke: Palgrave Macmillan.

Gavins, J. (2007) *Text World Theory: An Introduction*. Edinburgh: Edinburgh University Press.

Gavins, J. and Steen, G. (2003) *Cognitive Poetics in Practice*. London: Routledge.

Genette, G. (1983) *Narrative Discourse: An Essay in Method*, trans. Jane E. Lewin. New York: Cornell University Press.

Griffiths, N. (2002) *Kelly + Victor*. London: Vintage.

Herman, D. (2009) 'Narrative ways of worldmaking', in Heinen, S. (ed.) *Narratology in the Age of Cross-disciplinary Narrative Research*, pp. 71–87. Berlin: Walter De Gruyter.

Ishiguro, K. (1989) *The Remains of the Day*. London: Faber and Faber.

Leech, G. and Short, M. (2007) *Style in Fiction: A Linguistic Introduction to English Fictional Prose*. London: Routledge.

Lodge, D. (1990) *After Bakhtin: Essays on Fiction and Criticism*. London: Routledge.

Mason, J. (2014) 'Narrative', in Stockwell, P., and Whiteley, S. (eds) *The Cambridge Handbook of Stylistics*, pp. 179–95. Cambridge: Cambridge University Press.

McCabe, P. (1992) *The Butcher Boy*. London: Picador.

McLoughlin, N. (2016) 'Emergences: Towards a cognitive affective model for creativity in the arts', in Garrett, P. (ed.) *The Cognitive Humanities: Embodied Mind in Literature and Culture*, pp. 169–90. Basingstoke: Palgrave Macmillan.

Nash, W. (1980) *Designs in Prose*. London: Longman.

Palmer, A. (2004) *Fictional Minds*. Lincoln, NE: University of Nebraska Press.

Phelan, J. (2005) *Living to Tell About It: A Rhetoric and Ethics of Character Narration*. Ithaca, NY: Cornell University Press.

Pope, R. (2005) *Creativity: Theory, History, Practice*. London: Routledge.

Prince, G. (2001) 'A point of view on point of view or refocalizing focalization', in van Peer, W. and Chatman, C. (eds) *New Perspectives on Narrative Perspective*, pp. 43–50. Albany: SUNY Press.

Rimmon-Kenan, S. (1989) *Narrative Fiction: Contemporary Poetics*. London: Routledge.

Ryan, M. (1999) 'Immersion versus interactivity: Virtual reality and literary theory', *SubStance* 28(2): 110–37.

Scott, J. (2009) *The Demotic Voice in Contemporary British Fiction*. Basingstoke: Palgrave Macmillan.

Scott, J. (2013) *Creative Writing and Stylistics: Creative and Critical Approaches*. Basingstoke: Palgrave Macmillan.

Scott, J. (2016) 'Worlds from words: Theories of world-building as creative writing toolbox', in Gavins, J. and Lahey, E. (eds) *World Building: Discourse in the Mind*, pp. 127–45. London: Bloomsbury.

Scott, J. (2018) 'Cognitive poetics and creative practice: Beginning the conversation', *New Writing: The International Journal for the Theory and Practice of Creative Writing* 15(1): 83–8.

Semino, E. and Short, M. (2004) *Corpus Stylistics: Speech, Writing and Thought Presentation in a Corpus of English Writing*. London: Routledge.

Short, M. (2007) 'Thought presentation 25 years on', *Style* 24(2): 225–41.

Stockwell, P. (2002) *Cognitive Poetics: An Introduction*. London: Routledge.

Stockwell, P. (2009) *Texture: A Cognitive Poetics of Reading*. Edinburgh: Edinburgh University Press.

Swift, G. (1996) *Last Orders*. London: Picador.

Toolan, M. (1998) *Language in Literature: An Introduction to Stylistics*. London: Arnold.

Toolan, M. (2001) *Narrative: A Critical Linguistic Introduction*. London: Routledge.

Toolan, M. (2008) 'Narrative Progression in the Short Story: First Steps in a Corpus Stylistic Approach', *Narrative* 16(2): 105–20.

Werth, P. (1999) *Text World Theory: Representing Conceptual Space in Discourse*. London: Longman.

Whiteley, S. (2011) 'Text world theory, real readers and emotional responses to *The Remains of the Day*', *Language and Literature* 20(1): 23–41.Building a world from the day's remains

Part II

Readers' responses to stylistic manipulation

6

Manipulating inferences: Interpretative problems and their effects on readers

Billy Clark

1. Introduction

This chapter explores some of the ways in which fictional texts can be seen as manipulating the inferential processes of readers by making particular kinds of inferred conclusions ('explicatures' and 'implicatures') more or less easy to derive.[1] It focuses in particular on interpretative difficulties which texts can raise and the effects of these. These sometimes relate to relatively 'local' reader inferences derived from specific parts of texts (these have been the most common focus of work on pragmatic stylistics) and sometimes to relatively 'global' inferences based on representations of large parts of texts or texts as a whole.[2]

The chapter considers one novel which makes it relatively difficult for readers to represent the text as a whole (Rachel Cusk's *Outline*, 2014) and one which makes it hard for readers to make local inferences (Eimear McBride's *A Girl is a Half-formed Thing*, 2013). It contrasts these with a novel which does not seem to pose particular difficulties for readers in making either local or global inferences (Elif Batuman's *The Idiot*, 2017). Discussion of the texts is illustrated here by comments on the Goodreads website,[3] which encourages readers to share recommendations and reviews. These show readers focusing on questions about what worthwhile inferences can be drawn from each of the novels, as well as on the local and global interpretative difficulties raised by Cusk's and McBride's novels.

Clark (2014) suggests that particular kinds of local and global inferences play key roles in the evaluation of texts. Positive evaluations are more likely when readers find it relatively easy to represent parts of texts and texts as a whole, and when these can be used to derive further conclusions which readers consider worthwhile. Clark's model is used to organize the discussion here. The discussion focuses on questions about what worthwhile conclusions can be drawn from reading Batuman's novel, on how to represent Cusk's novel overall, and on difficulties in representing local parts of McBride's novel.

The chapter also considers how these texts vary with regard to how much they encourage an 'immersive' perspective and to how far they can be understood as realistic, relating this discussion to the interpretative difficulties they raise. Batuman's novel encourages a fairly detached perspective, presenting a narrative where events are packaged and presented as having happened in the past. While Cusk's novel shares these features, it can be seen as more realistic in some ways (in that the narrator presents fairly unmediated narratives told to her by others) but not in others (in that our real-life experience does not consist only of such unmediated narratives). McBride's novel encourages a less detached and more immersive reading experience. The linguistic style of the novel is highly marked and arguably not realistic, but this encourages an immersive response where readers feel that they are experiencing events from a perspective similar to that of the main character. These differences can be accounted for partly by considering the inferential processes of readers and by seeing work on pragmatics as complementing other approaches which have considered immersion and the details of reader experience, such as work on Text World Theory (Gavins 2007; Gavins and Lahey 2016; Lahey 2014) and work on narrative (see, e.g. Gerrig 1993; Ryan 2001). Batuman's novel can be understood as manipulating readers only in the very broad sense that it is designed to give rise to particular kinds of inferential processes and conclusions. Cusk's and McBride's novels are manipulative in a more restrictive sense in that they give rise to difficulties which lead to less overt effects. At a fairly explicit level, readers can consider the nature of both novels, assess their aims and evaluate their responses to them. Less overtly, each text encourages responses which are more experiential and less easy to describe or paraphrase. Cusk's novel can be understood as a series of summaries of the narrator's encounters and so lead to inferential paths which involve reflection on the nature of life and storytelling. McBride's novel moves further from the relatively detached perspective of Batuman's *The Idiot*, encouraging immersive responses which are far removed from the summaries of experience presented by Cusk.

A concluding argument is that the comments on Goodreads used as illustrations here provide evidence that readers treat works of prose fiction as communicative acts and so that pragmatic principles apply to them as they do to other communicative acts. While the discussion here does not require understanding of much technical material, the next section introduces the relevance-theoretic distinction between explicatures and implicatures which is presupposed in later discussion.

2. Explicatures and implicatures

The focus here is on how the responses of readers are affected by the ways in which writers have formulated their texts. This section discusses ideas about explicatures and implicatures which have been applied previously and are relevant in accounting for both what writers do when producing prose fiction and what readers do when responding to it.

The central focus of much work on pragmatics is the communication of implicatures, that is, of assumptions which are communicated implicitly and indirectly. Recent work in pragmatics also focuses on explicitly communicated assumptions. In relevance-theoretic work, these are termed 'explicatures' and, in common with other approaches, are seen as communicated partly explicitly.[4]

Clearly, fictional texts provide evidence for explicatures and implicatures. Naturally, then, much work in pragmatic stylistics has focused on accounting for these and for how the effects of texts can be partly explained with reference to them. We can illustrate with reference to the utterance produced in direct speech by a character in Rachel Cusk's novel *Outline* in the following passage (the narrator and the man who says this have just met and are sitting next to each other in a plane which is flying to Athens):

1) The man to my right turned and asked me the reason for my visit to Athens. I said I was going there for work.

> 'I hope you are staying near water', he said. 'Athens will be very hot.'
>
> (Cusk 2014: 6)

Pragmatic inferences involved in understanding what is explicitly communicated by the first part of the man's utterance here (its explicatures) include assumptions about the referents of pronouns (*I* and *you*), the time referred to in the utterance, and whether he is making a statement, asking a question or something else. Inferences about these might result in an explicature which we can represent, fairly simplistically, as:

2) The man on the plane is expressing his hope that the narrator will be staying near enough to the sea to make it relatively easy to cope with hot weather while in Athens after the flight they are both on.

The representation in (2) is simplified in several ways. It indicates that the narrator and readers need to make not only the inferences mentioned above but also an inference about how near to the water is intended and that the intended distance is partly vague. It does not offer a clear indication of what exactly is inferred.

One key implicature of the man's utterance is represented as follows:

3) The narrator will be uncomfortable during her stay if she is not staying somewhere near water.

If pragmatic stylistic analyses involved only the description of explicatures and implicatures like these, this research programme would have limited interest. In fact, researchers have focused on a range of complexities associated with them, including questions about the status and strength of explicatures and implicatures, about who is responsible for them, and about complexities in communicating and identifying them.

Both explicatures and implicatures can be communicated more or less strongly.[5] There are two ways in which the strength of communicated assumptions can vary. First, it can be more or less clear that an individual is intending to be communicative at all. A speaker might, for example, repeat a word for a particular effect or simply because they are thinking of what to say next. Second, it can be more or less clear that particular inferable conclusions are being intentionally communicated. We can illustrate this by considering some other possible implicatures of the man's utterance in (1), some of which are listed below:

4) a. The man cares about whether the narrator is comfortable during her stay in Athens.
   b. The man cares about the narrator's well-being.
   c. The man is knowledgeable about Athens.
   d. The man is knowledgeable about Greece.
   e. The man will be able to help with other kinds of advice.

These are only some of the possible implicatures of the man's utterance. One thing to notice about them is that there is less evidence for them than for the implicature in (3) above (they are also more plausibly deniable). Further, if the narrator (or readers) did not recover any of them, we could still say that they have understood the utterance. If they did not recover the implicature in (3), we would be likely to say that they had missed the point of what the man said.

Utterances in general convey more than one implicature. Some are fairly weakly evidenced and unlikely actually to be inferred. Utterances also vary with regard to how many implicatures they support and how strongly. Within relevance theory, the term 'poetic effects' has been used to refer to utterances which achieve relevance by giving rise to a wide range of fairly weak implicatures (for discussion, see Sperber and Wilson 1986: 217–24; Pilkington 2000).

Another area of pragmatic uncertainty was identified in early work on pragmatic stylistics (see, e.g. Leech and Short 1981: 237–54). This concerns how readers think about the sources of explicatures and implicatures. While the text as a whole is created by an author who is (to varying degrees) responsible for its explicatures and implicatures, some conclusions are understood as being communicated by narrators and some by characters.

For example, when the man in Cusk's novel produces the utterance in (2), we infer that he is communicating the explicatures and implicatures mentioned above. The narrator is telling us that he said this and so his utterance is embedded within her account of what happened (explicatures here are embedded within other explicatures). Her narration is in turn embedded in the author Cusk's communicative act in writing the novel. Of course, things can be more complicated with multiple 'levels' of communication involved, and various kinds of explicit and implicit attitudes communicated along the way. To take one well-known example, when characters speak in the central parts of *Wuthering Heights*, their utterances are conveyed by Nelly Dean, whose utterances are being conveyed by the narrator Lockwood, whose utterances are being conveyed by the author Emily Brontë.

Clearly, writers can formulate texts in ways which affect assumptions about attitudes towards and the reliability of narrators and characters (and themselves as authors, although this is not a topic for this chapter). They can also make it more or less easy for readers to come to conclusions about these and to feel confident about their conclusions. The next section focuses on the three novels considered here, which vary with regard to the kinds of interpretative difficulties they give rise to.

3. Understanding the novels: Three kinds of difficulties

Arguably, a key aim in reading a fictional text is to derive interpretations from the text as a whole. As Clark (2009: 199–201) points out, these 'global' inferences can include fairly formal literary ones, for example, concluding that *Wuthering Heights* is about 'the problems of evil in this world', a view attributed to some critics by Shunami (1973: 452), and more personal ones, for example, deciding that a friend is or is not likely to enjoy reading the text.[6] Clark (2014) suggests that local and global inferences play key roles in positive evaluations. Discussing Chekhov's story *The Lady With The Little Dog* (Chekhov 2002) he suggests that the ease of recollecting individual parts of the story and of the story as a whole makes it relatively easy for readers to continue thinking about the story after they have read it and to derive further inferred conclusions from these representations.[7] It is also important that these further conclusions seem to be worth the effort involved in deriving them.

The novels discussed here vary with regard to how easy it is to reach inferential conclusions based on them. Here are the opening passages of each novel.

5)   FALL

I didn't know what email was until I got to college. I had heard of email and knew that in some sense I would 'have' it. 'You'll be so fancy', said my mother's sister, who had married a computer scientist, 'sending your e, mails.' She emphasised the 'e' and paused before 'mail'.

That summer, I heard email mentioned with increasing frequency. 'Things are changing so fast', my father said. 'Today at work I surfed the World Wide Web. One second, I was in the Metropolitan Museum of Modern Art. One second later, I was in Anıtkabir.' Anıtkabir, Atatürk's mausoleum, was located in Ankara. I had no idea what my father was talking about, but I knew there was no meaningful sense in which he had been 'in' Ankara that day, so I didn't really pay attention.

(Batuman 2017: 3)

6)   **Outline**
                        I

Before the flight I was invited for lunch at a London club with a billionaire I'd been promised had liberal credentials. He talked in his open-necked shirt about the new software he was developing, that could help organisations identify the employees most likely to rob and betray them in the future. We were meant to be discussing a literary magazine he was thinking of starting up; unfortunately I had to leave before we arrived at that subject. He insisted on paying for a taxi to the airport, which was useful since I was late and had a heavy suitcase.

(Cusk 2014: 3)

7) For you. You'll soon. You'll give her name. In the stitches of her skin she'll wear your say. Mammy me? Yes you. Bounce the bed, I'd say. I'd say that's what you did. Then lay you down. They cut you round. Wait and hour and day.

Walking up corridors up the stairs. Are you alright? Will you sit, he says. No. I want she says. I want to see my son. Smell from dettol through her skin. Mops diamond floor tiles all as strong. All the burn your eyes out if you had some. Her heart going pat. Going dum dum dum. Don't mind me she's going to your room. See the. Jesus. What have they done? Jesus. Bile for. Tidals burn. Ssssh. All over. Mother. She cries. Oh no. "Oh no no no.
(McBride 2013: 2)

Readers unfamiliar with these texts are likely to see the opening of McBride's novel as significantly different from the others. It is much easier to come up with representations of explicatures (directly communicated assumptions) and implicatures (indirectly communicated assumptions) of the first two extracts, even if some of these are incomplete at least at first (in these cases, readers will assume that they can flesh out representations as they discover more by reading on). In reading the passages from Batuman's and Cusk's novels, we do not yet know who the referent of *I* is in each case, but we know that this person is narrating the story. In the passage from Batuman's novel, we know that the narrator is telling us about beginning college, about being about to have access to email, and so on. In Cusk's novel, we know that the narrator is telling us about having lunch with a billionaire before getting on a flight. In the passage from McBride's novel, things are much less clear. We do not know who is speaking or thinking the thoughts or utterances represented or even whether the same person is the thinker or speaker of each part. We cannot assign clear referents for the various pronouns and can only develop much less clear representations of what might be happening as we read through the passage. Readers of McBride's novel are far more likely than readers of the other three passages to make assumptions that they correct later as they read on.[8]

There is a significant difference between uncertainties about implicatures of relatively clear explicatures (e.g. implicatures about what exactly the girl in Batuman's novel is thinking about email and her father's reports on visiting Ankara via the World Wide Web) and uncertainties about explicatures themselves (e.g. about who is speaking or thinking at the start of McBride's novel, what is for who, who will soon do what and so on) which lead in turn to uncertainties about implicatures.

The rest of this section indicates some of the difficulties the novels pose for readers, illustrated by comments on Goodreads and in other reviews, and considers how inferential processes contribute to the experiences of readers. The texts can be seen as differing both in degree of difficulty and in how difficulties arise. For *The Idiot*, the issues are mainly about what worthwhile inferences can be inferred from the novel as a whole. For *Outline*, it is also hard for readers to represent the novel as a whole. For *A Girl is a Half-formed Thing*, it is difficult even to recover explicatures and implicatures of individual parts of the novel, and representations of these.

3.1. Looking for worthwhile conclusions: *The Idiot*

In *The Idiot*, a first-person narrator, Selin, tells us about her first year at Harvard University in the early 1990s, the classes she attends and the people she meets, including Ivan, a slightly older maths student. She is fascinated by language (studying linguistics and Russian) and by questions about the relationship between language and thought, disagreeing with a linguistics tutor who says that language does not shape thought.[9] She finds she can communicate with Ivan much more positively by email than in person and her relationship with him has connections with an eccentric story used in Russian class which contains only words learners should already know at the stage at which they read each section. Eventually, she follows Ivan to Hungary in the summer and takes on a temporary language teaching job there.

There are no significant difficulties in working out explicatures or implicatures of this novel. It is also fairly easy to represent the novel as a whole. Where some readers struggle is in deriving conclusions which seem worthwhile from their local and global representations.

A simple summary of the novel would say that it tells the story of a young woman's first year at university in the mid-1990s, the relationships she has with other characters and with ideas about language, literature and the world. One reviewer on Goodreads summarized it by saying, 'this is Selin's account of her freshman year at Harvard (c. 1995) and the summer of travel in Paris, Hungary and Turkey that follows' (Rebecca Foster, goodreads.com). A more detailed representation would include representations of her character ('highly strung', according to the book's cover), of her concerns about herself, relationships, her place in the world, and academic topics, of some of the people she interacts with, including her friend Svetlana and Ivan, with whom she has a complex relationship which never becomes an established romantic one, and of what she does, including teaching English and going to Hungary in the summer to teach and to be near Ivan.

Some readers respond positively to the novel, clearly finding worthwhile conclusions to draw from it:

8) Extracts from 'positive' reviews of *The Idiot* on Goodreads:

   a. I can't think of another book I've enjoyed more than this one in my adult life.
   (Madison)
   b. The Idiot is a comic masterpiece about a portrait of the young woman as a budding intellectual, someone who (wilfully? or not?) misunderstands social codes and what things mean.
   (Li Sian)

For others, there seems to be little worth concluding from reading the novel:

9) Extracts from 'negative' reviews of *The Idiot* on Goodreads:

   a. Around the 90-page mark I realized I was retaining next to nothing. I was pretty much zoning out while reading. From boredom. I pushed through, but admittedly started skimming about 70% in. I never got into it, and I never figured out what it was I was reading.
   (C.M. Arnold)
   b. I suppose it's appropriate that one of the recurring themes in Elif Batuman's *The Idiot* is the sensation of being trapped – in conversation, in a situation, in a location. Because about two-thirds of the way through this frustrating and tedious novel, I realized I too was trapped – too curious to simply jettison the story, all too aware that the plot was heading into ever more stagnant territory. In the end, I couldn't help but feel that the title, although ostensibly a reference to the Dostoyevsky classic, was actually referring to me.
   (Paul)

Some readers take a negative attitude in summarizing what happens in the novel:

10) Negative comments on what happens in *The Idiot* on Goodreads:

   a. This is a novel in which nothing truly happens: nothing good, nothing bad, and nothing exciting. At over four hundred pages of what read like a rambling stream of consciousness, I never felt invested in the story or connected with any of the characters.
   (Kimberly V)
   b. NOTHING REALLY HAPPENS. IT'S LIKE KNAUSGÅRD BUT WITH HUNGARIANS.
   (Bruno)[10]

Some readers report beginning negatively (and some report 'DNF', i.e. that they 'did not finish' the book). Some who begin negatively change their mind and move on to more positive responses:

11) Extracts on Goodreads from reviews which report a change of mind when reading *The Idiot*:

   a. I was ready to give up on *The Idiot* at page 100. There was no distinct plot – nothing major seemed to be happening except for a girl describing her classes at university. But I persisted. Thank god for that.
   (Barry Pierce)
   b. I went into this book with hesitation, because I have seen some harsh reviews. But, after 100 pages I became utterly consumed by it.
   (Yanira)

Reviews overall suggest that readers do not have difficulties following what Selin reports in the novel but that there is variation with regard to what readers make of this. There are some minor disagreements about what the characters are like and readers also vary in what they make of them. While most readers have negative attitudes to Ivan, readers vary with regard to Selin. Readers seem broadly to agree about what she is like but vary with regard to whether they respond positively or negatively to her personality. More significant variations are about what readers infer from the novel as a whole. Some readers derive significant conclusions based on what they have read while others struggle to find any worthwhile conclusions. The positive responses focus on what it is like to be a young person coming into adulthood, often connected with memories of their own lives, and some on ideas about language, literature and life.

Arguably, most if not all readers of fiction are looking to infer conclusions which justify the effort involved in reading the book. While it seems that readers of *The Idiot* find it fairly easy to make local and global inferences, it seems that some readers find it hard to make further inferences from these which justify the effort involved in deriving them.

3.2. Problems with global representations: *Outline*

The Idiot is a fairly standard first-person narrative and readers can fairly easily represent it as a whole. *Outline* (the first novel in a trilogy) creates more difficulties, arising largely from the relative indistinctness of the narrator and the fact that the book mainly consists of the relatively unmediated narratives of people she interacts with. The French translation of the novel is *Disent-ils*.

A word-for-word translation of this back into English would be 'say they'. More idiomatic translations might be 'do they say', treating the inversion as an interrogative marker, 'so they say' or, more loosely, 'supposedly'. An arguably better translation would simply be 'they say', given that inversion is common in reporting speech in French. The French translator seems to have picked up on the fact that most of the novel consists of the narrator's reports of what other characters say to her and to have chosen to reflect that in the title. Moore (2018) suggests that the novel can be understood as an exercise in representation using 'negative space', comparing Cusk's narrative technique to that of negative-space drawing exercises where 'students … are asked to draw everything surrounding a figure, filling up the page, until the blank shape of the figure emerges'.

Like *The Idiot*, *Outline* has a first-person narrator, a writer who tells us about a number of encounters she has as she travels to Greece to teach on a creative writing course. She meets many people who tell her about themselves. She says some things about herself, and reveals some of her thoughts, but a key feature of the book is that the narrator does not reveal much about herself. Her name (Faye) occurs only once, around four-fifths of the way through the book, used by another character when speaking to her. As the novel develops, our sense of the narrator arguably becomes less clear as what we discover about her is accompanied by the many stories coming from others. The narrator seems not to have been selective in choosing particular events or people, nor to have packaged them into a clear and clearly interpretable narrative (though, of course, Cusk has made decisions about this). Some commentators have suggested that the novel can be understood as a kind of outline (so we can understand the original English title, as well as the title of the French translation, as reflecting salient features of the novel). One example comes in this review from Goodreads:[11]

12) To live as a detection device in the middle of a busy street is a legitimate choice – and a tempting one to make. To observe the world as it leisurely unfolds without your interference means to avoid the difficulties of constant selection. If you are just a passive receiver, all bits of the ceaseless flow of information fit your narrative; there's no need to shape them in accordance with your purposes. In exchange for cohesion, you get all kinds of bypassing, unfinished, often interesting stories. In other words, you get an outline.

(Frona, goodreads.com)

This line of interpretation suggests ideas about the narrator herself being an outline and the other characters providing outlines, each of which could be developed into one or several more traditional stories. This can lead to interpretations which focus on the nature of life, writing, experiences and so on, including the idea that Cusk has presented us with an outline which could be the first step towards developing a novel (we might wonder whether the novel is a kind of first rough outline sketched by the author who is herself a creative writer). This is supported to some extent by a scene in the novel where another novelist, Angeliki, takes out a pen and notepad and makes a note of something the narrator has just said to her (we are not sure exactly what she notes but the narrator has been talking about marriage in general, her own marriage, and then about her mother).

One of the most common observations about the style of *Outline* (and the other books in the trilogy) focuses on the passivity of the narrator who, in Lockwood's (2018: 11) words, 'practises a torrential listening'. The novel mainly consists of the narrator, Faye, telling us what others have told her. This view is sometimes overstated. The narrator does tell us some things about her own utterances, thoughts and feelings. As just noted, for example, the narrator tells Angeliki some things about her marriage and her relationship with her mother which Angeliki finds interesting enough to make a note of. It is true, though, that we find out very little about the narrator's life and personality. Like the other characters, we discover only as much about her as she reveals by telling us what she says and thinks at particular moments.

Overall, then, the novel presents a number of narratives, some of them including expressions of what the narrators of the stories think/thought or feel/felt at particular moments. Many readers comment on the sense that these narratives are quite unmediated. Having read the novel, then, we have read a number of narratives, relatively unmediated, and not connected into one overall narrative (except in that they are the series of narratives Faye has heard during her trip to Greece).

What are the effects of this? One is that it is not easy for readers to represent the novel as a whole in a way that makes it easy to draw conclusions from, except as a very simple summary such as the one in the first sentence of the summary on Goodreads ('A woman writer goes to Athens in the height of summer to teach a writing course.') or a slightly longer one which comes from adding the second sentence of the summary ('Though her own circumstances remain indistinct, she becomes the audience to a chain of narratives, as the people she meets tell her one after another the stories of their lives'). By contrast, it would be very hard to represent a summary of the novel which included adequate representations of all of the things she hears (and sees and thinks). This is a greater level of difficulty than the one posed by *The Idiot* since readers find it hard even to represent the novel as a whole, which of course makes it hard to draw significant conclusions from such an overall representation. Two aspects of responses to the novel are that readers generally agree about what it does and that responses vary with regard to how positive or negative they are. The following extracts from reviews illustrate these responses:

13) Extracts on Goodreads from reviews of *Outline*:

   a. *Outline*, so aptly named, is a sketchbook of lives, charcoal drawings of souls captured in profile.
   (Julie Christine)
   b. The novel is a collection of conversations … I can already hear the criticisms of this book: 'It's boring.' (It isn't.) 'It's pretentious.' (It's actually the furthest thing from pretentious – it's not trying to be anything other than what it is.)
   (Julie Ehlers)
   c. In short, it's a novel that's much easier to admire than to love. It's very well written with some truly brilliant observations, it's intelligent, it holds its focus. It's also a novel that arouses the suspicion now and again that there might be a conceit involved, the presence of the emperor's new clothes factor. I enjoyed reading it; at the same time I have a feeling I'll remember nothing about it six months from now.
   (Violet Wells)
   d. mm I read the first 66 pages before setting this aside. I didn't dislike the writing; I even found it quite profound in places, but there's not enough story to peg such philosophical depth on. This makes it the very opposite of unputdownable.
   (Rebecca Foster)
   e. Like watching paint dry without the action of having paint run down the wall.
   (Brian)

Clearly, some readers struggle to find conclusions worth deriving from the novel, as they do for *The Idiot*. Some readers do manage this, though. Here are three quotes indicating lines of interpretation:

14) Extracts on Goodreads from reviews of *Outline*:

   a. This is a book about thought in its clearest and purest form.
   (Jaidee)

b. The subject of the conversations is the failure of the domestic relationship, mostly marital, occasionally filial. It is a brittle and lonely satire on self-scrutiny.
      (Julie Christine)
  c. Joan Didion once wrote that 'we tell ourselves stories in order to live.' Rachel Cusk's 'Outline' illustrates this love of storytelling.
      (Caitlin)

So far, then, we have considered a novel (*The Idiot*) with a first-person narrator whose significant interpretative problems mainly concern what can be concluded from the novel as a whole and another (*Outline*) which makes it hard for readers to represent that text as a whole. Next, we consider a novel which makes interpretation hard at the (local) level of individual explicatures and implicatures.

3.3. Problems with local inferences: *A Girl is a Half-formed Thing*

Eimear McBride's *A Girl is a Half-formed Thing* is a significantly more challenging novel.[12] As the passage in (7) shows, it is much harder to make inferences about what is being said (including about the referents of pronouns and other aspects of explicatures), who is speaking or thinking the content of individual parts, and what is happening at each stage. Many readers report negative responses and many report giving up on it. Others carry on and provide very positive evaluations. Clark (forthcoming) outlines some of the difficulties and develops arguments about how different ways of responding to them lead to different kinds of evaluations.

What is a reader to make of the opening passage quoted in (7)? They can tell that someone is saying or thinking that something is for someone (whoever is referred to by *you* in the first orthographic sentence), that the referent of the second *you* (maybe the same person) will soon do something and so on. They cannot tell who is saying or thinking the thoughts or utterances represented by each phrase. As Clark (forthcoming) points out, the opening passages of novels often contain indeterminacies of various types. To take just one example, readers of the opening of Mark Haddon's *The Curious Incident of the Dog in the Night-Time* (which begins with chapter 2) do not know which dog is dead, who Mrs Shears is, or where the events being described have taken place:

15)   2

It was 7 minutes after midnight. The dog was lying on the grass in the middle of the lawn in front of Mrs. Shears' house.

(Haddon 2003: 1)

They expect, however, (and are right in this case) that they will soon find out more. This turns out not to be the case for McBride's novel. Readers can eventually piece together more about what is happening and some of this will emerge naturally through reading. But the novel never makes it easy to make inferences about its explicatures and implicatures. Clark (forthcoming) discusses some of the effects of this and argues that readers who continue to read the novel without taking trouble to try to infer explicatures, details of what is happening when and so on, have an experience closer to what McBride intended for them, and are more likely to respond positively to the book than readers who put in extra effort to make inferences such as these.

We can compare these three novels, then, by considering how they vary with regard to how difficult they are. *The Idiot* is the easiest to follow, raising difficulties about interpretations as a whole. *Outline* makes it harder for readers to represent the novel as a whole as well as to derive conclusions from such representations. *A Girl is a Half-formed Thing* makes it hard for readers even to understand what is going on throughout the book.

As mentioned earlier, the claim is not that readers cannot get to a stage where they have a representation of each novel in mind and can make inferences based on this. Rather, the novels vary with regard to how difficult they are, the nature of the difficulties, and the different kinds of effects these difficulties give rise to for readers.

4. Experiencing the novels: Immersion and realism

Work in pragmatic stylistics has not said much about how texts can encourage more or less 'immersive' or 'realistic' reading experiences or about how writers use particular techniques to support these. Immersion and the nature of reading experiences have been explored more fully in other approaches to stylistics, notably in Text World Theory (see, e.g. Gavins 2007; Gavins and Lahey 2016; Lahey 2014) and in work on narrative (see, e.g. Gerrig 1993; Ryan 2001). Immersion and a sense of realism are not exactly the same thing, of course. A reader might feel immersed in an experience which is quite far from reality or feel detached from something that seems realistic. This section considers the inferential experiences of reading the novels considered here, and to what extent they provide an 'immersive' or 'realistic' experience. It argues that *The Idiot* encourages a fairly detached response, treating the novel as a fairly 'packaged' representation of the events the novel presents; that *Outline* also encourages a fairly detached perspective, but a distinctive one which is realistic in some ways (presenting fairly unmediated narrative from the narrator and from the characters, the latter embedded in the narrator's narrative); and that *A Girl is a Half-formed Thing* encourages an immersive response and a reading experience which feels quite realistic (one which encourages readers to feel that they are sharing the experience of the girl whose story it represents). McBride has said that one of her aims was for readers to feel close to the perspective of the girl who is the main character and she seems to have succeeded in this. This section considers how she has done this and to what extent the different experiences of reading the novels can be accounted for by considering the inferential processes they each encourage.

4.1. 'Realism' and immersion

The experience of reading a novel is, of course, completely real in that the reader is interacting in the real world with a real object produced by one or more others and that real cognitive processes are caused by the experience. At the same time, the experience is different from other kinds of experiences and so there is a sense in which we understand our relationship to characters and events as 'unreal'. When we say that a reading experience is relatively 'realistic', therefore, we mean either that readers perceive it as such or that the nature of the experience is in some ways closer to experiences we have when not reading texts like these. Schaeffer and Vultur (2005: 238), for example, suggest that 'adopting the stance of immersion implies being absorbed in the mentally represented content in such a way as to treat it — up to a point — as if it were the actual object or situation'. We can consider our responses to a range of experiences, including 'fictional' ones such as the experience of reading a novel, reading poetry, viewing a film and looking at artworks, in this way. We can also think of the experience of understanding utterances in everyday interactions as more or less immersive. The use of the historic present, for example, can be seen as a technique for immersing listeners or readers more fully in a story, as in example (16):

16) A funny thing happened last night. I was out with my friends and we went to the cinema. We get in and somebody's sitting in our seats.

The change to historic present in the third sentence here encourages the listener to adopt a perspective close to that of the person telling the story at the time when she went into the cinema. The listener would be likely to adopt a more detached perspective if the speaker had produced (17):

17) A funny thing happened last night. I was out with my friends and we went to the cinema. We got in and somebody was sitting in our seats.

One difference between the two versions is that the historic present encourages a more 'immersive' perspective. Another is that the past tense suggests that the events have been arranged in packages of similar types. Pragmatically, we are more likely to treat the narrative in (17) as a whole, creating a representation of the whole sequence of events the speaker is telling us about and deriving inferences from that. In (16), we are more likely to treat the first two sentences as a separate 'scene-setting' component which provides contextual assumptions to help us respond to the section in present tense and perhaps to treat each part of that more separately than we would when understanding (17). Two ideas developed in this chapter are that readers often aim to arrive at a situation where they can treat novels as a whole and derive inferential conclusions from them and that novels vary in how much they facilitate this. *The Idiot* makes this easier than the novels by Cusk and McBride, each of which make this less easy in different ways.

Novels which are told in third person with a consistent past tense are generally easier to treat as reports of a whole packaged narrative from which we can draw conclusions. First-person narratives seem to encourage a more engaged response but can still lead to a representation of the novel as a whole from which inferences can be drawn. Novels which combine more than one perspective are more dynamic and lead to more complex representations and responses.

The Idiot uses first-person throughout and the story is more or less chronological, leading us through a period in the lives of the characters set in the past. Selin tells us her story, having chosen what to tell us, in what order and how. We follow the characters through their stories and can then make inferences about what they have told us. We have seen above that the novel nevertheless raises some interpretative difficulties for readers.

Cusk's and McBride's novels are also more or less chronological, but they are significantly different in how they tell their stories. In both cases, they make it less easy for readers to arrive at a representation of the whole package and to draw inferences from that. Cusk's novel is closer to *The Idiot* than McBride's. The narrator tells us about a lunch before her visit to Greece, the flight and then what happens to her there. What makes this less typical of first-person novels is that she mainly tells us what others have told her, not shaping the narrative as much as we might typically expect. McBride's novel is significantly different. Readers find it hard to identify referents, who is speaking or thinking, and what is happening. It is much harder for readers to follow the narrative and many readers give up without finishing the book.

The rest of this section considers the three novels in turn and suggests how we can account for the reading experiences they encourage, partly by considering what kinds of inferential processes they lead readers to carry out. Batuman's novel is unrealistic in presenting events and the thoughts and utterances of characters in structured prose. Cusk's novel is unrealistic in some ways but arguably more realistic in others. It can be understood as realistic in that the narrator does not do much to mediate what others say to her but also as unrealistic in that our daily experience is not reducible to what we hear others say. Like Batuman's novel, it is inevitably unrealistic in presenting events and the thoughts and utterances of characters in structured prose. However, we might argue that it is more realistic in that the narratives seem not to have been selected to form a coherent overall narrative. McBride's novel is unrealistic in that it is quite different from anything we encounter in everyday interactions or experience. However, its attempt to represent fairly unmediated and unorganized experience can be seen as representing something quite realistic.

4.2. Reading *The Idiot*

The opening extract from *The Idiot* is typical of the novel in that it does not pose special problems of pragmatic interpretation for readers. Some pragmatic inferences are very straightforward and those which cannot be resolved straight away will be resolvable before reading much further. Readers will recognize that the heading indicates that the opening passage takes place in Fall/Autumn and the reference to getting to college will indicate that the book begins at the start of an academic year. The reference to email being new will place the action around the 1990s. Readers will vary with regard to when they assume email first became available, of course. Anyone who researches the novel will discover that the author Elif Batuman went to Harvard in 1995 and so will place the events around then. There are some indications to help readers make inferences about specific parts of the story, for example, the inverted commas around *have* indicating the narrator's lack of confidence about what 'having' email meant, the comma in *e*, *mail* and further explanation of how her aunt uttered this phrase and so on.

Quite quickly, readers are likely to feel confident about what they are reading and to carry on making inferences about events and characters which they can use to make further inferences. The reader's experience will, then, largely consist of piecing together a fairly coherent story and then making inferences about what it is about and what to make of it (which some of them struggle with, of course). The overall experience, then, will be not much different from hearing an everyday oral narrative but extended over a longer period of time. As with all novels, readers can speed up and slow down, pause to think about things so far, and continue to make inferences about the novel while going about the rest of their lives. We might summarise this as a fairly straightforward and not very challenging reading experience, with difficulties associated with making global inferences about the point of the novel.

4.3. Reading *Outline*

As mentioned earlier, the most common kinds of observations about *Outline* focus on the narrator's passivity as she mainly tells us about what others have told her. There is far less shaping and packaging than we might expect in other novels (including *The Idiot*). Cusk has made some interesting comments about what she was aiming to do:

> 18) I wanted to try and close the gap between my experience of life and truth and how those things were represented in fiction.[13]

What is the effect of this style on readers and how can pragmatic theories help us to understand it? In what ways does the novel 'close the gap between' Cusk's 'experience of life and truth' and the way these are usually represented in fiction?

Readers who are expecting a packaged narrative which they can use to make inferences from will be disappointed. Instead, the novel appears to be fairly formless, shaped only by the fact that narratives come from whoever the narrator interacts with. The narrator herself becomes less salient as she is surrounded by what others tell us and our idea of her arguably becomes less clear (although some readers have suggested that we understand her in the light of how the others respond to her).

At the same time, individual passages seem to conform to what we might expect from typical prose fiction, as illustrated by the opening passage (6) quoted earlier. The narrator tells us that she was invited to dinner before a flight. The use of *the* before *flight* suggests a definite one we can access and we are likely to expect to discover what the referent is soon. We can infer that she is referring to a flight to Athens which she soon tells us about. The use of passive forms (*I was invited*, *I'd been promised*) is not problematic as we assume that it is not important for us to know who invited her or who said the person she dines with had liberal credentials. And so on. Difficulties arise when some of our likely expectations are not met. There are no special problems about assigning reference or deriving implicatures from each passage. However, characters come and go seemingly based only on the order in which the narrator encounters them and there is little sense of a connected overall narrative. The other character who appears most often is a man she meets on her flight to Athens and refers to often as 'my neighbour' even though he was only her neighbour during that flight in the sense that he was sitting next to her.

So there are no problems with individual parts of the novel. We can fairly straightforwardly infer explicatures and implicatures of each of them, but it is hard to connect these into an overall narrative. At each stage, the novel works quite straightforwardly but readers will find it hard to construct an overall representation of the novel.

One effect of this is that the implicatures supported by each section constitute a fairly wide range and are less strong than they would be if connected into an overall narrative. We could refer to the notion of 'mutual parallel adjustment' in describing this (for discussion of this notion, see Clark 2013: 142–54). This refers to the idea that the processes of inferring explicatures, contextual assumptions and implicatures affect each other as we infer them in online processing. We could illustrate this with reference to the utterance from the novel made by the narrator's neighbour mentioned earlier, reproduced here as (19):

19) 'I hope you are staying near water,' he said. 'Athens will be very hot.'
(Cusk 2014: 6)

One thing we need to infer when he says 'Athens will be very hot' is which sense of the ambiguous word *hot* he intends. To understand this, we need to infer that *hot* here refers to a high temperature and that it means that the general temperature of the city will be high for a European city in summer. This makes it possible to infer the implicature that being near water will make it easier to cool off. So the hypothesized implicature supports the inference about the intended sense of *hot* and the inference about the sense of *hot* supports the implicature.

Similarly, we can also think of global inferences supporting local inferences and vice versa. Clark (2009) suggests, for example, that local inferences about the group of characters in William Golding's (1955) novel *The Inheritors* possibly being able to communicate telepathically support global inferences about this group as a whole and the meaning of the novel and vice versa. Clark also points out that relatively global inferences can become more or less strongly supported as we read. This process is difficult for readers of *Outline* to the extent that they struggle to make global inferences.

The account developed so far is, however, too strong. It is not the case that readers cannot make global inferences from the novel. We saw above that some readers on Goodreads have developed more global inferences about the nature of life, relationships and writing. We might also pursue interpretative paths which are about life being a kind of 'outline' in that it is not definitively shaped and is constantly being shaped. We might also consider that the book is making comments about how novels in general present something quite detached, 'packaged' and unrealistic. This might also support inferences about this book being in some ways realistic (and in others not). Inferences about *Outline* being realistic can be thought of as fairly explicit and detached ones rather than ones which create or constitute a feeling that the book is realistic, that is, readers are likely to explicitly think about how realistic the novel is rather than simply to have an experience which can be described as realistic. As we will see, this is different from the ways in which *A Girl is a Half-formed Thing* can be seen as realistic.

4.4. Reading *A Girl is a Half-formed Thing*

McBride's novel is significantly different from *The Idiot* and *Outline* with regard to the inferential demands it makes on readers. The difficulties it poses are salient from the very beginning. In fact, earlier versions of the opening were more challenging, and McBride's editors persuaded her to make the opening easier for readers. In an interview for the *Guardian* in 2014, she described her editors' advice, her response to that, and some of her aims for the novel:

> 20) They thought I maybe needed to lower the reader into it a little more easily, and so I did that ... I wanted to try to give the reader a very different type of reading experience.[14]

Clark (forthcoming) discusses an interview with the critic and literary scholar John Mullan for the *Guardian*'s book club,[15] where McBride said that one aim of her style was for readers to experience the book from the perspective of the girl rather than to take a more detached perspective. McBride said this to Mullan in response to a question about why the girl has no name throughout the novel. Giving the girl a name, she said, would have encouraged a sense of detachment which she wanted to avoid. How would this work? Readers of *The Idiot* quickly discover the narrator's name. The name Selin first appears on page 12 (we learn the narrator's surname, Karadağ, on page 3, the first page of the first chapter). Some readers will know the narrator's name before they open the book (Selin is mentioned on the back cover). This means that they can think of the novel as being about Selin. Soon, they will be able to entertain thoughts such as these:

21) Possible thoughts before and during reading of *The Idiot*:
   a. This is a book about a young woman called Selin Karadağ told by Selin.
   b. Selin is telling us about experiences when she started to study at Harvard.
   c. Selin is Turkish-American.
   d. Selin is intrigued by email, which is a new technology at the time she is telling us about.

Readers can go on to make further inferences about the narrators and their personalities, including thoughts about how similar or different they and their experiences are to themselves and to other people they know.

Of course, readers can make similar assumptions about 'the narrator' of *Outline* (whose name is mentioned only once and in passing when uttered by another character) and 'the girl' of *A Girl is a Half-formed Thing* but, arguably, the lack of a name contributes to their less clearly defined status. However, the lack of a name is not the only thing which makes the narrators hard to represent. Faye not only has no name for most of the novel, but she is also not much described and we understand her mainly by how she responds to others (although, as mentioned earlier, it is not accurate to suggest that the novel only consists of what others say to her).

In the case of *A Girl is a Half-formed Thing*, there are far greater difficulties. We read representations of what characters (including the girl) say, and of thoughts of the girl, without clear guidance about who is responsible for each part. They are expressed in fragmented linguistic structures. Arguably, all of the book consists of incomplete thoughts, including representations of the words of others as they appear in the girl's consciousness. Collard (2016: 205–6) suggests that the book presents a 'stream of pre-conscious' and 'an attempt ... to represent thought at the point immediately **before** it becomes articulate speech, before it is ordered into rational utterance'(emphasis in original).

McBride's aim of giving readers access to the girl's consciousness means that our inferential experience is much like the girl's. We aim to make what we can of this 'stream of pre-conscious', as the girl herself does, but without access to all of the contextual assumptions available to her at each moment. Clark (forthcoming) suggests that readers vary with regard to how much effort they put in to try to work out explicatures and implicatures of passages in the novel. Readers might wonder who the speaker or thinker of each part is, what the referents of referring expressions are and so on, and they might put a lot of effort into this. Or they might continue with very partial representations. Here is a very simplified representation of what a reader of the first few sentences might end up with once they have gone to the effort of looking for evidence to flesh out what the sentences represent (I do not have complete confidence about each of these and other readers might recover different explicatures):

22) Fairly 'full' explicatures of opening sentences of *A Girl is a Half-formed Thing*:

The girl's mother is saying to the girl's brother that it is for him to decide what the girl will be called when she is born. The girl's mother is saying that her brother will soon decide this. The girl's mother is saying that her brother will give her a name (or 'give' in the sense of letting others know information on what her name will be).

Here is a much less complete representation:

23) Partial representation of opening sentences of *A Girl is a Half-formed Thing*:

Somebody is saying that something is for someone. Someone is saying that someone will soon do something. Someone is saying that someone will give the referent of *her* a name.

As Clark (forthcoming) points out, it is challenging and effortful to entertain representations like those in (23) and to carry on reading and drawing inferences based on representations like these. However, for many readers, carrying on like this leads to a rewarding experience. As the book develops, they begin to be able to draw more inferences and to piece things together more fully. Moving towards representations like those in (22) takes effort to find evidence to support inferences. Carrying on with representations like those in (23) involves effort in continuing to entertain such complex representations and trying to draw conclusions based on them. As readers move on, they begin to be able to draw a fuller range of inferences and to be more confident about what is happening.

Representations like those in (22) are similar to those we arrive at when reading *The Idiot* and *Outline*. They amount to 'packaged' representations of a type not easy to arrive at for books like this. Representations like those in (23) are significantly closer to inferences the girl would make as she experiences the events in the novel, and closer to the kinds of experiences we have in everyday life when not listening to or reading packaged stories.

Overall, then, we could see *A Girl is a Half-formed Thing* as encouraging a fairly immersive experience and one that feels quite realistic. And we can understand this to some extent by considering the nature of the inferential processes it encourages for readers.

Eventually, we can end up with a representation of the book as a whole, which will include thoughts about its form and inferences we have made while reading. These might include assumptions about experience and about reading. Such interpretations are similar to some of the possible interpretations of *Outline* mentioned earlier.

5. Fictional texts as communicative acts

This section considers one more point which these texts provide evidence for, which is about the status of novels as communicative acts. In discussing the relevance of pragmatic theories in general, and of relevance theory in particular, to accounts of the interpretation of literary texts, Wilson (2011, 2018) points out that the behaviour of readers provides at least some evidence that they make inferences about what texts intentionally convey so that we should not completely accept the view that author intentions are never relevant in considering texts, a view associated with Wimsatt and Beardsley's (1946) discussion of the 'intentional fallacy'. Wilson points out that readers make inferences which help them to work out explicatures, for example, about the referents of pronouns, which partly involve assumptions about intentions, while also considering that, of course, readers also derive some inferential conclusions which authors could not have intended.

The responses of readers when discussing texts also provide evidence that readers treat fictional texts such as these novels as communicative acts. The comments on Goodreads discussed earlier show that many readers are asking what the point is of the texts they read and what significant conclusions they might derive from them. Of course, as mentioned earlier, readers who discuss books on Goodreads are clearly prepared to look for interpretations and to discuss possible interpretations. This does not mean that all readers respond in similar ways. However, the comments do provide evidence that readers look for effects from reading which will justify the effort involved in reading and deriving interpretations. This fits with relevance-theoretic assumptions about what we expect from intentional communication (enough effects to justify the effort involved in deriving them).

Ideas from narrative theory also seem relevant here. Labov and Waletzky (1967) suggest that oral narratives often include an 'evaluation' which indicates the point of a story or the value in processing it. Lambrou (2014) provides evidence from narratives told by the same individual at different points in time which suggests that evaluations (and complicating actions) are perceived as important elements of narratives. Comments on Goodreads suggest that readers are also looking to see what makes narratives worthwhile, although authors of prose fiction rarely provide any explicit indications of this and we might not treat them as reliable if they did. Some authors do provide some help with this, though. Clark (2009) discusses the epigraph in William Golding's (1955) novel, which suggests some lines of interpretation. Batuman's *The Idiot* also begins with a suggestive epigraph from Proust:

> But the characteristic feature of the ridiculous age I was going through – awkward indeed but by no means infertile – is that we do not consult our intelligence and that the most trivial attributes of other people seem to us to form an inseparable part of their personality. In a world thronged with monsters and with gods, we know little peace of mind. There is hardly a single action we perform in that phase which we would not give anything, in later life, to be able to annul. Whereas what we ought to regret is that we no longer possess the spontaneity which made us perform them. In later life we look at things in a more practical way, in full conformity with the rest of society, but adolescence is the only period in which we learn anything.
> Marcel Proust: *In Search of Lost Time, Volume II: Within A Budding Grove*

This surely guides readers to look for interpretations which consider both positive and negative ways of thinking about Selin, as well as thoughts about the time of her life which the novel is about and how we should think about that.

Both Golding's and Batuman's novels, then, provide further evidence that some authors and readers expect texts to have a point by giving some indications of what it might be. It is also noticeable that neither of them give strong or very definite indications. Neither Cusk's nor McBride's novels do this. It seems, then, that considering the inferential processes of readers, and what their comments reveal, suggests that they are perceived by authors and readers, at least to some extent, as communicative acts.

6. Conclusions

This chapter has considered some ways in which texts can cause interpretative difficulties for readers, considering difficulties associated with three aspects of interpretation: deriving conclusions seen as worthwhile from texts, representing texts as a whole and understanding local parts of texts. It considered how these relate to the extent to which reader experiences can be understood as realistic or immersive. Some kinds of interpretative difficulties lead to experiences which feel more realistic, more immersive, or both. While the chapter did not look in systematic detail at what readers have said about how they respond to the novels, the comments used for illustration here provide some evidence about how readers treat texts and support the view that novels are generally treated as communicative acts with some concern for the intentions of their authors. This means that they fall within the scope of pragmatic theories. As well as further developing accounts of the role of inferential processes in the production, interpretation and evaluation of texts, future research would benefit from making connections with other approaches which focus on the experience of readers, such as Text World Theory and a range of approaches which have been applied in work on narrative.

Notes

1. I am very grateful to members of the audience at the Symposium on Manipulating Readers in Fiction at Université Aix-Marseille, Aix-en-Provence in 2017 for helpful comments and suggestions. I am also grateful to Sandrine Sorlin for organizing the symposium and for the opportunity to contribute here.
2. Clark (2009) considers the distinction between relatively local and relatively global inferences in reading William Golding's *The Inheritors*. For a discussion of the distinct but related notion of global coherence, see Unger (2006).
3. https://www.goodreads.com/book/show/30962053-the-idiot
4. For discussion, see Carston (2002); Clark (2013); Sperber and Wilson (1986).
5. This section focuses only on the strength of implicatures to illustrate this but questions about the strength of explicatures are also relevant in accounting for some of the interpretative difficulties discussed later.

6 This latter, of course, goes beyond what an author is likely to have intentionally communicated and so is likely to be a non-communicated implication rather than a communicated implicature.
7 While readers of texts which are harder to represent might also spend time thinking about further inferences, the amount of effort involved in doing so is considerably higher.
8 In the first published review of the book, David Collard (2013) mistakenly referred to the 'two-year-old female narrator', a mistaken assumption I also made on first reading the novel (in fact, the girl who narrates the story is not yet born at this stage).
9 Readers familiar with ideas in linguistics are likely to recognize that this refers to debates about the misleadingly labelled and much-discussed 'Sapir-Whorf' hypothesis (see discussion, for example, in Gumperz and Levinson 1996).
10 Bruno nevertheless gave the book 4 stars. This is his entire review.
11 https://www.goodreads.com/book/show/21400742-outline
12 For a very useful discussion of the novel, including discussion of how McBride wrote it, how she found a publisher, its reception, and details of its form, see Collard (2016).
13 Why Rachel Cusk avoided plot when writing her latest novel. The Next Chapter, CBC Radio, Canada, 27 November 2017. Available at: https://www.cbc.ca/radio/thenextchapter/full-episode-july-28-2018-1.4414510/why-rachel-cusk-avoided-plot-when-writing-her-latest-novel-1.4414612 (accessed 7 November 2018).
14 Rustin (2014).
15 https://membership.theguardian.com/event/book-club-with-eimear-mcbride-26195584699

References

Batuman, E. (2017) *The Idiot*. London: Jonathan Cape.
Carston, R. (2002) *Thoughts and Utterances*. Oxford: Wiley-Blackwell.
Chekhov, A. (2002) 'The lady with the little dog', in *The Lady with the Little Dog and other stories, 1896–1904*, trans. Ronald Wilks, pp. 223–40 (first Russian version published 1899, revised version 1903). London: Penguin.
Clark, B. (2009) 'Salient inferences: Pragmatics and *The Inheritors*', *Language and Literature* 18(2): 173–213.
Clark, B. (2013) *Relevance Theory*. Cambridge: Cambridge University Press.
Clark, B. (2014) 'Before, during and after Chekhov: inference, literary interpretation and literary value', in Chapman, S. and Clark, B. (eds) *Pragmatic Literary Stylistics*, pp. 55–69. Basingstoke: Palgrave Macmillan.
Clark, B. (forthcoming) "Lazy reading" and "half-formed things": indeterminacy and responses to Eimear McBride's *A Girl Is Half-formed Thing*, in Chapman, S. and Clark, B. (eds) *Pragmatics and Literature*. Amsterdam: John Benjamins.

Collard, D. (2013) 'Eimear McBride: Gob impressive', *Times Literary Supplement*, 17 June 2013. Available at: https://www.the-tls.co.uk/articles/public/eimear-mcbride-gob-impressive/ (accessed 7 November 2018).

Collard, D. (2016) *About a Girl: A Reader's Guide to Eimear McBride's 'A Girl Is A Half-formed Thing'*. London: CB Editions.

Cusk, R. (2014) *Outline*. London: Faber and Faber.

Gavins, J. (2007) *Text World Theory: An Introduction*. Edinburgh: Edinburgh University Press.

Gavins, J. and Lahey, E. (eds) (2016) *World Building: Discourse in the Mind*. London: Bloomsbury.

Gerrig, R. (1993) *Experiencing Narrative Worlds: On the Psychological Activities of Reading*. New Haven, CT: Yale University Press.

Golding, W. (1955) *The Inheritors*. London: Faber and Faber.

Gumperz, J. J. and Levinson, S. C. (1996) *Rethinking Linguistic Relativity*. Cambridge: Cambridge University Press.

Haddon, M. (2003) *The Curious Incident of the Dog in the Night-Time*. London: Jonathan Cape.

Labov, W. and Waletzky, J. (1967) 'Narrative analysis: Oral versions of personal experience', in Helm, J. (ed.) *Essays on the Verbal and Visual Arts*, pp. 12–44. Seattle, WA: University of Washington Press.

Lahey, E. (2014) 'Stylistics and Text World Theory', in Burke, M. (ed.) *Routledge Handbook of Stylistics*, pp. 284–96. London: Routledge.

Lambrou, M. (2014) 'Narrative, text and time: Telling the same story twice in the oral narrative reporting of 7/7', *Language and Literature* 23(1): 32–48.

Leech, G. and Short, M. (1981) *Style in Fiction*. London: Longman.

Lockwood, P. (2018) 'Why do I have to know what McDonald's is?' *London Review of Books* 40(9): 11–12. Available at: https://www.lrb.co.uk/v40/n09/patricia-lockwood/why-do-i-have-to-know-what-mcdonalds-is

McBride, E. (2013) *A Girl is a Half-formed Thing*. Norwich: Galley Beggar Press. Republished 2013. London: Faber and Faber.

Moore, L. (2018) 'The Queen of Rue (review of *Kudos* by Rachel Cusk)', *New York Review of Books*, 16 August 2018. Available at: https://www.nybooks.com/articles/2018/08/16/rachel-cusk-queen-of-rue/ (accessed 7 November 2018).

Pilkington, A. (2000) *Poetic Effects*. Amsterdam: John Benjamins.

Ryan, M-L. (2001) *Narrative as Virtual Reality: Immersion and Interactivity in Literature and Electronic Media*. Baltimore, MD: Johns Hopkins University Press.

Rustin, S. (2014) 'A life in . . . Eimear McBride', *The Guardian*, 16 May 2014. Available at: https://www.theguardian.com/books/2014/may/16/eimear-mcbride-girl-is-a-half-formed-thing-interview (accessed 7 November 2018).

Schaeffer, J-M. and Vultur, I. (2005) 'Immersion', in Herman, D., Jahn, M. and Ryan, M.-L. (eds) *Routledge Encyclopedia of Narrative Theory*, pp. 237–9. London: Routledge.

Shunami, G. (1973) 'The unreliable narrator in *Wuthering Heights*', *Nineteenth Century Fiction* 27(4): 449–68.
Sperber, D. and Wilson, D. (1986; 2nd edition 1995) *Relevance: Communication and Cognition*. Oxford: Wiley-Blackwell.
Unger, C. (2006) *Genre, Relevance and Global Coherence: The Pragmatics of Discourse Type*. Basingstoke: Palgrave Macmillan.
Wilson, D. (2011) 'Relevance theory and the interpretation of literary works'. *UCL Working Papers on Linguistics* 23: 47–68.
Wilson, D. (2018) 'Relevance theory and literary interpretation', in Cave, T. and Wilson, D. (eds) *Reading Beyond the Code: Literature and Relevance Theory*, pp. 185–204, Oxford: Oxford University Press.
Wimsatt, W. K., Jr and Beardsley, M. C. (1946) 'The intentional fallacy', *The Sewanee Review* 54: 468–88.

7

Surprise and story ending: Readers' responses to textual manipulation in a short story by J. D. Salinger

Laura Hidalgo-Downing

1. Introduction

The present chapter explores the relation between textual features and how real readers respond to the unexpected ending of the short story 'A Perfect Day for Bananafish', by J. D. Salinger (1953) and how they interpret the whole story in the light of the ending. The motivation for the study arises from my personal reading of the short story, as I was indeed surprised by the ending. This led to my interest, as a stylistician, in exploring the way in which specific textual strategies employed in the story had successfully led to this surprising resolution. The importance of story endings has been pointed out in the literature (Prince 2003; Rabinowitz 2002; Richardson 2002; Toolan 2009, 2016). Within the stylistics literature on short stories, most studies have focused on the analysis of textual features which characterize narrative sequences and on the phenomenon of closure (or lack thereof), with hardly any research on readers' responses to narrative development and story endings (for exceptions, see Sanford and Emmott 2012; Toolan 2016). Specific research within stylistics and cognitive poetics has focused on the rhetorical manipulation techniques in genres such as detective fiction (Emmott and Alexander 2010; Emmott, Sanford and Alexander 2010; Emmott and Alexander 2019) and political thriller fiction (Sorlin 2016). Some experimental research has been carried out on readers' anticipation of closure in short stories (Lohafer 2003). Although the need to establish connections between the observation of textual features in fiction and the responses by readers has been pointed out (see, e.g. Toolan 2016) hardly any research has been carried out from this integrative perspective. Following research into the narrativity of short stories (Toolan 2009, 2013, 2016), the present chapter contributes to the study of the narrative significance of a story ending by bridging the gap between these two complementary approaches to the study of narrative fiction in a short story, namely, the study of textual features of the text and the effect of such strategies on real readers. The present study focuses on some textual features which require increased reader attention, such as the title and the ending, and those which perform a manipulating function in distracting the reader and leading her to the final surprising effect.

For this purpose, the short story is first analysed briefly by focusing on the manipulation techniques that can be observed, and this is followed by an experimental study with a group of students, who read the story in two stages. The objectives of the study are to explore (1) students' anticipations of the ending, (2) their emotional response to it, (3) their interpretation of the story in the light of the ending, (4) the metaphoric interpretations of the story in relation to the title, and (5) their ethical considerations regarding the topic touched upon in the ending, the protagonist's suicide. Students are asked to provide justification of their interpretations by referring to textual clues in the story. Additionally, the experimental study combines questions which elicit responses of the students' reactions to the literary text as readers, while others elicit responses from the students as analysts of the literary text. This distinction is based on Stockwell's (2013) observation that readers can engage with texts either by means of natural reading or by analysing the text, and that these two activities cannot happen simultaneously though they are complementary.

'A Perfect Day for Bananafish' is a short story by J. D. Salinger which was first published in *The New Yorker* in 1948, and was subsequently published in the collected volume *Nine Stories*, in 1953. It has been pointed out that the short story is obscure and open to symbolic interpretation (Gwynn and Blotner 1962: 110), though the interpretation itself may vary depending on the features which are perceived as being more relevant, namely, the protagonist's inner troubles as derived from his traumatic experience at war, a familiar topic in Salinger, or an indirect criticism of materialistic post-war American society (Wiegand 1962: 123–5). It has also been observed that each of the short stories in the *Nine Stories* collected volume poses a riddle which involves an underlying problem or conflict related to the protagonist (Gwynn and Blotner 1962: 110).

The story takes place during the honeymoon holiday of the young couple Seymour and Muriel in a hotel at the seaside. There are four consecutive scenes, of which the first two happen simultaneously and are followed by the very brief scene three and the ending. While scenes one and two are considerably long, both scene three and the ending are comparatively very short, and the ending thus comes through as very abrupt. The scenes are summarized below:

- The telephone conversation between Muriel, Seymour's wife, and her mother in the hotel room. The conversation focuses on trivial topics, such as fashion, but Muriel's mother also expresses her concerns regarding Seymour's alleged mental instability and regarding Muriel's possible safety.
- Seymour on the beach talking to 5-year-old Sybil. Seymour tells Sybil the bananafish tale.
- Seymour's encounter with a woman in the elevator back in the hotel, in which Seymour seems to be very nervous.
- Ending with Seymour back in the hotel room, Muriel asleep, and Seymour's suicide.

The short story is written mostly in the form of dialogue, which contributes to the surprising effect of the ending, condensed in a short narrative paragraph.

2. Theoretical background

The present chapter contributes to research on reader response to a short story within the tradition of stylistics and cognitive poetics (see, e.g. Burke 2014; Stockwell and Whiteley 2016; Sorlin 2016) and, more specifically, of recent works on the narrative of the short story and readers' responses to literary texts (Emmott 1997; Miall and Kuiken 1998; Sanford and Emmott 2012; Caracciolo 2013; Miall 2014; Peplow and Carter 2014; Toolan 2009, 2016; Whiteley 2016). With regard to the relevance of this study within the more specific theme of the present volume, manipulation of readers, I address this topic on two levels. First, manipulation understood as the use of textual strategies on the part of the author in order to distract readers. Second, manipulation understood as a strategy used by an analyst in order to elicit responses from readers by means of instruments such as questionnaires.

With regard to the use of rhetorical manipulation strategies in fiction to guide readers' interpretations, I make use of the definition of manipulation in detective fiction in Emmott and Alexander (2010) and Emmott, Sanford, and Alexander (2010) and apply and adapt some of the strategies mentioned in their model to the analysis of the present short story. With regard to the concept of reader manipulation with reference to the design of a questionnaire, this will be mentioned in the section on data and methodology.

The present section provides an overview of various relevant theoretical concepts, namely, manipulation in fiction, the nature of the modernist short story as a genre, together with the role of endings and of emotion in the interpretation of short stories, and textual strategies for manipulation and linguistic/textual resources.

2.1. Manipulation in fiction

The term 'manipulation' is used by Emmott and Alexander (2010: 328) to explain how authors of detective fiction, such as Agatha Christie (see Chapter 9, this volume), use specific textual strategies as techniques to misdirect the reader's attention during the reading process and thus prevent them from guessing who is the murderer. Emmott and Alexander argue that Agatha Christie 'uses her rhetorical skills to control readers' attention, hence cognitively misdirecting readers' (2010: 329). It is the author's skill at controlling the reader's attention which determines the success of the reading process as convincing and entertaining.

It may be argued that some of these techniques of misdirection are also exploited in other genres such as the short story. Before considering the manipulation techniques that can be observed in the short story under study, I wish to make some clarifications regarding the notion of manipulation and the way it is understood in the present chapter. First, manipulation techniques are stylistic strategies or choices which, as mentioned earlier, are aimed at misdirecting the reader, and, additionally, have potential cognitive effects on readers (see Sorlin, Chapter 1, this volume), for example by triggering emotions such as suspense or surprise. The relative success of a story will depend on the extent to which such effects are observable in real readers. This means that, ideally, in order to have a complete picture of manipulation, an analyst needs to study both the features in the text which have a potential for manipulation and the responses of real readers to such features during the reading process (also see Toolan 2016). This dependency on the effect of the reader justifies the identification of strategies as potentially manipulative, since the performance of such manipulation depends on the actual effect on the reader (see Sorlin this volume). Not all potential strategies may have an effect or the same effect in all readers. Second, manipulation seems to be a genre-dependent phenomenon, that is, generic conventions of specific literary forms, like detective fiction or the short story, will lend themselves more easily to the exploitation of certain manipulative techniques, while other genres may require different ones or variations. For this reason, I focus only on those strategies which are potentially relevant within the genre of the short story. Third, it can be argued that manipulation techniques designed to distract readers interact dynamically with other strategies which require increased attention from the reader, such as titles and endings, which are addressed later.

2.2. The short story as a genre

The short story arose as a modernist genre with some specific conventions which make it different from full-length narratives such as novels (Lohafer 2005: 528; Toolan 2009, 2016). Some of the features pointed out as characteristic of short stories are its focus on one or two characters, typically one, and its brief extension, designed to make it possible to read the story in one sitting. Lohafer describes the short story as follows:

> A sojourn within the extraordinary consciousness of an ordinary character, unfolding through the cumulative effect of meaningful imagery rather than through the linear logic of goal-directed action, and leading to a deepening of perception rather than to a resolution of problems. (2005: 529)

The short story thus focuses on the revelation of some kind of insight concerning the protagonist, rather than on the development of a sequence of narrative actions. In this respect, Toolan (2016: 33) points out that in the short story there will be references to the protagonist's mental states, to his or her antecedents (childhood, traumatic experiences, love relations, etc.) and 'probably a Problem or Complication will emerge, at least partly of the character's making and at least partly – seemingly – within their power to modify if not to resolve' (Toolan 2016: 33). The short story typically ends on a note of failure, out of which, however, an insight or 'expansion in understanding' arises (Toolan 2016: 112).

Titles and endings occupy privileged positions in nineteenth- and twentieth-century European and American fiction (Rabinowitz 2002: 300), and possibly more so in short stories. Rabinowitz (2002: 302) summarizes the key role of titles as follows:

> Titles not only guide our reading process by telling us where to concentrate; they also provide a core around which to organize an interpretation. As a general rule, we approach a book with the expectation that we should formulate an interpretation to which the title is in fact appropriate.

According to Rabinowitz, readers of *Anna Karenina*, for example, are led by the title of the novel to focus on this character and not on other characters. In their search for narrative coherence and an interpretation of a story (Toolan 2013), readers take into account the role of the title as well as the ending.

Endings in particular are sites of increased readerly attention (Toolan 2016: 219). Prince (2003: 26) explains the importance of endings as follows:

> The end occupies a determinative position because of the light it sheds (or might shed) on the meaning of the events leading up to it. The end functions as the (partial) condition, the magnetizing force, the organizing principle of narrative: reading (processing) a narrative is, among other things, waiting for the end.

Rabinowitz similarly argues that endings play a crucial role in narrative because they 'often serve to scaffold our retrospective interpretation of the book' (2002: 303). Thus, when we finish reading a narrative, the ending may often lead us to revise and reinterpret the story. In this respect, Rabinowitz spells out his rule of conclusive endings: 'The ending of a text is not only to be noticed; there is also a widely applicable interpretive convention that permits us to read in a special way, as a conclusion, as a summing up of the work's meaning' (2002: 304).

Ending needs to be distinguished from closure. While the ending refers to the final textual section of a narrative, closure is a controversial concept. Perhaps the most enlightening definitions of closure are those that relate it to the reader's fulfilment of expectations regarding the narrative development (see Abbott 2005). Rabinowitz (2002: 307) distinguishes between two types of closure:

> On the one hand, closure can refer to the way a text calls on readers to apply rules of signification; in this sense a text is 'open' if its symbolic meanings are not restricted. ... But closure can also refer to the way that a text utilizes rules of configuration; in this sense, a work is 'open' when, for instance, the plot remains unresolved and incomplete even at the end.

The first definition of closure has to do with the expectations readers have regarding the possible integration of meaning into one interpretation, while the second one has to do with the sense of completeness of a narrative, more specifically, whether the plot has a resolution. In this light, it may be argued that 'A Perfect Day for Bananafish' is open in the first definition, since the reader has available a set of possible metaphoric interpretations of the story arising from suggested possibilities, while it is closed according to the second definition since the plot ends with the death, the suicide, of the protagonist.

Endings, especially in short stories, often bring about an emotion of surprise in the reader. Surprise in actual readers may indicate that the manipulation techniques of distraction from relevant information have worked. Surprise arises when a reader's expectations regarding what is going to happen is defeated by what actually happens (Prince 2003: 96; Pyrhönen 2005: 578; Toolan 2009: 8). Surprise is also the response to the way in which suspense may be resolved. Short stories typically develop through a tension between sustained suspense and a sense of imminent closure, which, when resolved, may result in surprise. As explained in Section 4.1, by manipulating information, withholding some facts and (partially) revealing others, short stories guide the reader's expectations regarding the unfolding narrative and create emotions such as suspense, uncertainty and surprise (Prince 2003: 96; Schneider 2005: 136; Toolan 2009: 8). As pointed out by Abbott (2013), curiosity, suspense and surprise are the three master forces of narrative. Surprise is successful if there is a balance between the anticipation of possible outcomes and the defeat of the reader's expectations regarding such outcomes (Prince 2003: 96; Toolan 2009, 2016). Surprise is also 'a solution to a narrative's central enigma' (Pyrhönen 2005: 579).

Before continuing on to manipulation techniques, mention has to be made of the role of metaphor in the interpretation of short stories such as 'A Perfect Day for Bananafish'. Numerous short stories can be read as metaphors or allegories, while others may ask for an ironic interpretation. In numerous cases, the metaphoric, allegoric or ironic interpretation will arise as an option only when the reader reaches the end of the story. In this sense, the metaphor or allegory will be contributing to narrative coherence (Toolan 2013) by providing the means of bringing together parts of the story which were not explicitly connected in the text. However, metaphors are tricky resources, in the sense that they both constitute a challenge to narrative coherence by requiring a greater processing effort on the part of the reader and contribute to narrative coherence if the metaphoric interpretation is successful (Hidalgo-Downing 2019).

2.3. Textual strategies for manipulation and linguistic/textual resources

Emotions such as suspense and surprise arise in the reader from textual clues provided by the narrative itself, which guides the reader concerning the development of expectations in narrative progression (Toolan 2009: 2). To explain the process of reading a short story, Toolan uses the metaphor of walking through a forest with many potential routes. In this process, 'the reader is "led" without being able fully to foresee what will happen next, later, and finally' (Toolan 2016: 32). The text uses a series of resources in the narrative progression, among which repetition and what is unsaid play crucial roles (Toolan 2009, 2016). Thus, as argued by Toolan (2016), through repetition there is a process of arresting and holding back the narrative, creating suspense. By means of withholding information from the reader, by leaving things unsaid, the reader has to make an extra effort to fill in the gaps left in the narrative and anticipate their possible significance. Repetition and the withholding of information need to be balanced against the pressure 'to advance to a new situation, perhaps a crisis and a resolution' (Toolan 2016: 28). In addition to repetition and withholding of information, it may be argued that the extensive use of dialogue, as in 'A Perfect Day for Bananafish', may be a plot-arresting strategy, since the narrative sequence which typically leads to a resolution is delayed.

Following Emmott, Sanford and Alexander (2010: 345), the following techniques of textual manipulation may be used in the short story to distract the reader's attention and hinder her interpretation:

- Burying information: information which is relevant to the understanding of the plot may be buried in the text by various means, which typically involve the backgrounding of this information. This can be done by grammatical means, such as introducing relevant information in a subordinate clause or other non-prominent position, or by placing important information together with other non-relevant details in such a way that at the moment of reading the reader cannot distinguish the significance of some details as contrasted to others.
- Red herrings or foregrounding less important details: while red herrings or misleading clues are a prototypical technique in detective fiction, variations of this strategy may be used in other genres such as the short story. Certain details may be foregrounded by repetition, drawing the reader's attention to them and distracting her from the more relevant clues.
- Spilt frames and reconstruction: Emmott, Sanford and Alexander (2010) explain how readers complete information on reading detective fiction by filling in slots in schematic constructs, such as a dinner on a special occasion. The authors observe that the interpretation of the story may be rendered more complex when frame knowledge regarding the main event is split across two frames of reference in two different situations, for example, the situation in which the murder took place and the reconstruction of the murder in a similar scenario. Emmott, Stanford and Alexander (2010) observe that readers have to reconstruct the frame knowledge they had

activated in the first situation, often revising and modifying assumptions that had been made initially. In the short story, such split frame distribution of knowledge may focus, instead of on clues regarding a murder, on features which enable us to understand the main character and the possible underlying conflict.
- Underspecification of main characters: Emmott, Stanford and Alexander (2010) observe that the underspecification of attributes of characters and their roles also contributes to hindering interpretation by withholding important information regarding the roles of main characters.

3. Data and method

The data is, first, the short story 'A Perfect Day for Bananafish' by J. D. Salinger, and, second, questionnaires completed by thirty-six female and male Spanish university students of the third-year course in the English Studies degree at Universidad Autónoma of Madrid during the academic year 2017/18. Students had a background in North American literature as part of their curriculum, but had not read the short story before. Students were familiar with Salinger, mostly as being the author of *The Catcher in the Rye*. The task was completed by the students in a two-hour in-class session, in which they were given the short story and the questions in two stages. Students handed in their completed questionnaires at the end of the two-hour session. The questionnaires were coded with an F for female participants and an M for male, and each was assigned a number. Of the thirty-six students, only seven were male, so the distribution between female and male was not sufficient in order to carry out a gender-based analysis.

In the first stage, the final paragraph of the short story was removed and students were asked to anticipate and write an ending. They were also asked to justify their decision by making reference to specific information mentioned in the text. In the second stage, students were given the ending to the short story and were asked the following questions:

Q1. Do you find the ending of the story shocking? Yes/No.
Q2. Why/Why not?
Q3. Why does Seymour Glass commit suicide?
Q4. Do you think that Seymour committing suicide is the less expected ending? Yes/No

Q5. Does it make sense in terms of the story development? Yes/No.
Q6. Is it related to a traumatic experience? Yes/No
Q7. If so, which?
Q8. Why is the short story called 'A perfect day for bananafish'?
Q9. Do you think suicide is a social taboo?

The questionnaire is inspired by studies on the difficult task of questionnaire design (Rasinger 2010). Before describing in detail the questionnaire, I turn to the concept of manipulation as a strategy used by the analyst to elicit information from the reader. Reader manipulation may be understood at this level as the process by which the analyst guides the reader of a text by means of questions which are designed to focus on specific aspects of the text rather than others. In this sense, as an analyst, I was interested in exploring three dimensions of the readers' responses: their emotional responses, their interpretation of the story from textual clues and their ethical position towards the topic of suicide. In order to focus on these dimensions, some of the questions are designed as leading readers to focus on specific aspects of the text, rather than others. This, in part, is what makes an experiment with a questionnaire different from naturalistic reading experiments, for example, in which readers are free to discuss the text.

The questionnaire has the purpose of eliciting information from students to both closed and open questions. While the closed questions provide answers which make it possible to quantify some of the results, the open-ended questions are a good source of data regarding students' opinions and explanations. The study is of a qualitative nature, though quantitative results are also included, in particular regarding key issues such as the emotional reaction to the story ending. While stage one and question one address students' anticipation of and responses to the ending as readers of the short story, the rest of the questions elicit their responses to the literary text both as readers and analysts.

The first stage, the anticipation of the story ending, is designed to make students work on the expectations they have built on reading the story and finding clues in the text for the conclusions they may have drawn. Questions 1–8 address various aspects of the response to the story and its interpretation, while question 9 requires the readers to take up an ethical stance with regard to the topic of suicide which is introduced in the story.

The questions thus aim to investigate in what way students make connections between textual clues of the short story, their anticipation of the story ending, their emotional reaction to it, their interpretation of the whole story in terms of the ending and their ethical considerations regarding the topic of suicide.

The discussion of the results is organized according to the following research questions:

1. To what extent do students anticipate the story ending? (stage one)
2. What is the emotion experienced by the readers on reading the story ending? (questions 1 and 2 in the questionnaire)
3. What are the explanations provided by students regarding the story ending? (questions 3 to 7 in the questionnaire)
4. To what extent do students provide metaphoric explanations of the title and the story? (question 8)
5. What is the ethical position of the students regarding the taboo nature of the topic of suicide? (question 9)

The hypotheses guiding the research questions are the following:

1. A higher frequency of students will not anticipate the ending of the story.
2. The ending of the story will be considered shocking by most students.
3. The ending of the story will be considered the less expected ending.
4. Students' explanations of the story ending will focus on Seymour's internal troubles, rather than on external problems.
5. Students' explanations of the title will be based on a metaphoric interpretation of the story.
6. The topic of suicide will be considered taboo.

As mentioned in the introduction, following Stockwell (2013), a distinction is made between responses which readers make as readers of a literary piece of work and responses made by readers as analysts. According to Stockwell (2013), these two dimensions exclude each other, as one cannot read and at the same time analyse a text.

4. Results and discussion

4.1. A brief analysis of the manipulation techniques in the short story

The textual strategies for manipulation which can be identified in 'A Perfect Day for Bananafish' are the following:

- Burying information: the relation between Seymour's mental instability and his experience at war is not mentioned explicitly. In scene 1, the telephone

conversation between Muriel and her mother, the mother makes numerous references both to Seymour's possible mental instability and to the war, but these themes are presented among a list of other topics which are the object of their conversation, many of them of a very trivial nature, such as the weather or fashion. By using repetition, the mother seems to place particular emphasis on her concern for Muriel's safety, thus foregrounding the possible connection between Seymour's mental instability and Muriel's safety rather that other connections.
- Split information regarding the main character across frames. The main information regarding Seymour, the protagonist, comes to the reader through the dialogues which take place in the two main scenes, scene 1 and scene 2, and, very briefly, in scene 3, each of which presents Seymour in a different light.
- Character underspecification. Although information about Seymour comes through in the main scenes of the short story, such information remains sketchy and superficial.

It may be argued that in 'A Perfect Day for Bananafish' suspense is created by means of delayed outcome of the resolution in a narrative which has a dialogue format and presents numerous cases of repetition and withholding of information. Thus, in scene 1, Muriel's mother repeats several times her concerns regarding Seymour's alleged mental illness, though many of her sentences are left unfinished, leaving the reader to infer the suggested information and to take up one or more threads of interpretation of the story. In scene 2, the story of the bananafish which Seymour tells Sybil is mysterious, and requires an extra processing effort on the part of the reader, who realizes it must be significant because it gives the title to the short story. On reaching the abrupt ending of the protagonist's suicide, the reader has to revise and reinterpret the story in such a way as to find a coherent thread which brings together the suggested concerns in the first scene and the metaphoric meaning of the bananafish tale in the second scene.

4.2. The reader response study

In stage 1, students read the story without the final five lines. They provide an ending to the story and explain reasons for their choice. Table 7.1 shows the main types of endings provided by the students according to the topic and also depending on whether they choose to continue with the dialogue format followed in most of the story or whether they choose a narrative ending.

Table 7.1 Endings to the short story written by the students

Endings	Number	%
The couple stays together (dialogue)	9	25
The couple separates	8	22.22
Seymour kills himself	3	8.33
Seymour kills Muriel	3	8.33
Seymour kills Muriel and kills himself	1	2.77
Muriel kills herself	3	8.33
Other	9	25
Total	36	99.98

As can be observed in Table 7.1, the endings which expand on the fact that the couple stays together are developed in the form of dialogue, thus providing a continuity with the dialogue format which characterizes the rest of the story. The rest of the options are in narrative form. Within the former, most dialogues focus on intimate scenes between Seymour and Muriel once he returns to the hotel room, in some cases making reference to Seymour's mental instability, in other cases, making reference to the bananafish, typically as an imagined story in Seymour's mind. These endings offer a perspective of the couple as one with some problems but able to overcome them. As observed in Section 2, these endings are in line with the modernist short story as a piece of writing which focuses on the protagonists' consciousness rather than on a sequence of events.

Most students make reference to Seymour's mental instability and justify their conclusion from clues provided in Muriel's conversation with her mother. The endings written with regard to Seymour's mental illness lack closure of plot, since they focus on the protagonists' problems, though in three cases a tragic outcome is suggested but not explicitly stated. Indeed, some students point out that there are clues in the text which make the reader aware that there is something wrong or that something tragic is imminent.

With regard to research question 1, 'To what extent do students anticipate the ending of the story', only five students anticipate Seymour's suicide, with one student writing that Seymour commits suicide by eating too many bananafish. The results thus confirm the first hypothesis, that most students will not anticipate the story ending. Among the other topics which are mentioned, there is a tendency to focus either on the relationship of the couple, mainly whether there is a final separation or a reconciliation, or on the bananafish theme. The endings telling of a separation focus mostly on Muriel abandoning Seymour to return to her parents, except for one student who pictures Seymour as leaving Muriel to never appear again. These choices are justified by making reference to the concerns expressed by Muriel's mother regarding her safety during their telephone conversation. These responses seem to confirm that the manipulation technique of burying information (and foregrounding less important information) has an effect on readers.

Table 7.2 shows the distribution of endings according to their violent or non-violent ending. It is worth noticing that students most frequently anticipate a non-violent ending. As pointed out above, these focus on scenes in which the couple is separated or reunited and in which the topic of Seymour's mental illness plays an important role.

Research question 2 explores the emotional response of the readers to the story ending (questions 1 and 2 in the questionnaire). Table 7.3 shows the results of the answers to question 1 'Do you find the ending shocking?' Students more frequently find the ending shocking than not shocking, thus confirming the second hypothesis, that the ending would cause shock in the reader.

When asked to justify their answers (question 2), students who find the ending shocking explain that they did not expect the ending (twelve responses) and that the text did not provide sufficient clues to anticipate this ending. Students use evaluative expressions such as 'crazy', 'not logical', 'unexpected',

Table 7.2 Violent versus non-violent endings in the students' endings

Endings	Number	%
Violent	9	25
Non-violent	27	75
Total	36	100

Table 7.3 Responses to the question 'Do you find the ending shocking?'

Do you find the ending shocking?	Number	%
Yes	24	66.66
No	12	33.33
Total	36	99.99

'a bit hard for the end', 'too sudden' to describe the ending, as in examples (1) to (6) below.

(1) I did not expect a suicidal ending. But looking at the date of the story was published, it makes sense since he probably was a soldier during WWII. (F2)
(2) I wasn't expecting him, to actually kill himself. (F3)
(3) I thought he'd have a madness attack and would have killed her. (F6)
(4) Because you can't expect after the whole story the die of someone. (M8)
(5) It is much too sudden compared to the rest of the story. (M12)
(6) Death is always shocking, and also if the short story is based in mental diseases. (M13)

With regard to the lack of clues in the text, some students point out that the character is not presented as one with a serious problem which would lead to such an outcome, as in examples (7) and (8) below:

(7) Because although we knew there was something wrong with him, he's not presented as a character who has a problem with himself. (F4)
(8) I did not expect this ending since I thought he was comfortable with his life, being the girl the one who was upset and angry. (M14)

The replies to questions 1 and 2 suggest that manipulation techniques of withdrawing important information and underspecifying features of the protagonist in combination with a dramatic ending have been successful.

Research question 3 addresses students' explanations of the story ending by eliciting answers to questions 3–7 in the questionnaire.

With regard to question 3 'Why does Seymour Glass commit suicide?' results in Table 7.4 show that most students take up the thread of Seymour's alleged mental illness as a reason for his suicide, a fact that is mentioned by Muriel's mother in the telephone conversation in scene 1.

Table 7.4 Responses to the question 'Why does Seymour Glass commit suicide?'

Theme	Number	%
Mental illness	14	38.88
War	11	30.55
Problems in life and communication	7	19.44
Other	4	11.11
Total	36	99.98

Related to this is the theme of Seymour not being able to overcome his experience at war. Finally, other students point at more general problems of communication in Seymour, thus trying to find a coherent thread which runs through the various scenes in the short story. These choices thus reveal that students follow two different types of strategy in their search for narrative coherence. For some students, the suggestions regarding Seymour's possible mental illness or traumatic experience at war mentioned in scene 1 are perceived as more foregrounded than other features in the story and are used as scenarios in terms of which the rest of the scenes in the story and the ending itself are understood. Other students, on the other hand, find textual clues in the four scenes which provide a thread for a common, unifying scenario, one in which Seymour has a more general problem of communication which manifests itself in different situations. Examples (9), (10) and (11) below illustrate the scenarios of the mental disorder, war and problems with communication, respectively:

(9) He has a mental disorder and he can't stand life anymore when you have problems and you feel alone. You think you can't communicate with anybody. (F5)
(10) Perhaps war had a huge impact on him. Some soldiers usually go mad after having been fighting at wars. (F21)
(11) I think because he feels that nobody understand him and his thoughts. (F23)

While questions 1 and 2 address the emotional response of the readers to the ending when first reading it, questions 3 and 4 require the reader-analyst to interpret the textual role of the ending in the light of the development of the whole story once it is read. In question 3, students are asked whether they think that Seymour committing suicide is the less expected ending. Table 7.5 shows the answers to this question and Table 7.6 collects the answers to the question 'Does it [the ending] make sense in terms of the story development?'

While most students feel an emotion of shock and surprise on reading the ending, most students find the ending congruent with the development of the story, as revealed by the results in Tables 7.5 and 7.6. Thus, the ending is considered to be more expected in terms of story development by most students (Table 7.5) and the ending is considered to make sense in terms of the story development because it has been anticipated early on in the story (Table 7.6). These results do not support hypothesis 3, which predicted that students would consider the ending of the story the less congruent ending. Reasons for the lack of fulfilment of this expectation may be that students are aware of the difference between their emotional responses as readers to the short story and

Table 7.5 Answers to the question 'Is Seymour's suicide the less expected ending?'

Is Seymour's suicide the less expected ending?	Number	%
Yes	12	33.33
No	24	66.66
Total	36	99.99

Table 7.6 Answers to the question 'Does the ending make sense in terms of story development?'

Does the ending make sense in terms of story development?	Number	%
It is mentioned explicitly in scene 1 and/or reference to mental disorder	21	63.6
Structure of the short story	5	15.1
I don't know, it doesn't make sense	4	12.1
Other	3	9

their interpretation of the story ending in view of the narrative development as discourse analysts. This result would confirm research carried out in this area which highlights the different roles played by readers of literary texts as readers and as analysts (Stockwell 2013). These results also confirm studies on the role on story endings mentioned in Section 2, that is, that endings provide an interpretive frame according to which the whole story is interpreted retrospectively. This means that certain previously held assumptions, typically activated by distracting manipulation techniques, are finally discarded in favour of an interpretation which arises when reading the end.

Examples (12) to (15) provide illustrations of why students think the ending makes sense in terms of story development and is congruent with the rest of the story. The most frequent reasons provided are, first, a metaphorical interpretation of the story, in which the story of Seymour is understood in terms of the bananafish story, as in example (12). Second, students find that the references to Seymour's alleged mental instability by Muriel's mother anticipate the ending, as in example (13). Finally, some students observe that the story development and the ending follow conventions of the genre and the topic of alleged mental illness, as in examples (14) and (15).

(12) You can see a comparison between his and the bananafish's life. (F4)
(13) Because from the first moment that Muriel and her mother talk, you start thinking about what crazy thing Seymour could do. (F31)

(14) I don't know, it just fits, it is like he is living a mental breakdown and she is trying to help but she can't, nobody can and he knows it, so he just do it. (F7)

(15) Because this short story tries to shock you, and to do that in those times, death and suicide was the best option to do. (M13)

Examples (16) and (17) illustrate the negative responses of two students to the question whether the ending was not less expected in terms of story development. The reasons provided have to do with the narrative progression, in the sense that the ending is anticipated earlier on in the text, and also because of the theme as characteristic of a short story. This last point seems to confirm the observation mentioned in the Section 2 that modernist short stories end on a note of failure. It is worth noting that these students had previously answered that they had found the ending shocking:

(16) No, it is somehow latent in the story (M12)
(17) Even though I find it shocking I think it would be less expected to see them like a happy couple. (F15)

Table 7.5 also shows that four students have difficulties finding textual clues which will help them find a coherent interpretation of the story, as for them the ending 'does not make sense'.

Students are next asked question 6 'Is it [the ending] related to a traumatic experience? Yes/No, and question 7. 'If so, which?'. Results are collected in Tables 7.7 and 7.8.

The question 'Is it related to a traumatic experience?' may be considered to lead students towards a specific interpretation, thus revealing a process of manipulation on the part of the analyst. However, the question is justified as a way of trying to elicit the connection between mental illness and war experience in Seymour.

Table 7.7 Answers to the question 'Is Seymour's suicide related to a traumatic experience?'

Is it [the ending] related to a traumatic experience?	Number	%
Yes	29	80.5
No	4	11.11
I don't know	2	5.55
No answer	1	2.77
Total	36	99.88

Table 7.8 Answers to the question 'If so, which [traumatic experience]?'

If so, which (traumatic experience)?	Number	%
War	22	75.8
Other	7	24.13
Total	29	99.93

Responses in Table 7.7 and Table 7.8 show that when students are asked explicitly whether they think that Seymour's suicide is related to a traumatic experience, most think it is, namely, his experience as a soldier in the Second World War. If we compare these answers to the answers to question 3 'Why do you think Seymour Glass commits suicide?' it can be observed that students more frequently answered that the suicide was related to Seymour's mental problems in the first place, and only to war in the second place, though of course the argument that Seymour had mental problems could be related to his war experience. It seems that students are now establishing connections between Seymour's possible mental problems and his experience at war when elicited to do so.

Considering now research question 3, 'What are the explanations provided by students regarding the story ending?' responses to questions 3–7 confirm hypothesis four, that students will interpret the outcome in the ending as being related to Seymour's internal troubles (his possible mental illness, his traumatic experience at war, his problems with communication) rather than external problems (with his wife or with his mother-in-law). These results confirm research carried out on Salinger's stories.

Research question 4 asked to what extent students search for metaphoric explanations of the story as prompted by the title and is connected to question 8 in the questionnaire, 'Why is the story called "A perfect day for bananafish"'? The possible interpretations of the story are collected in Table 7.9.

Most students are able to find a metaphoric interpretation, thus confirming hypothesis five, which anticipated that most interpretations of the story would be metaphorical. This shows that most students are aware of the role of the metaphoric interpretation in the search for narrative coherence and an interpretation to the story which encompasses the ending and the title of the story.

Because the title focuses on the bananafish story which Seymour tells the five-year-old girl Sybil on the beach, the readers are pressed to establish a metaphorical connection between the development of Seymour's story and the story of the bananafish mentioned in the title. Most students are aware that the bananafish story is significant in the interpretation of Seymour's story,

Table 7.9 Answers to the question 'Why is the story called "A perfect day for bananafish"'?

Why is the story called 'A perfect day for bananafish'?	Number	%
Parallelism between bananafish and Seymour's life	19	52.77
Imagination	4	11.11
Irony	3	8.33
Not answered or does not know	7	14.44
Other	3	8.33
Total	36	94.98

though seven are unable to provide an answer. Among those who provide an interpretation, most establish a metaphorical connection between Seymour's life and the bananafish, others consider that the bananafish story represents the role of imagination and lack of contact with reality on the part of Seymour, and still others interpret the story as ironic, as 'meaning something else' or 'opposite' to what it seems to set out initially. Examples (18) to (24) illustrate the metaphoric interpretations of the story:

(18) He explains how bananafish kill themselves and he did the same so it could be like a symbol for suicide. (F7)

(19) Probably the bananafish are a metaphor of soldiers, that end up fed up of killing (bananas) that they can't come out of the war (the hole) and die. (M12)

(20) It could be considered as a metaphor, since all the factors made the protagonist to find death, not to fish some bananafish. Also, the fish makes the character to die, so basically the title could be "it is a perfect day for dying", because of the bananafish. (M13)

(21) Because as well as Seymour, 'they led a very tragic life' and once they are introduced in the water 'they behave like pigs' just like Seymour behaves when he is introduced in society. (F21)

(22) Because when he is telling the story about the bananafish, he says how bananafish die, so we feel that was the perfect day to die. (F30)

(23) Because it makes the reader think it is going to be a happy story with a happy ending and not a short story where someone is so done that he wants to commit suicide. Also, 'bananafish' probably stands for something else (like 'death' or 'suicide') but since it is a taboo topic in our society, the writer didn't want to be politically incorrect. (F33)

(24) I think is because he feels identified with one of them and finally he decides to kill himself (as bananafish which die). (F34)

The examples above illustrate some of the resources that students use to indicate that their interpretations are metaphoric, such as the explicit mention of the story as metaphoric (examples (19) and (20)), the use of comparative expressions such as 'like', 'the same' (examples (18) and (21)) or equivalence, such as 'how' and 'feels identified' (examples (22) and (24)). The metaphor which underlies these interpretations can be spelled out as 'Seymour's life and death is interpreted in terms of the life and death of the bananafish'.

Four students interpret the bananafish story as the way in which Seymour's imagination compensates for his difficulties in communication, as in example (25).

(25) I think that the story is called this way because the 'bananafish' is an animal that he has created in his imagination in order to not feel alone. Because he feels that nobody understands him. (F17)

This interpretation is also metaphoric, though the metaphor is different. It can be spelled out as follows 'Seymour's problems of communication can be understood in terms of the imaginary story of the bananafish'. Possibly the first interpretation, in which it is Seymour's life and death that are interpreted in terms of the tale, constitutes a more successful attempt in the search for narrative coherence, since a clear connection is established between the title, the bananafish tale and the story ending. The second interpretation, in which the metaphoric interpretation accounts for Seymour's problems of communication, focuses on an interpretive thread which identifies common topics throughout the subsequent scenes in the story but does not foreground the role of the ending. Finally, three students interpreted the title as meaning 'something else' ironic or sarcastic. This interpretation highlights the students' awareness that a figurative interpretation to the story is necessary and, possibly, that this involves a defeat in reader's expectations, hence the ironic effect.

Research question 5 elicited students' ethical position regarding the taboo nature of the topic of suicide. Results are shown in Table 7.10.

Table 7.10 Answers to the question 'Do you think suicide is a social taboo'?

Do you think that suicide is a social taboo?	Number	%
Yes	16	44.4
No	7	19.4
Yes and no	1	2.7
No answer	12	33.3
Total	36	99.83

This question is designed in order to elicit a response from readers from an ethical perspective, thus complementing their emotional responses and their responses to textual observations. From the perspective of manipulation within a questionnaire, readers are here led into adopting ethical positions with regard to the topic of the story.

Results show that the number of students who believe that suicide is a social taboo doubles the number of students who do not agree. However, the number of students who choose not to answer the question is also high thus suggesting that the topic is indeed a delicate one, as pointed out by some of the students who do provide responses. Examples (26) to (31) illustrate some of the positive responses, while examples (32) to (35) illustrate negative responses.

(26) Yes, but I think it shouldn't be since suicidal thoughts are a part of so many persons' lives. I think it still is because some people rather deny it as a problem rather than facing reality. (F2)

(27) It is a delicate topic and most people don't know how to talk about it, so they don't, and they prefer to ignore it. (F3)

(28) Religion and moral have a lot of influence in our society: if you commit a suicide it is considered a sin and you have not power to provoke your own death. (M13)

(29) Because it is one of the most frighting [sic] things of the world. So, we try to avoid it and try not to think about it. (F19)

(30) Because nobody talks about the tough stuff. It doesn't even appear in the newspaper, the media, etc. (F22)

(31) Yes. In a sense that for example people are ashamed to admit that sbdy in their family committed suicide or that they have suicidal thoughts. (F24)

(32) Not exactly, I think nowadays we're used to it both because we see it in movies and because of real life events. (F4)

(33) There are people committing suicide every single day and it's a topic discussed very often because of many problems we have nowadays, such as bullying, economic crisis … (M9)

(34) No in the sense that it's not a taboo for the media. (F24)

(35) No, because many stories end up in a suicide. (F25)

Among the explanations provided for the taboo nature of the topic of suicide, some students argue that it elicits a strong emotional response, such as fear or shame, and thus most people avoid talking about it or ignore it. Some students mention that moral and religious beliefs account for the taboo nature of suicide and one student argues that suicide does not even appear in the news. This contrasts with students who think that suicide is not a social taboo since they consider that it is a topic that is dealt with recurrently in the media in connection to situations of crisis such as the economic crisis or bullying, and it also forms part of the generic conventions of fiction. These results seem to suggest that suicide is perceived as a social taboo by most students, in particular because it is a topic that tends to be avoided or is not given sufficient attention in the media. However, both positive and negative responses show that there is a social awareness of the importance of suicide as a social problem and also as a topic which plays a role in contemporary narrative fiction.

5. Conclusions

The present chapter set out to explore the way in which the responses to a questionnaire by real readers could be said to relate to manipulation techniques of the author of the short story and of the analyst as the designer of the questionnaire. With regard to the relation between the responses to the questionnaire and the manipulation features observed in the short story, the following conclusions can be suggested: first, the lack of anticipation of the ending and the emotional response of shock in most readers seem to support the claim that manipulation strategies of burying information, red herrings and character underspecification have been effective. The students' explanations of the reasons for their shock also seem to confirm that these manipulation techniques are at play. Second, students' responses to the question whether the ending was the least expected have provided an interesting angle on their interpretation of the story. Thus, while they did not anticipate the ending as readers and they reacted with surprise and shock, retrospectively, most students concluded that the ending was congruent with the narrative development of the story. This shows that a distinction may be drawn between their role as readers, who are indeed surprised by the story ending, and their role as observers of the text or analysts, who are able to interpret the connection between genre conventions, manipulation techniques and ending of a story. Third, it may be concluded that the present study provides support to the claims that titles and endings are sites for increased reader attention and act as clues for the interpretation of short stories. In their responses to the questionnaire, students showed they were able to reconstruct the interpretation of the story in the light of the outcome of the ending together with the clue provided by the title. Most students identified the metaphorical interpretation of the story which was elicited by the title. It may be observed that such metaphoric interpretation will be carried out or confirmed once the ending was read, and a complete parallelism between the life and death of the protagonist and the life and death of bananafish could be established.

Results show that though the readers are learners of English as a foreign language, their own background knowledge and training in the degree in English Studies enables them to find adequate interpretations for a complex piece of fiction. All in all, the present study points to the need to carry out further research which explores the relations between readers' anticipation and reaction to aspects of a literary texts and their interpretations and explanations of the textual features of the piece of fiction.

References

Abbot, H. P. (2005) 'Closure', in Herman, D., Jahn, M., and Ryan, M. L. (eds) *The Routledge Handbook of Narrative Theory*, pp. 67–8. London: Routledge.

Abbott, H. P. (2013) 'Narrativity', Paragraph 16, in Hühn, P. et al. (eds) *The Living Handbook of Narratology*. Hamburg: Hamburg University. Available at: http://www.lhn.uni-hamburg.de/article/narrativity (accessed 8 March 2018).

Burke, M. (ed.) (2014) *The Routledge Handbook of Stylistics*. London: Routledge.

Caracciolo, M. (2013) 'Phenomenological metaphors in readers' engagement with characters: The case of Ian McEwan's *Saturday*', *Language and Literature* 22(1): 60–76.

Emmott, C. (1997) *Narrative Comprehension: A Discourse Perspective*. Oxford: Oxford University Press.

Emmott, C. and Alexander, M. (2010) 'Detective fiction, plot construction, and reader manipulation: Rhetorical control and cognitive misdirection in Agatha Christie's Sparkling Cyanide', in McIntyre, D. and Busse, B. (eds) *Language and Style: In Honour of Mick Short*, pp. 328–46. Houndmills, Basingstoke: Palgrave Macmillan.

Emmott, C. and Alexander, M. (2019) 'Reliability, unreliability, reader manipulation and plot reversals: Strategies for constructing and challenging the credibility of characters in Agatha Christie's detective fiction', in Page, R., Busse, B. and Nørgaard, N. (eds) *Rethinking Language, Text and Context: Interdisciplinary Research in Honour of Michael Toolan*, pp. 177–90. Abingdon: Routledge.

Emmott, C., Sanford, A., and Alexander, M. (2010) 'Scenarios, characters' roles and plot status: Readers' assumptions and writers' manipulations of assumptions in narrative texts', in Eder, J., Jannidis, F., and Schneider, R. (eds) *Characters in Fictional Worlds: Understanding Imaginary Beings in Literature, Film and Other Media*, pp. 377–99. Berlin: Mouton De Gruyter.

Gwynn, F. L. and Blotner, J. L. (1962) 'A slight case of incest', in Grunwald, H. A. (ed.) *Salinger: The Classical Critical and Personal Portrait*, pp. 86–114. New York/London: Harper.

Hidalgo-Downing, L. (2019) 'Metaphoric interpretations of a short story by J.D. Salinger: A reader response study', in Page, R., Busse, B., and Nørgaard, N. (eds) *Rethinking Language, Text and Context. Interdisciplinary Research in Stylistics in Honour of Michael Toolan*, pp. 191–206. London: Routledge.

Lohafer, S. (2003) *Reading for Storyness: Preclosure Theory, Empirical Poetics and Culture in the Short Story*. Baltimore, MD and London: The John Hopkins University Press.

Lohafer, S. (2005) 'Short story', in Herman, D., Jahn, M., and Ryan, M. L. (eds) *The Routledge Handbook of Narrative Theory*, pp. 528–30. London: Routledge.

Miall, D. S. (2014) 'Emotions, feelings and stylistics', in Stockwell, P. and Whiteley, S. (eds) *The Cambridge Handbook of Stylistics*, pp. 424–38. Cambridge: Cambridge University Press.

Miall, D. S. and Kuiken, D. (1998) 'The form of reading: Empirical studies of literariness', *Poetics* 22: 327–41.

Peplow, D. and Carter, R. (2014) 'Stylistics and real readers', in Burke, M. (ed.) *The Routledge Handbook of Stylistics*, pp. 440–54. London: Routledge.

Prince, G. (2003 [1987]) *Dictionary of Narratology (Revised Edition)*. Lincoln: University of Nebraska Press.

Pyrhönen, H. (2005) 'Suspense and surprise', in Herman, D., Jahn, M., and Ryan, M. L. (eds) *The Routledge Handbook of Narrative Theory*, pp. 578–80. London: Routledge.

Rabinowitz, P. (2002) 'Reading beginnings and endings', in Richardson, B. (ed.) *Narrative Dynamics*, pp. 300–13. Columbus, Ohio: The Ohio State University Press.

Rasinger, S. M. (2010 [2008]) *Quantitative Research in Linguistics*. London and New York: Continuum.

Richardson, B. (ed.) (2002) *Narrative Dynamics: Essays on Time, Plot, Closure, and Frames*. Columbus: Ohio State University Press.

Salinger, J. D. (1953) 'A perfect day for bananafish', in *Nine Stories*, pp. 3–18. Boston, MA: Little, Brown and Company.

Sanford, A. J. and Emmott, C. (2012) *Mind, Brain and Narrative*. Cambridge: Cambridge University Press.

Schneider, R. (2005) 'Emotion and narrative', in Herman, D., Jahn, M., and Ryan, M. L. (eds) *The Routledge Handbook of Narrative Theory*, pp. 136–7. London: Routledge.

Sorlin, S. (2016) *Language and Manipulation in House of Cards: A Pragma-Stylistic Perspective*. Basingstoke: Palgrave Macmillan.

Sorlin, S. (2020) 'Manipulation in fiction', in Sorlin, S. (ed.) *Stylistic Manipulation of the Reader in Contemporary Fiction*, pp. 1–21. London: Bloomsbury.

Stockwell, P. (2013) 'The positioned reader', *Language and Literature* 22(3): 263–77.

Stockwell, P. and Whiteley, S. (eds) (2014) *The Cambridge Handbook of Stylistics*. Cambridge: Cambridge University Press.

Toolan, M. (2009) *Narrative Progression and the Short Story: A Corpus Stylistic Approach*. Amsterdam: John Benjamins.

Toolan, M. (2013) 'Coherence', Paragraph 24, in Hühn, P. et al. (ed.) *The Living Handbook of Narratology*. Hamburg: Hamburg University. Available at: http://www.lhn.uni-hamburg.de/article/coherence (accessed 16 February 2018).

Toolan, M. (2016) *Making Sense of Narrative Text: Situation, Repetition, and Picturing in the Reading of Short Stories*. London: Routledge.

Whiteley, S. (2016) 'A cognitive poetic approach to researching the reading experience', in Otterholm, K., Skjerdingstad, K. I., McKechnie, L. E. F., and Rothbauer, P. (eds) *Plotting the Reading Experience: Theory, Practice, Politics*, pp. 99–114. Waterloo: Wilfred Laurier Press.

Wiegand, W. (1962) 'The cures for banana fever', in Grunwald, H. A. (ed.) *Salinger: The Classical Critical and Personal Portrait*, pp. 115–36. New York/London: Harper.

8

Manipulating metaphors: Interactions between readers and 'Upon Opening the Chest Freezer'

Sara Whiteley

1. Introduction

In the title of this volume, the phrase 'stylistic manipulation of the reader' portrays readers as recipients of manipulation. The implication is that stylistic features designed by an author, or simply present in a text, manipulate the reader in order to produce certain effects. This characterizes one important dimension of literary reading. But, of course, it has long been recognized in reader response theory, stylistics and most recently cognitive stylistics, that reading involves both top-down and bottom-up processes, and that the reader also plays an active role in literary interpretation. From a cognitive stylistic perspective, reading is an act of conceptualization, influenced by both textual and contextual factors. Thus, at its core, the act of reading is an *inter*action, and readers are agents performing manipulation as well as the target of manipulative strategies.

One way to access examples of the readerly manipulation of texts is to examine the way readers use texts in particular contexts. After offering a stylistic analysis of the poem 'Upon Opening the Chest Freezer' by Simon Armitage (2010), this chapter examines the discourse of two groups of readers as they discuss the poem, and considers how these readers 'manipulate' conceptualizations of the text in the production of context-specific, interactional interpretations. Specifically, it examines the way readers use the imagery of the poem to construct metaphors and extend those metaphors across the turns of their discussion as they interpret the poem together. As well as providing an insight into the effects of the poem's stylistic features, the reading group talk illustrates the flipside of literary manipulation: that is, readers' manipulation of the text for particular purposes.

The stylistic features of the poem, including its use of point of view, register, deixis and metaphor, are discussed in Section 2. Section 3 introduces the reading group data. Section 4 considers extracts from the discussions of one all-male and one all-female reading group. Overall, the approach taken in this chapter posits that an examination of the language of the poem, in conjunction with the language readers use to discuss the poem, can provide insights into the multi-directional manipulation involved in the act of reading.

2. 'Upon Opening the Chest Freezer': Stylistic analysis

The poem 'Upon Opening the Chest Freezer' (see Appendix) is written by contemporary British poet Simon Armitage, and was published as part of his *Seeing Stars* collection in 2010. The collection features several narrative poems about domestic marital relationships. This poem is a darkly humorous representation of marital discord: it represents the habitual actions of an artist named Damien, before revealing Damien's wife's decision to leave him, and the farewell note she leaves in the freezer for him to find. As the stylistic analysis below will demonstrate, the poem presents a relatively complex blend of voices and perspectives as it narrates the ending of the relationship. It also connects the end of the relationship with the chest freezer in the couple's home. The significance of the chest freezer is highlighted by the title of the poem, and this connection provides the basis for metaphorical interpretations of the text.

The first stanza describes Damien's habitual actions in the simple present and future tenses ('Damien *likes* to roll up' (2), '*he'll* drive out in the van' (7)). Each year, Damien saves a large ball of winter snow in the chest freezer in the pantry and then, in high summer, he dumps it in a public place as a 'stunt' and photographs peoples' reactions to it. This stunt is actually very similar to the work of an existing British artist named Andy Goldsworthy, who is famous for making crop circles and other kinds of natural art. Armitage is known to be fond of Goldsworthy's work, and this link is recognized by both of the reading groups discussed below (as evident in Extract 4, Turn 42 when a member of Susan's group makes a joke about crop circles).

The first stanza of the poem is narrated in the third person which suggests an external narrative viewpoint. However, some deictic markers such as the use of definite reference in 'the chest freezer in the pantry' (3–4) and the mix of poetic and prosaic registers make the voice represented appear more complex.

A literary register is present in phrases such as 'the last snowfall of winter' (1) or 'the thin membrane of night which divides one long day from the next' (5–6) and is also evident in intertextual links to Shelley's 'Ozymandias' in the phrase 'look upon such mighty works bewildered and amazed' (14). A more prosaic register is present in phrases such as 'one of his little stunts' (4), 'a ginormous snowball' (2–3) and 'snap away with the Nikon' (10). This clash of registers makes the first stanza appear to be an example of free indirect discourse, where narrator and character voices are blended, and we are being presented with a partially focalized third-person account of the scene. The clash of registers also hints at the focalizing character's disdain for Damien's artwork. The members of the public who admire the work are described rather hyperbolically as 'awestruck citizenry who swarm around his miracle of meteorology' (12–13) while Damien's elaborate efforts are portrayed bathetically as a 'little stunt' (4). The specific identity of the focalizing character does not become clear until the second stanza, however.

The second stanza involves an abrupt point of view shift from third person to first-person direct address: 'Damien, I'm through playing housewife to your "art" and this brief story poem is to tell you I'm leaving' (15–17). The inverted commas around 'art' signal the same disparaging tone that was present in the first stanza and suggests that it is the wife's voice that is present throughout the poem. As well as a shift in point of view, the second stanza creates several shifts in temporal location. Lines 15–18 use the present tense to represent the wife's actions in the narrative present as she sticks the story poem to the lid of the chest freezer: 'I'm gaffer taping it to the freezer lid'. Lines 18–22 depict a future hypothetical time zone in which Damien is reading the note: 'If you're reading it, you're ... ' (18). Lines 22–29 use the past tense to depict Damien's ball of snow being used up for various household purposes such as feeding guests and family. Agency deletion in the syntax of these lines means the wife's responsibility for decimating Damien's snowball is implied rather than stated: 'At first it was just a scoop here, and a scraping there ... ' (22–23), 'the day dawned when there wasn't so much as a snowflake left' (28–29). As I shall discuss below, this agency deletion seems to be influential in the interpretative difficulty which some readers experienced in their reading of the poem. Finally, the poem returns to the narrative present: 'I need for you now to lean into the void' (29–30). The temporal shifts across stanza 2 create an association between the gradual diminishment of the snowball in the past, and the wife's current actions: now that there isn't 'so much as a snowflake left' in the freezer, the wife has decided to write Damien a note and leave.

The deictic complexity of the second stanza is intensified with the textually deictic reference to 'this story poem' in lines 16 and 18 ('if you're reading *it*'), and the use of the second person. To a certain extent, the second person implicates the reader, as both we and Damien are being addressed as readers of the poem. The textual deixis suggests that the poem we are reading might be the poem the wife has written: rendering the entire second stanza an instance of free direct writing (Semino and Short 2004). However, the poetic narratorial register established in the first stanza is also present here (e.g. 'steaming abyss' (19), 'bruised purple by frost' (22)), so the poem doesn't seem to be a straightforward portrayal of the note itself. Despite this ambiguity, the shift to the first-person, the textual deixis and the direct address creates a sense of increased proximity to the action as the poem progresses.

Perhaps unsurprisingly, inferencing is needed by the reader in order to connect the scenes being portrayed and blend the voices as part of interpreting the poem. The shifts in narrative voice seem to position readers in various character perspectives: in the first stanza we experience a blend of narrator and character voices representing the wife's perspective, before there is a shift into the wife's voice and perspective in stanza 2. However the use of 'you' and the textual deixis in stanza 2 also positions the reader with Damien as addressees or readers of the note. Participants in the reading groups discussed in Section 4 express confusion and interpretative differences in relation to some of the details of this poem. As I shall demonstrate in Section 4, the reading groups end up focusing on the metaphorical aspects of the poem as a way of interpreting the scenes it portrays.

The cognitive approach to metaphor adopted in this chapter regards metaphor as a conceptual process, not simply an ornamental feature of language (Lakoff and Johnson 1980; Stockwell 2002). Metaphor involves the mapping of features from one conceptual domain to another; from a source to a target domain. A conceptual domain is a 'body of knowledge within our conceptual system that contains and organises related ideas and experiences' (Evans and Green 2006: 14). In his elucidation of the cognitive stylistic approach to metaphor, Stockwell (2002: 107–8) draws a graded distinction between 'visible' and 'invisible' metaphors. Visible metaphors are those in which source and target domains are explicitly mentioned in the language of a text, for instance, in metaphorical expressions such as: 'Juliet is the sun', or similes such as: 'The brain is like a city' (Stockwell 2002: 107). These sentences make the metaphorical target domains (JULIET, BRAIN) and source domains (SUN, CITY) linguistically explicit (conceptual domains are denoted by the use of small capitals, see Lakoff and Johnson 1980; Stockwell 2002). Metaphors can be less visible, however, if one of the domains is less explicitly mentioned. More invisible renderings of the metaphor THE BRAIN IS A CITY would be expressions such as: 'In the streets and on the corners of my mind' (where 'streets' and 'corners' imply the CITY source domain); or 'This is the nerve-centre of the body' (where 'centre' implies the CITY source domain); or an allegory which represents psychoanalytical archetypes as the landmarks and inhabitants of a city (where the BRAIN target domain is implied) (Stockwell 2002: 108). Thus, invisible metaphors are woven into the text more obliquely, and require greater creative input on the part of the reader, as well as creating more potential for ambiguity (Stockwell 2002: 107).

'Upon Opening the Chest Freezer' does not contain many visible metaphors: the most visible is the simile 'as hard as bullets' (21). Less visible metaphors include the genitive expression 'that thin membrane of night' (5), the grammatical metaphor 'citizenry who swarm' (12), and the comparison of the cold air of the freezer to a 'steaming abyss' (19) and 'the true scald of Antarctica's breath' (31). But otherwise, the actions described in the poem are quite literal. The chest freezer, for instance, is referred to as an actual object in the couple's home: it is something into which Damien puts his snowball (3) and to which the wife gaffer tapes her note (18). Interestingly, despite the literal quality of the text, metaphorical connections between the chest freezer and the couple's relationship are a key part of the interpretations developed in the reading group discussions shown in Section 4. As I shall go on to demonstrate, the readers construct and manipulate mappings between the source domain CHEST FREEZER and target domain RELATIONSHIP in their interpretations of the poem.

The readers' construction and use of this metaphor has interesting implications for the study of reader-text interaction in interpretation. While it can be said that the poem evokes the conceptual domains of RELATIONSHIP and CHEST FREEZER through its language – it represents a co-habiting relationship ('housewife', 'I'm leaving') and a chest freezer ('Upon opening the chest freezer', 'the freezer lid') – the text itself does not contain any visible or invisible metaphors which link these domains metaphorically. It could perhaps be argued that the poem *invites* such metaphorical connections: for instance, it establishes a strong narrative association between the emptiness of the freezer and the wife's decision to leave (lines 28–30), and the chest freezer features in the title of the poem. Genre is a crucial framing device in the perception and interpretation of metaphors (e.g. see Forceville 2002: 11), and readers schooled in poetry will know to look to the title for 'clues' about overall poetic meaning. However, beyond introducing the conceptual domains, the metaphorical association between the CHEST FREEZER and the RELATIONSHIP is not specifically enacted by the poem's language; it is instead an interpretative possibility upon which the reading groups capitalize in their discussion.

3. Reading group talk

Reading groups (also known as book clubs or reading circles) are groups of people who come together to talk about a literary work. Such groups customarily meet in living rooms, cafes, libraries, workplaces, prisons or schools, or interact online through discussion boards. Studies in the United States and the United Kingdom in the early 2000s, such as Long (2003) and Hartley (2002) noted an 'explosive growth' (Long 2003: 19) in reading group membership, which continues to be evident today (Peplow et al. 2016: 2). As a very popular and culturally salient form of social engagement around literature, reading groups have attracted increasing academic interest in a number of fields including cultural studies (e.g. Long 2003; Rehberg Sedo 2011), discourse analysis (e.g. Peplow 2016; Swann and Allington 2009) and stylistics (e.g. Nuttall 2015; Peplow et al. 2016: 30–60; Whiteley 2011a, 2016a). In stylistics, reading group discussion is regarded as a site for the observation of readers' responses to literary texts, and such talk is typically used to inform the close stylistic analysis of the effects of a particular work.

Peplow et al. (2016: 30) argue that reading group discussion is a form of 'social reading' in which multiple interactants share, compare, debate and co-construct their interpretations of literary texts. Reading groups also talk beyond the text, about a wide range of personal, social, cultural, historical and moral issues (Peplow et al. 2016: 21). The emphasis is often not upon reaching an agreed interpretation of a work, but rather exploring possible interpretative avenues: reading groups 'press texts into service for the meanings they transmit and the conversations they can generate' (Long 2003: 147–8). As such, reading groups are an interesting site for the examination of readerly manipulations of texts. As Swann and Allington (2009: 250) note, the interpretations generated in reading groups are entirely 'contingent upon aspects of the contexts in which they read' and are 'closely embedded within sets of social and interpersonal relations'.

The reading group data discussed in Section 4 was recorded in 2011, as part of the 'Creative Writing in the Community' project at the University of Sheffield. One strand of the project was an exploratory study of the way poetry is discussed in different contexts in Sheffield, and involved the recording of group discussions of poetry both within and outside of the university (see also Whiteley 2011b,

2016b). Reading groups were asked by the researcher to read and discuss the same three poems, which enabled the collection of comparative data across a range of groups. The two groups I discuss in this chapter – named Andy's group and Susan's group – are domestic reading groups who regularly meet in each others' homes in an affluent area of Sheffield. Andy's group has eight participants, all male, aged in their 50s–70s, who meet monthly to discuss (in their words): 'A rotation of modern and classic novels, poetry and factual books.' At the time of the recording the group were mainly retired or semi-retired from professional jobs (the three non-retired members worked in town planning, psychotherapy and university project management), and had secondary school or A-level academic qualifications in English. Susan's group also has eight regular participants, all female, aged in their 40s–70s, who meet monthly to discuss novels that are 'challenging, thought provoking, and material of good quality'. The majority of Susan's group were in professional employment at the time of the recording, as a university manager, English teacher, artist, accountant, solicitor and publications manager (two of the group were retired). The majority of the group have academic qualifications in English at either secondary school or A-level, but two also have degrees in English.

These local reading groups volunteered to take part in the 'Creative Writing in the Community' project after hearing an announcement at the project launch, which involved a reading by the poet Simon Armitage in a local cinema. I supplied Andy and Susan with copies of three poems from Armitage's latest collection and a digital recorder, and they liaised with their groups to supply the texts and make the recording. The researcher was not physically present during these group discussions. While this was an effort to mitigate the impact of the research context on the interactions, it also made it difficult to disambiguate individual speakers in the subsequent recording, and this is why some speakers in the transcripts reproduced below are marked '?'. Both groups talked about 'Upon Opening the Chest Freezer' last, around an hour into their meetings (preferring to discuss the other poems, 'I'll Be There to Love and Comfort You' and 'An Accommodation' first). Andy's group spoke about the poem for around fifteen minutes and Susan's group for around twenty-five minutes. Participants in both Andy and Susan's group express confusion or uncertainty about the poem's meaning at points in their discussion, and at these points metaphorical interpretations of the text become particularly relevant. The analysis below focuses on four extracts of reading group talk, three short extracts from Andy's group and one longer extract from Susan's group. Extracts 1 and 2 come from the beginning of Andy's group's discussion, and Extract 3 comes from the end (for discussion of the intersubjectivity exhibited in Andy's group discussion, see

Peplow and Whiteley, forthcoming). Extract 4 is taken from midway through Susan's group discussion, at a point where interpretational difficulties are also raised by the group.

In Extract 1, from Andy's group (Section 4), Mike says that he 'had difficulty' with this text and 'didn't get it' (Extract 1, Turn 1) – especially the part which describes the ice being removed from the freezer, and later in Extract 3 Simon suggests that he's gained a 'different perspective' on the poem from the others and that his understanding was incomplete ('I wasn't quite there with [it]', Extract 3, Turn 14). As the group discuss the poem, however, Mike and Simon increasingly appear to attach meanings to the text, building on the metaphors introduced by other members. By the end of the meeting these two participants report that they've developed important understandings of the poem, that they 'get it' more than they did at the outset (Extract 3, Turns 12–22). Andy's group use the metaphor as a way of building deeper understanding of the poem.

Similarly, in Susan's group shown in Extract 4, Rachel poses a question about 'Upon Opening the Chest Freezer' by asking: 'Did he have a thing with the freezer then?' and citing lines 22–23 ('At first it was just / a scoop here, and a scraping there', Extract 4, Turns 1 and 3). The other members of Susan's group respond to Rachel's question as though it was a misreading of the poem: Kate, Lucy and Marion correct Rachel by pointing out that the wife is the agent responsible for using the snowball, not Damien (Extract 4, Turns 4–16). Following this correction, Sandra also expresses surprise which suggests that she also hadn't realized who was removing ice from the freezer (Extract 4, Turn 9). As noted in the stylistic analysis in Section 2, the agency deletion in the poem could be seen as the source of these interpretative differences, and the diversity in readers' initial responses demonstrates how much the poem leaves to reader inference. Rachel's group then go on to use metaphors as a way of elaborating the scenes depicted in the poem and 'mind-modelling' the characters (Stockwell 2009: 140). Sections 4.1 and 4.2 consider the ways the reading groups construct and manipulate metaphors in more detail.

4. Manipulating metaphors in the reading group talk

4.1. Metaphor in Andy's reading group

Extract 1 comes from the beginning of Andy's group's discussion of 'Upon Opening the Chest Freezer'. Following Mike's opening expression of uncertainty (Turn 1) Andy is the first to propose a metaphorical interpretation of 'Upon Opening the Chest Freezer' (see Appendix for transcription conventions).

Extract 1 (01.10.30 – 01.13.08)

1	Mike:	I had difficulty with this one I didn't get it really [...] it's this what seems to be a diminishing snowball being used for other things "a scoop here and scraping there slush puppies for next door's kids a lemon sorbet an ice pack margaritas" it's all the use of ice for other things other than the art until it's all gone and I didn't get that bit
2	Andy:	I wondered actually - this is about the 17th time I've read it I think probably because I didn't get it first time at all other than it sounded quite funny [...] and then I wondered about the freezer really and - someone's leaving by the sound of it she [leaves him a note
3	Ron:	[his wife yeah
4	Andy:	[...] she's just so fed up of it and it feels like the chicken thighs and the petit pois are all that remains of the relationship or you could say that the diminishing snowball as it disappears is all that's left you know until there's actually nothing left and then she leaves
5	Simon:	there's nothing left in the chest freezer which represents their [relationship
6	Ron:	[relationship
7	Andy:	yeah
8	Simon:	is that what you're saying
9	Andy:	yeah

In Turn 4, when he says: 'The petit pois are all that remains of the relationship' and 'the diminishing snowball ... is all that's left ... until she leaves', Andy establishes mappings between the conceptual source domain of the CHEST FREEZER and the target concept of the poetic characters' RELATIONSHIP. More specifically, his expressions create a metaphor in which the CONTENTS OF THE FREEZER are mapped onto the QUALITY OF THE RELATIONSHIP; so an empty or emptying freezer becomes representative of a weak or damaged relationship. Simon reiterates the metaphor established by Andy to make it even more visible: 'There's nothing left in the chest freezer that represents their relationship, is that what you're saying' (Turns 5 and 8).

Simpson (2014: 95-8) draws a useful distinction between 'novel' and 'conventional' metaphors, pointing out that literary metaphors operate in relation to a background of more conventional, everyday metaphorical thought (see also Lakoff and Johnson 1980: 139). He points out that when literary writers create metaphors, they may seek to establish new connections between target and source domains, or elaborate and extend upon existing conventional metaphors in various ways (Simpson 2014: 96; see also Lakoff and Johnson 1980: 152). The RELATIONSHIP IS A CHEST FREEZER metaphor which Andy creates makes quite novel associations between conceptual domains: it is unusual to compare relationships to freezers. However, it is also grounded in more conventional, structural associations between conceptual domains. States or relationships are regularly conceptualized as containers; the RELATIONSHIP IS A CONTAINER metaphor underpins everyday expressions such as being 'in' or 'getting out' of a relationship, for instance (Lakoff and Johnson 1980: 29–32; Lakoff 2014). As Lakoff and Johnson point out (1980: 30), containers are conceptualized as bounded objects that can be quantified in terms of amount of substance they contain. Here, Andy maps from the chest-freezer-container to the container-of-the-couple's-relationship in order to represent certain qualities. The implication that an empty freezer signals a damaged relationship also draws on conventional orientational mappings, such as MORE IS UP and GOOD IS UP, so an empty freezer seems indicative of a bad relationship (Lakoff and Johnson 1980: 16).

The RELATIONSHIP IS A CHEST FREEZER metaphor which Andy establishes in Extract 1 is elaborated throughout the group's discussion in slightly different configurations, which capture different aspects of the source domain. The particular properties of chest freezers, such as their contents and the way they are used by their owners, are mapped onto the couple's relationship. The mappings between source and target domains across the discussion seem to reflect the participants' developing interpretations of the poem. About a minute after Extract 1, Ron and Simon have the following exchange, which both reiterates and extends Andy's initial metaphor.

Extract 2 (01.13.32 – 01.14.15)

```
1 Ron:   for every bit of creative work outside there's
         something that happens at home and essentially
         the person who's actually with him at home >and
         let's say it's his wife for the sake of argument<
         erm (1.5) has got sick to death of the fact
         that (2.0) wh- (1.0) what is in the freezer (.)
         essentially in the heart (.) the heart of the
         relationship (.) is his thinking about the outside
         world and she's been looking after some of the
         domestic things and gradually she's drawing and
         drawing and drawing away from this until there's
         actually (.) there's actually nothing left as far
         as she's concerned so she's leaving
```

```
2 Simon:  =well she's been supporting him in doing that
          [housewife things to his art
3 Ron:    [supporting him in doing that yeah
```

Ron's utterance in Turn 1 partially repeats the metaphorical mappings established by Andy, as the wife's 'drawing away' from the contents of the freezer symbolizes the reduction of the quality of the couple's relationship until 'there's actually nothing left'. However, in Andy's articulation of this metaphor in Extract 1 no one was represented as being responsible for the emptying freezer. In contrast, here Ron portrays the wife as the agent drawing the contents of the freezer away as she 'look[s] after some of the domestic things'. Indeed, Ron and Simon extend the RELATIONSHIP IS A CHEST FREEZER metaphor by giving further metaphorical weight to the precise nature of the contents of the freezer, and the way the respective partners interact with the freezer. These extensions of the metaphor begin to apportion blame for the condition of the relationship to Damien rather than his wife.

For instance, Simon's addition to Ron's utterance in Turn 2, which receives support from Ron in Turn 3, seems designed to reduce the blame apportioned to the wife for the damage done to the relationship. She has been drawing things away from the chest freezer, but she has been doing so in order to 'support' Damien. Thus, the wife's interaction with the freezer is conceptualized as representative of the effort she has put into the relationship, creating the following associations: INTERACTION WITH FREEZER IS EFFORT PUT INTO RELATIONSHIP.

Damien, on the other hand, is represented as interacting with the freezer quite differently. In Turn 2, Ron represents Damien's addition to the contents of freezer in the following way: 'What is in the freezer (.) essentially in the heart (.) the heart of the relationship (.) is [Damien's] thinking about the outside world'. While the wife has been taking things out of the freezer in her efforts to be a supportive partner, Damien is represented here as putting things in the freezer which symbolize his disregard for the relationship. This extension of the RELATIONSHIP IS A CHEST FREEZER metaphor draws once more on the CONTAINER domain by making a distinction between the 'inside' of the relationship and 'the outside world'.

The implication is that a relationship-container – here the chest freezer – should be a private space, containing the shared resources of participants. By putting public things into the freezer, which only he uses, Damien is damaging the relationship by not showing his partner enough awareness. This elaborates the CONTENTS OF THE FREEZER IS THE QUALITY OF THE RELATIONSHIP metaphor established by Andy by making new elements of the source domain reflect new elements of the target.

In Extract 3, five minutes later (and towards the end of the group's discussion), Mike also reiterates the CONTENTS OF THE FREEZER IS THE QUALITY OF THE RELATIONSHIP metaphor first established by Andy and continued by Ron. After expressing confusion at the beginning of the discussion (Extract 1, Turn 1), here Mike adopts and elaborates the metaphor which the group has been using to interpret the poem, and explicitly acknowledges that his understanding of the poem has developed across the course of the discussion (Turns 15–22).

Extract 3 (01.20.15 – 01.21.48)

1	Mike:	and (0.5) i-(.) if you take one of his (.) big snowballs in the freezer as (.) as (0.5) as representing their relationship (0.5) she's then saying actually rather than *revere* it and she's already [criticised his work
2	Andy:	[yeah
3	Mike:	rather than *revere* that she's actually been nibbling away at it she's had a couple of scoops out for slush puppies for the kids
4	Andy:	(*laugh*)
5	Mike:	she's used (.) made a lemon sorbet out of a bit of it and she's used it for an ice pack and then <suddenly> she's realised there's not even any of it left not even a snowflake and that's like a metaphor for their (0.5) relationship and (0.5) you know opens the freezer one night and there's just a few bruised peas and some (1.0) over date err (0.5) chicken thighs and she's like 'right I'm off' hehe you know (.) >it's almost a metaphor for there's nothing left< in [the relationship
6	Andy:	[in the relation[ship yeah
7	Mike:	[yeah yeah
8	Andy:	=exactly yeah I think so
9	Mike:	but- [but-
10	?:	[bitter? [yeah
11	Andy:	[she's angry she's angry
12	Simon:	[I- agh – I think I've had a different perspective of this thank you [that's helped me a lot I I I think that was
13	Mike:	[I've only I've only

```
14  Simon:    the one I err yeah that I wasn't quite
              there with but err no it's err put all of
              that [into perspective
15  Mike:          [well earlier I said I didn't get it
              and it's only [while we've been discussing
              this
16  ?:                       [yeah
17  Simon?:                  [yeah
18  Mike:     that I've thought of that and it seems to
              fit for me now
19  Simon?:   yes
20  Mike:     so I get it more than I did
21  Simon:    =yes yes
22  Mike:     =when we started talking which is (.) always
              shows its worth talking about it as well as
              rereading
```

Interestingly, though Mike's utterances in Turns 1, 3 and 5 uses the same conceptual resources established in Extracts 1 and 2, the mappings created here indicate a slightly different interpretation of the poem than that established by Ron and Simon in Extract 2. Ron and Simon characterized the female protagonist's interactions with the freezer as being supportive of her partner, whereas here Mike portrays the wife actions more negatively: she is 'nibbling away' at the contents of the freezer rather than 'rever[ing]' them (Turn 3). In Mike's construal of the metaphor, the wife is portrayed as the agent reducing the contents of the freezer and thus as the person responsible for damaging the relationship. Her interaction with the freezer is an extension of her lack of respect for Damien, which also evident in her critical attitude to Damien's work ('she's already criticised his work', Turn 1).

Across Extracts 1 to 3 participants in Andy's group establish and develop various configurations of the RELATIONSHIP IS A CHEST FREEZER metaphor. The mapping scope of this metaphor is rich, as evidenced by the multiple potential mappings between the domains (Stockwell 2002: 108). Andy's group seem to agree that this metaphor is an appropriate interpretative resource for understanding the poem, and it is both reiterated and construed slightly differently across the turns of the discussion in the expression of related but distinct interpretations. In particular, Andy's group explore the mappings of the CONTENTS OF THE FREEZER IS QUALITY OF THE RELATIONSHIP and INTERACTION WITH THE FREEZER IS EFFORT PUT INTO THE RELATIONSHIP metaphors in order to apportion different levels of blame to the parties portrayed in the poem. As noted in Section 2, reading groups tend not to reach one single agreed interpretation of a work, but instead explore possible interpretative avenues as they 'press' the text 'into service' for conversational purposes (Long 2003: 147–8). These extracts demonstrate the way in which readers adopt conceptual domains introduced by 'Upon Opening the Chest Freezer' and create metaphors from them in order to develop understanding of the poem and explore its possible meanings.

4.2. Metaphor in Susan's reading group

The extract from Susan's reading group begins in a similar way to Extract 1, as participants identify some interpretative difficulty in their responses to the poem (Turns 1–17, Extract 4). Susan's group do not develop the RELATIONSHIP IS A CHEST FREEZER metaphor as explicitly or visibly as Andy's group, but their discussion does still revolve around the way the characters interact with the freezer and the way such interactions stand for other aspects of the couple's relationship. The characters' behaviour around the freezer is used to make mind-modelling inferences about the characters' views and feelings, and the group engage in playful elaborations of the scenes represented in the poem. Thus, while Andy's group manipulate metaphors in the service of forming coherent interpretations of the poem, Susan's group appear more concerned with manipulating metaphors in order to create humorous contributions to their discussion.

Extract 4: Susan's Group (01.12.29 – 01.14.22)

```
1   Rachel:   what what do you think it was did he have a
              thing with the freezer then?
2   Mary:     a thing? What do you mean a thing?
3   Rachel:   Well all this "at first it was a scoop
              here a scraping there a slush puppy
              [there"
4   Kate:     [No she's taking she's stealing his
              snowball
5   Lucy:     [she's taking his snowball she's destroying
              his [snowball
6   ?:            [bit by bit by bit
7   Marion:   she's taking bits of [his snowball
8   Lucy:                          [it's brilliant
9   Sandra:   oh she's using his snowball
10  Marion:   he was expecting it to be there
11  ?:        yeah
12  Marion:   and when he finally looks in its already
              been used up for bits of this
13  Sandra:   ooh right so she's using it for the
              margaritas and everything else
```

14	Kate:	and everything else yeah
15	Mary:	she's [getting she's using it until 'there wasn't so much as a snowflake left'
16	Marion:	[so he'll open the freezer and expect a snowball to be there but all he'll find is these [petit pois and chicken thighs
17	?:	[I love that
18	Rachel:	is that because it's happened umpteen times before and she's just so sick of it that she's decided she's leaving?
19	Mary:	yes she wants somewhere to put her sausages well she says she's leaving though doesn't she
20	?:	yes she does
21	?:	she's off she's off
22	Mary:	you can push a woman so far but fill up her freezer!
23	?:	*(Laughs)*
24	Marion:	but I could imagine her pushing him into the chest freezer
25	?:	yes
26	?:	absolutely
27	Marion:	into the empty space where his snowball was
28	?:	into where there's only those snowflakes
29	Kate:	and she says "I need you now to <u>lean</u> into the void"
30	?:	yeah
31	Marion:	yes it does feel as though she might push him in
32	Kate:	=and gaffer tape it on
33	Marion:	*(Laughs)*
34	Rachel:	But also he never goes in the freezer that's all he does
35	Marion:	no he does
36	Rachel:	no he [puts his snowball in
37	?:	[all he does is put his snowball in
38	Rachel:	and takes it out again so he's not getting the peas out for the dinner [or he's not
39	Marion:	[no but he would be going there expecting to find his snowball
40	Mary:	but what Rachel's saying is that in the in the [interim
41	Rachel:	[in the interim he hasn't been in the freezer so [he's not interested
42	Lucy:	[he's been doing his crop circles or something
43	*(Group laughter)*	

Across Turn 1–17, participants are involved in reconstructing the poem and identifying who is responsible for the reduction of the snowball. Mary, Kate, Lucy and Marion explain to Rachel and Sandra that the wife is the one scooping and scraping away from the snow. The discussion is initially concerned with the literal details of the poem's narrative, but from Turn 18 it becomes more metaphorical.

After Rachel questions why the wife is removing the snowball (Turn 18) Mary offers a potential justification for her behaviour: 'She wants somewhere to put her sausages' (Turn 19) and quips 'you can push a woman so far but fill up her freezer!' (Turn 22). While Andy's group conceptualized the freezer as a shared space, here Mary portrays the freezer and its potential contents as the woman's possessions, shown by the possessive pronouns 'her freezer' and 'her sausages'. Like Andy's group, however, Mary's utterance also creates a metaphor which is grounded in conventional, structural connections between conceptual domains. Mary's quip in Turn 22 depicts the chest freezer as a source of conflict by drawing on the conventional metaphorical source domain of WAR, which is often used to structure our understanding of aspects of relationships such as ARGUMENTS and LOVE (Kövecses 2000: 26; Lakoff and Johnson 1980: 61–8). The notion of 'push[ing] a woman so far' uses the physical action of pushing, and the sense that ground can be lost or gained, to represent opposing forces in a conflict. Thus, Mary's utterances also link the RELATIONSHIP IS A CHEST FREEZER metaphor to other related metaphorical source domains: the chest freezer becomes territory in the war between the two people in a relationship. Damien's snowball is an invasion of the wife's territory, and her use of the snowball is a counter-attack in order to reclaim the space. Ultimately, the wife will end the war by leaving. The connection Mary makes between the imagery of the poem and more conventional metaphorical understandings of relationships creates humour and receives laughter from the group (Turn 23).

In Turns 24–33, Marion and Kate develop the concept of WAR introduced by Mary in another humorous direction. While Mary's utterance represented the freezer as a territory in a metaphorical war between the couple, Marion and Kate's turns co-construct a more literal representation of the freezer as a potential weapon in an actual physical conflict between the wife and Damien. Marion notes that she could 'imagine her pushing him into the chest freezer' (Turn 24). Kate develops Marion's suggestion with textual evidence, citing lines from the poem: 'She says "I need you now to lean into the void"' (Turn 29) and suggesting that the wife could 'gaffer tape' the lid on using the tape with which she affixed the poem (Turn 32, see also line 17 of the poem). Here Marion and Kate imaginatively elaborate the scenes of the poem, creating a hypothetical extension to the narrative. This imaginative 'replotting' (Gerrig 1993: 90–6) is a common feature of reading group discussion and a result of readers 'mind-modelling' (Stockwell 2009: 140) the literary characters so that they are able to imagine how they would behave in scenarios beyond those represented in the text (see also Peplow et al. 2016; Whiteley 2011a). Kate and Marion's co-constructed scene is interesting because it reverses the movement from the literal to the metaphorical which has typified the reading group talk considered thus far. This movement between the literal and the metaphorical mirrors the style of the poem. It is also a further example of the manipulation of metaphors in the reading groups: as well as manipulating the source and target domains of the RELATIONSHIP IS A CHEST FREEZER metaphor, readers can choose to adopt or abandon metaphorical approaches in order to perform different types of interpretative and interactional moves. One result of the move to the literal here is more laughter (Turn 33).

Across Turns 34–43, Rachel, Mary and Lucy re-establish a metaphorical approach to the poem, developing a metaphorical interpretation of the freezer which evokes the mappings that were performed in Andy's group, specifically the INTERACTION WITH CHEST FREEZER IS EFFORT PUT INTO THE RELATIONSHIP metaphor. When Rachel says that Damien 'never goes in the freezer' and that 'all he does [is] puts his snowball in and takes is out again' (Turns 34, 36, 38), her utterances suggest that his behaviour with the freezer signals things about his investment in the relationship. This connection is made more explicit when she explains that Damien's treatment of the freezer suggests that he is 'not interested' in the relationship (Turn 41). Lucy elaborates Rachel's point by playing on the connection between Damien and the artist Andy Goldsworthy, suggesting that Damien is too busy 'doing his crop circles or something' (Turn 42). This receives a big laugh from the group. In contrast, the wife 'getting the peas out for the dinner' (Rachel, Turn 38) appears to represent the attention she is devoting to the relationship. Rachel's utterances perform similar metaphorical mappings to Ron and Simon in Extract 2, where the wife's regular contact with the freezer is contrasted with Damien's annual visit and is used to stand for their relative investment in their relationship. As with Ron and Simon's interpretation, the implication of Rachel and Lucy's utterances is that Damien's concern for his art is largely responsible for the dysfunction in the couple's relationship.

In Extract 4, Susan's group can also be seen to 'press' the poem 'into service' for conversational purposes (Long 2003: 147–8). Like Andy's group, they create metaphors from conceptual domains introduced by 'Upon Opening the Chest Freezer' in order to explore possible interpretations of the poem. Susan's group also capitalize on the potential to shift between metaphorical and literal portrayals of the poem in order to create humour as part of a playful interaction.

The reading group discussions examined in this section demonstrate the way readers manipulate conceptualizations of the poem in order to generate conversation within their respective interactional contexts.

5. Conclusion

This chapter has used reading group discussion as a source of insight into the manipulative interactions between readers and texts. I have argued that the stylistic features of 'Upon Opening the Chest Freezer' work to establish certain interpretative possibilities, and that readers' interactions with these possibilities is evident in their talk about the poem. Reading group discussions demonstrate the active roles which readers play in interpretation, as opposed to being passive recipients of the 'manipulations' of the text. In the extracts considered above, reading group participants conceptualize the poem in different ways by manipulating and metaphorizing the conceptual domains evoked by the poem (RELATIONSHIP IS A CHEST FREEZER). Across the turns of their talk, the source and target domains are elaborated, refined, weighted differently and related to the main events of the poem in different ways. In generating this novel metaphor, readers draw on more conventional, culturally specific metaphors used to conceptualize relationships. They also switch between metaphorical and literal readings of the poem. Neither group arrives at a single interpretation of the poem, preferring instead to explore potential conceptualizations of its meaning. In the reading group context, the poem is manipulated in order to produce conversation and perform social action: Andy's group seem particularly concerned with developing an understanding of the poem as a literary artefact, while Susan's group also seem interested in generating humorous and playful interaction. The examples discussed in this chapter demonstrate some of the multi-directional dimensions involved in the act of reading, including authors/texts interacting with readers; readers interacting with texts, and readers interacting with other readers.

Acknowledgements

This research was funded by the Higher Education Innovation Fund at the University of Sheffield as part of the 'Creative Writing in the Community Project'. The author would like to thank Jessica Mason, Louise Nuttall and Peter

Stockwell for their comments on an earlier version of this chapter presented at the Poetics and Linguistics Association conference 2018.

Appendix

Upon Opening the Chest Freezer

1   From the last snowfall of winter to settle on
    the hills Damien likes to roll up a ginormous
    snowball then store it in the chest freezer in
    the pantry for one of his little stunts. Come
5   high summer, in that thin membrane of night
    which divides one long day from the next,
    he'll drive out in the van and deposit his
    snowball at a bus stop or crossroads or at the
    door of a parish church. Then from a discreet
10 distance, using a telescopic lens, he'll snap
    away with the Nikon, documenting the
    awestruck citizenry who swarm around his
    miracle of meteorology, who look upon such
    mighty works bewildered and amazed.
15 Damien, I'm through playing housewife to your
    'art' and this brief story-poem is to tell you
    I'm leaving. I'm gaffer-taping it to the inside
    of the freezer lid; if you're reading it, you're
    staring into the steaming abyss where nothing
20 remains but a packet of boneless chicken thighs
    and a scattering of petit pois, as hard as bullets
    and bruised purple by frost. At first it was just
    a scoop here, and a scraping there, slush puppies
    for next door's kids, a lemon sorbet after the
25 Sunday roast, an ice pack once in a while for my
    tired flesh, then margaritas for that gaggle of
    sycophants you rolled home with one night,
    until the day dawned when there wasn't so
    much as a snowflake left. And I need for you
30 now to lean into the void and feel for yourself
    the true scald of Antarctica's breath.

Simon Armitage (2010)

Transcription conventions

(.)   brief pause, untimed
(2.0)   longer timed pause, timing in seconds
[single square brackets mark the beginning of overlapping speech
=   latching - where an utterance follows a previous utterance with no perceptible gap between them
ob-   a sharp cut off sound or syllable
" "   cited text
> <   speech that is more rapid than surrounding speech
< >   speech that is slower than surrounding speech
[...]   excision - part of longer transcript omitted

References

Armitage, S. (2010) 'Upon Opening the Chest Freezer', in *Seeing Stars*, p. 17. London: Faber and Faber.

Evans, V. and Green, M. (2006) *Cognitive Linguistics: An Introduction*. Edinburgh: Edinburgh University Press.

Forceville, C. (2002) 'The identification of target and source in pictoral metaphors', *Journal of Pragmatics* 34: 1–14.

Gerrig, R. J. (1993) *Experiencing Narrative Worlds*. Boulder, CO: Westview Press.

Hartley, J. (2002) *The Reading Groups Book: 2002-2003 Edition*. Oxford: Oxford University Press.

Kövecses, Z. (2000) *Metaphor and Emotion: Language, Culture and Body in Human Feeling*. Cambridge: Cambridge University Press.

Lakoff, G. (2014) 'Mapping the brain's metaphor circuitry: Metaphorical thought in everyday reason', *Frontiers in Human Neuroscience* 8: 958. Available at: https://www.frontiersin.org/articles/10.3389/fnhum.2014.00958/full (accessed 15 May 2018).

Lakoff, G. and Johnson, M. (1980) *Metaphors We Live By*. Chicago: University of Chicago Press.

Long, E. (2003) *Book Clubs: Women and the Uses of Reading in Everyday Life*. Chicago: Chicago University Press.

Nuttall, L. (2015) 'Attributing minds to vampires in Richard Matheson's *I Am Legend*', *Language and Literature* 24(1): 23–39.

Peplow, D. (2016) *Talk About Books: A Study of Reading Groups*. London: Bloomsbury.

Peplow, D, Swann, J., Trimarco, P. and Whiteley, S. (2016) *The Discourse of Reading Groups: Cognitive and Sociocultural Approaches*. London: Routledge.

Peplow, D. and Whiteley, S. (forthcoming) 'Interpretation in interaction: Approaching style and response dialogically', in Bell, A., Browse, S., Gibbons, A. and Peplow, D. (eds) *Style and Response: Minds, Media, Methods*. Amsterdam: John Benjamins.

Rehberg, S. (ed.) (2011) *Reading Communities from Salons to Cyberspace*. Basingstoke: Palgrave Macmillan.

Semino, E. and Short, M. (2004) *Corpus Stylistics: Speech, Writing and Thought Presentation in a Corpus of English Writing*. London: Routledge.

Simpson, P. (2014) *Stylistics: A Resource Book for Students*. Second Edition. London: Routledge.

Stockwell, P. (2002) *Cognitive Poetics: An Introduction*. London: Routledge.

Stockwell, P. (2009) *Texture: A Cognitive Aesthetics of Reading*. Edinburgh: Edinburgh University Press.

Swann, J. and Allington, D. (2009) 'Reading groups and the language of literary texts: A case study in social reading', *Language and Literature* 18 (3): 247–64.

Whiteley, S. (2011a) 'Text World Theory, real readers and emotional responses to *The Remains of the Day*', *Language and Literature* 20(1): 23–42.

Whiteley, S. (2011b) 'Talking about "An Accommodation": The implications of discussion group data for community engagement and pedagogy', *Language and Literature* 20(3): 236–56.

Whiteley, S. (2016a) 'Building resonant worlds: Experiencing the text-worlds of *The Unconsoled*', in Gavins, J. and Lahey, E. (eds) *World Building: Discourse in the Mind*, pp. 165–81. London: Bloomsbury.

Whiteley. S. (2016b) 'A cognitive poetic approach to researching the reading experience', in Otterholm, K., Skjerdingstad, I., McKechnie, L. E. F. and Rothbauer, P. (eds) *Plotting the Reading Experience: Theory, Practise, Politics*, pp. 99–114. Ontario: Wilfred Laurier Press.

Part III

Genre-specific and multimodal manipulation

Manipulation in Agatha Christie's detective stories: Rhetorical control and cognitive misdirection in creating and solving crime puzzles

Catherine Emmott and Marc Alexander

1. Introduction

Detective stories are a highly manipulative genre, where the key aims are to create an apparently insoluble puzzle, baffle the reader during the investigation, then provide the detective's solution in a way that both surprises and satisfies the reader. Agatha Christie, the 'Queen of Crime' (e.g. Haining 1990: 11f.), is so successful at achieving these acts of manipulation that she is currently the bestselling novelist of all time and her plots have significant cultural influence in films, television dramas and on stage. Literary critics sometimes baulk at imputing intentions to an author, but there can be no doubt that Christie intended to manipulate her readers. In her autobiography, she discusses manipulative plotting in her first thoughts about how to write a detective story (Christie 1978 [1977]: 261–2) and she comments on her own 'very elaborately worked out plot' in relation to one of her later books (Author's Foreword, Christie 2014 [1937]).[1] The intricate nature of plotting is evident throughout her detective fiction, to the extent that critics sometimes argue that she subordinates everything (e.g. background description, characters, themes) to plot.

Some of Christie's plot manipulations are extremely famous and have been much discussed[2] – our primary aim here is not to look specifically at her plotting overall, but to show some of the devices which are used to control readers, to prevent them from guessing the solutions to her mysteries. In this chapter, we focus particularly on two of Christie's techniques. We will look firstly at how she carefully handles descriptions of the evidence in crimes, manipulating small details to withhold or underplay information at the puzzle stage of stories, then using strong rhetoric to support surprise revelations at the solution stage. Secondly, we will examine Christie's cognitive misdirection in relation to the way in which suspects are dealt with. In this second type of strategy, rather than manipulating details of the language, Christie cognitively misdirects her characters and her readers, giving them erroneous puzzle-solving tasks to deflect their attention from consideration of the real culprit(s).

The discussion will include examination of specific plot-handling devices in one of her short stories ('Sing a song of sixpence') and five of her novels (*One, Two, Buckle my Shoe*; *The Mirror Crack'd from Side to Side*; *Peril at End House*; *Death on the Nile*; and *Murder on the Orient Express*). We have discussed other plot-handling devices in previous work (e.g. Emmott and Alexander 2010, 2014, 2019), so we do not aim to provide a comprehensive survey of devices here, but we suggest that the examples provided give a good indication of Christie's manipulative strategies generally. The examples discussed cover two very important aspects of detective stories, the evidence and the suspects, and two quite different methods, language-based manipulation of descriptions and the deflection of attention by control of the puzzle-solving task.

Christie's characters often comment on the complexity of the crimes they are trying to solve. In *The Moving Finger* (1961 [1943]), the detective, Miss Marple, remarks to one of the other characters, as follows:

> 'To commit a successful murder must be very much like bringing off a conjuring trick.' [...] 'You've got to make people look at the wrong thing and in the wrong place – Misdirection, they call it, I believe.' (p. 124)

Although, this comment is made within the text-world (Werth 1999) about the design of the crime, it is, nevertheless, a highly appropriate description of the art of manipulation practised by the author.

2. Handling the evidence: Controlling descriptive details

In previous work (e.g. Emmott and Alexander 2014), we have discussed how Christie buries details which appear not to be of great importance but are in fact plot-significant. Such details are sometimes hidden in background descriptions (e.g. scene-setting passages), so that they are not obviously seen as relevant. In this section, we look instead at handling of the evidence relating to the crime.

We might expect the main focus of attention to rest on the items discussed (e.g. in taking witness statements and describing the crime scene), so this is very different from just hiding the items in general background description. The strategy we will examine here is where Christie adjusts the description of the evidence so that only a low level of detail is given in relation to a specific crucial point and, hence, the relevance of information to solving the crime is unclear. Cognitive scientists and linguists (Hobbs 1985; Talmy 1983, 2000) refer to this as adjusting the *granularity* of a description, using the metaphor of the grain of a photograph, that is, the amount of detail apparent in an image.

One way of adjusting granularity is simply to provide a superordinate expression which has no obvious plot significance instead of a more specific description which might be more clearly plot-relevant. We will see this in Section 2.1 where a superordinate expression relating to money ('silver change') in the victim's handbag is used in 'Sing a song of sixpence' in the puzzle stage, without details of the number or types of coin in the handbag until later. Likewise in Section 2.3, in *The Mirror Crack'd from Side to Side*, there are descriptions at the puzzle stage which could relate to many illnesses (e.g. having a temperature), but the exact nature of the illness is left unstated until the solution stage. Characters in the text-world can subsequently claim that they have observed something at the more specific level, but this may not have actually been shown to the reader at all. Christie might be accused of not 'playing fair' with the reader, but the technique nevertheless allows her to stop the reader from guessing the significance of information at the puzzle stage, leaving her investigator to reveal this significance later.

Another way of handling descriptions is to provide the relevant detail, but only very briefly and without the significance of it being highlighted. Over long stretches of text, a small detail may be forgotten, particularly if it has been omitted in later descriptions of the same object or if it is presented in a context where there is a significant distraction, such as a brutal murder. In addition, the reader may not even engage with the full semantic meaning of the description in the first place. Psychology work (Sanford 2002; Sanford and Sturt 2002; Sanford et al. 2006) has shown that readers may sometimes read with 'shallow processing', failing to fully notice certain semantic aspects of a word unless attention is overtly drawn to those features. So when, in experiments, a story about an air crash is presented and readers are asked 'Where should the survivors be buried?,' they are often so focused on the task of answering the question that they fail to notice that survivors are, by definition, alive and hence would not be buried (see Sanford and Emmott 2012 for a summary of this type of work).

Christie herself was aware of this manipulative effect since her detective, Miss Marple, actually refers in one of the short stories ('Motive v. opportunity' (1977b [1932]: 61)), to the type of example that originally prompted the Psychology work ('Teacher, do you say yolk of eggs *is* white or yolk of eggs *are* white?' – the teacher explains the linguistic point, but fails to notice that the yolks are yellow not white). We will look in Section 2.2 at how Christie briefly alludes to a detail about the appearance of a shoe in *One, Two, Buckle my Shoe* at the puzzle stage, in a situation where the reader may be distracted by the gruesome crime being described. It is only subsequently that the detective uses heavy rhetorical presentation to fully highlight the semantic significance of this detail in relation to the solution to the crime.

Hercule Poirot, in *The ABC Murders* (1962 [1936]), makes a general comment about how evidence is presented:

> 'telling everything you know always implies *selection*. [...] One cannot tell *everything*. Therefore one *selects*. At the time of a murder people select what *they* think is important. But quite frequently they think wrong!' (p. 95–6, Christie's italics)

Our concern here is not just with what the characters say, but with how physical evidence is described by the narrator. The point above is important, but in this chapter we will focus primarily on how a selected item is described at a low level of granularity or very briefly, rather than complete omission.

2.1. 'Sing a song of sixpence': Control of granularity to hide incongruities

The short story 'Sing a song of sixpence' (1970 [1934]) provides a simple example of how the granularity of key items is presented at different levels of specificity at the puzzle stage of the story to prevent the reader from seeing an incongruity in two pieces of evidence.

The sixpence is mentioned in an answer to the investigator's question to a maid, Martha, about what her murdered mistress said to her before her death. At this stage, the granularity is relatively high, with a fair amount of detail included in her evidence about the denomination of the coin, its newness and its design. Overall, Martha's speech might appear somewhat over-specified as evidence (she interprets the second question literally and talks about all the household conversation rather than selecting points that are obviously relevant to the crime).

'And she said nothing to you that could lead you to believe that she was expecting anybody?'

'No, sir.'

'You're quite sure? What exactly did she say?'

'Well,' Martha considered, 'She said the butcher was nothing more than a rogue and a cheat, and she said I'd had in a quarter of a pound of tea more than I ought, and she said Mrs Crabtree was full of nonsense for not liking to eat margarine, and she didn't like one of the sixpences I'd brought her back – one of the new ones with oak leaves on it – she said it was bad, and I had a lot of trouble to convince her. And she said – oh, that the fishmonger had sent haddocks instead of whitings, and had I told him about it, and I said I had – and, really, I think that's all, sir.' (p. 76)

Information is generally viewed in the context in which it occurs and here the overall discourse focus is on household matters and the personality of the dead woman. The investigator, Sir Edward, suggests that she was 'Rather a difficult mistress to please' and the maid agrees that she was 'A bit fussy' (p. 76). The information about the sixpence is placed in the middle of the list of what the mistress said, and it does not obviously have any relevance to the crime at this stage.

Shortly afterwards, the maid takes Sir Edward to the drawing-room, the scene of the crime, and shows him the evidence of the murdered woman's handbag. Money is mentioned here again, but it is at a much lower level of granularity, so the reader is given the general superordinate description that there is silver change without any details about specific coins. This is only a page later than the description of the sixpence, so if more detail had been given a discrepancy might have been noticed by the reader, but here a key fact in the text-world is obscured:

> There was some odd silver change, two ginger nuts, three newspaper cuttings [...], a trashy printed poem about the unemployed, an *Old Moore's Almanack*, a large piece of camphor, some spectacles and three letters. (p. 77)

Sir Edward examines the items in the handbag, but concludes with the evaluation that 'I'm afraid there isn't much there' (p. 77). Sir Edward subsequently leaves the house, but has a sudden revelation and returns to examine the contents of the bag again, looking specifically at the money this time:

> Sir Edward tumbled out the silver change on the table. Then he nodded. His memory had not been at fault. (p. 78)

Again the description for the reader does not specify particular coins, but the subsequent text makes clear that Sir Edward has himself observed them.

Sir Edward, who is a renowned retired criminal barrister, then uses a technique that Morley (2009: 175–6) introduces in a handbook for real courtroom barristers, what Morley refers to as 'the lever':

> [The lever] is notionally what drops the witness through the evidential trapdoor when pulled. [...] For almost any witness there is some feature of evidence which is just not quite right. It leaves him open to attack, to being undermined, or to mild embarrassment [...] I mean the sort that creates a moment of silence and everyone realises something is wrong: like [...] when someone overstates how good they are at speaking French, but then cannot follow what you say in the language. It is the embarrassment which follows when you catch someone out.

Morley's (2009: 178–84) suggested technique is to bring together two pieces of contradictory evidence from a witness's earlier statements (ideally asking the witness to reaffirm what has been said), then explicitly point out the contradiction. This drives 'an unanswerable rhetorical wedge' (p. 183) between the two statements and the barrister can even ask the witness which is the lie. In Christie's story, Sir Edward contrasts the maid's earlier verbal evidence about the new sixpence (which he asks her to reaffirm in the example below) with the actual physical evidence from the handbag. At this point, the granularity of the 'silver change' is raised to reveal the two old sixpences that Sir Edward has observed among the contents of the handbag, detailed information which has not previously been disclosed to the reader.

> 'You told me, Martha, if I remember rightly, that you had a slight altercation with your late mistress over one of the new sixpences.'
> 'Yes, sir.'
> 'Ah! But the curious thing is, Martha, that among this loose change, *there is no new sixpence. There are two sixpences, but they are both old ones.*' (p. 78, Christie's italics)

Sir Edward then pulls the evidential lever on the maid, challenging an earlier piece of evidence from her, that no-one visited the house that evening:

> 'You see what that means? *Someone did come to the house that evening – someone to whom your mistress gave sixpence ...*' (p. 78, Christie's italics and ellipses)

The effect of this is to immediately force a confession from Martha, since it is clear that the supposedly reliable maid[3] has been lying.

What this story shows is that information is sometimes withheld from the reader until the revelation stage, to avoid the reader guessing the plot twist.

The description of Sir Edward's earlier examination of the handbag did not specify the type of coins and this detailed information is only provided at the point where Sir Edward wants to pull the evidential lever. This lack of explicitness is particularly important in this short story where the two earlier mentions of the money (the maid's verbal evidence and the description of the physical evidence of the handbag) are in relatively close proximity (only a page apart), so any discrepancy might be more easily noticed than in a full-length novel, hence removing the surprise from the denouement and reducing the apparent cleverness of the investigator.

2.2. *One, Two, Buckle my Shoe:* Relying on shallow processing of semantic features

When Christie employs the evidential lever in a full novel, different mentions of an item at the puzzle stage can be spread over many pages. Hence, the reader's attention may be focused less on any potential discrepancy in a full novel than in a short story, particularly if there are distractions from the discourse context in which the information is presented.

The handling of descriptions over a longer text can be seen in Christie's novel *One, Two, Buckle my Shoe* (1959 [1940]). The plot twist in the story depends on the reader initially believing that a shoe observed on a woman in the street is the same shoe subsequently found on a woman's dead body, hence implying that the woman is the same (although in fact there has been some impersonation, with similar but not identical shoes being worn to fit the shoe size of the impersonator). When we first see the shoe, we perceive it through Hercule Poirot's eyes, as he watches a lady's foot appear out of a taxi:

> Poirot surveyed the foot with gallant interest.
> A neat ankle, quite a good quality stocking. Not a bad foot. But he didn't like the shoe. A brand new patent leather shoe with a large gleaming buckle. He shook his head.
> Not chic – very provincial!
> The lady got out of the taxi, but in doing so she caught her other foot in the door and the buckle was wrenched off. It fell tinkling on to the pavement. Gallantly, Poirot sprang forward and picked it up, restoring it with a bow.
> Alas! Nearer fifty than forty. Pince-nez. Untidy yellow-grey hair – unbecoming clothes – those depressing art greens! She thanked him, dropping her pince-nez, then her handbag.
> Poirot, polite if no longer gallant, picked them up for her. (p. 18)

The information that will be drawn on later in the story is mentioned here – the fact that the shoe is new. However, rather than focusing on this feature of the shoe, the continuing discourse puts the emphasis on the buckle (which is also highlighted in the title of the book) and on the negative aspects of the woman's appearance, including Poirot's critical appraisal of her.

In a subsequent encounter with the lady, supposedly Miss Sainsbury Seale, Poirot continues to notice the shoe, focusing again on the buckle's absence, but making no mention of other features, such as the age of the shoe:

> Poirot noticed, with sorrow, that she had not yet sewn the buckle on her shoe. (p. 46)

Miss Sainsbury Seale vanishes and Poirot later encounters what appears to be the same buckled shoe in a very different context:

> In the middle of [the room] was a big metal chest of the kind used for storing furs. The lid was open.
> Poirot stepped forward and looked inside.
> *He saw the foot first*, with the shabby shoe on it and the ornate buckle. His first sight of Miss Sainsbury Seale had been, he remembered, a shoe buckle.
> His gaze travelled up, over the green wool coat and skirt till it reached the head.
> He made an inarticulate noise.
> 'I know', said Japp, 'It's pretty horrible.'
> The face had been battered out of all recognisable shape. Add to that the natural process of decomposition, and it was no wonder that both men looked a shade pea green as they turned away. (p. 92, Christie's italics)

There is a minor incongruity here since the shoe is described as 'shabby', but was previously new. This is not, however, drawn attention to and no contrast is made with the original description of the shoe as 'new' over seventy pages previously. Christie can, perhaps, rely on a reader's lack of memory for an earlier small detail and shallow processing of this current minor detail to obscure these differences, particularly when there is the distraction of the gruesome crime.

As Poirot later considers the clues, the main emphasis is still on buckles, just before he recognizes the solution to the case:

> It was like a kaleidoscope – shoe buckles, 10-inch stockings, a damaged face [mention of other clues] all rose up and whirled and settled themselves down into a coherent pattern.
> For the first time, Hercule Poirot was looking at the case *the right way up*. (p. 141, Christie's italics).

Having solved the case in his own mind, Poirot subsequently presents his solution. At this point, he pulls the evidential lever:

> 'I shall begin, I think, where the matter began for me. With a *shoe!*'
> Blunt said blankly:
> 'With a *shoe?*'
> Hercule Poirot nodded.
> 'Yes, a buckled shoe. [He describes the first time he saw the shoe.] I did not like the shoe. It was a new, shining patent leather shoe with a large ornate buckle. Not chic – not at all chic!' […] 'As she descended a *contretemps* occurred – she caught the buckle of her shoe in the door and it was wrenched off. […]
> 'Later, on that same day, I went with Chief Inspector Japp to interview the lady. (She had not as yet sewn on the buckle, by the way.) […]
> 'Part Two began when Chief Inspector Japp summoned me to King Leopold Mansions. There was a fur chest in a flat there, and in that fur chest there had been found a body. I went into the room, I walked up to the chest – and the first thing I saw was a shabby buckled shoe!'
> 'Well?'
> 'You have not appreciated the point. It was a *shabby* shoe – a *well-worn* shoe. [He explains that the lady was last sighted on the same day as he first observed her, the day of the murder]. In the morning the shoes were *new* shoes – in the evening they were *old* shoes. One does not wear out a pair of shoes in a day, you comprehend' (p. 171–2, Christie's italics)

Here, Poirot brings together the two evidential details (previously distant in the text), driving the 'rhetorical wedge' between the two. The shoe is not just shabby, it is further highlighted as old, in direct contrast to its earlier newness – hence, it is argued that it is not the same shoe. 'Shabby' ('well-worn') does generally imply oldness (*OED* Online 2018), but it can also refer more broadly to something that is negatively evaluated as unkempt (which might apply to a shoe in poor condition because the buckle has fallen off). Oldness is perhaps less central as a semantic feature of shabbiness than the aliveness of survivors in the earlier-mentioned Psychology research or the yellowness of Miss Marple's egg yolks, which people often miss in the shallow processing questions quoted earlier. The mention of the shabby shoe may have been read with shallow processing at the puzzle stage (if Christie is successful in manipulating the reader), but it is foregrounded (Mukařovský 1964) at this solution stage, so that the reader cannot possibly miss the point. In addition to the repetition of 'shabby' and Christie's use of italics, plus the close contrast in the final paragraph, Poirot uses explanatory devices such as 'You have not appreciated the point' and 'you comprehend'.

The addressee, who is the guilty party, does not give way immediately and there is further discussion of the significance of the shoe in terms of its role as identificational evidence. The lever here does, nevertheless, play its role in suggesting physical evidence to support the solution in a way which at least sounds persuasive whether or not the contradiction in the physical evidence is really convincing in itself.

2.3. *The Mirror Crack'd from Side to Side:* Withholding suggestive details

In the above examples, the reason for withholding or underplaying details at the puzzle stage was simply that otherwise two descriptions might be seen to be contradictory. Information can also be withheld because it is too inherently suggestive in its own right and might lead to the reader making a plot-significant inference prior to the revelation. An example of this is in *The Mirror Crack'd from Side to Side* (1965 [1962]) where the plot twist rests on an actress committing murder because her unborn child has been damaged by contact with a fan carrying the illness German measles (Rubella) which is known to cause damage to the foetus. According to Curran (2010: 404), the publisher's initial reader guessed the ending when the illness was specified, so the manuscript had to be revised and the nature of the illness withheld until the end of the book.

Christie, in the example below, initially conveys the illness to the reader by mentioning words from this semantic field such as 'temperature' and 'doctor', but there is no mention of the specific nature of the illness. Here, the fan, Heather Badcock, tells of her encounter with the actress, Marina Gregg. This story is told as general chat prior to the day that the crime is committed, so has no obvious relevance to the future crime at this stage.

> 'I've always been a terrific fan of hers. When I was a teenager I used to dream about her. The big thrill of my life was when there was a big show in aid of the St. John's Ambulance in Bermuda, and Marina Gregg came to open it. I was mad with excitement, and then on the very day I went down with a temperature and the doctor said I couldn't go. But I wasn't going to be beaten. I didn't actually feel too bad. So I got up and put a lot of make-up on my face and went along. I was introduced to her and she talked to me for quite three minutes and gave me her autograph. It was wonderful. I've never forgotten that day.' (p. 19)

The main discourse context here is a conversation about Marina Gregg and Heather's excitement that she is coming to live locally. Christie relies on the fact that it is common in everyday conversation not to give full medical details in certain contexts (speakers may not always know or remember the precise nature of an illness, may not want to disclose it or may not feel that it is relevant to their current discourse).

Subsequently, Heather meets Marina again on the day of the crime, just before Heather is murdered. Heather recalls her previous meeting with Marina, linking it to the Bermuda event many years ago. In the example below, the reader hears only fragments of the conversation, as if from the perspective of Mrs Bantry who can hear Heather's story in the background as she talks to Mrs Allcock.

> Heather was continuing in a determined manner with her story.
> [Conversation between Mrs Bantry and Mrs Allcock]
> ' – I didn't feel really ill – and I thought I just must –'
> [Conversation between Mrs Bantry and Mrs Allcock]
> ' – I said to myself; I won't be beaten! I put a lot of make-up on my face –'
> [Conversation between Mrs Bantry and Mrs Allcock]
> She turned back to hear Heather Badcock's triumphant peroration.
> 'I've never forgotten how wonderful you were that day. It was a hundred times worth it.'
> Marina's response was this time not so automatic. Her eyes which had wavered over Heather Badcock's shoulder, now seemed to be fixed on the wall midway up the stairs. She was staring and there was something so ghastly in her expression that Mrs Bantry half took a step forward. (pp. 39–40, Christie's dashes)

The fragmentary presentation style, interlocking portions of Heather's speech with the conversation of Mrs Bantry and Mrs Allcock, allows Christie to withhold Heather's mention of the exact form of her previous illness. Heather's story appears to be just in the background and witnesses subsequently trivialize it ('her rather silly story' (p. 52), 'a long spiel' (p. 65), 'what a bore' (p. 65)), focusing on Marina's shocked expression and assuming that it has been caused by something else (e.g. other guests arriving). In fact, the story was significant – we are told at the solution stage (p. 180) that Heather had revealed at this point that she had met her in Bermuda when infected with German measles and Marina's shock (due to the effects of that infection on her unborn child) derives from that information and provides the motive for murdering Heather.

During the investigation stage of this crime, witnesses continue to report Heather's comments in general terms, such as mentioning 'sickness' (p. 52). Only later do characters start to bring the description to a more specific level, preparing the way for Christie to introduce the actual illness. Marina's husband, telling a deliberate lie to protect her, refers to 'flu' (p. 79) and another witness inaccurately mentions 'chicken pox' and 'nettlerash' (p. 171, p. 175). These erroneous descriptions do, nevertheless, allow Miss Marple to start questioning the exact form of the illness (p. 175), hence prompting the revelation that it was actually German measles.

Christie's initial underspecification of the nature of the illness in the reports of the event and subsequent inaccurate reporting of it does not really 'play fair' with readers since inadequate or erroneous clues are provided, but nevertheless provides a manipulative strategy for Christie to avoid readers guessing the solution until the end.

3. Controlling the suspect list: Task-based inattentional blindness

In the previous section, the manipulative strategy related to handling the evidence and the method for misleading the reader derived from the underspecified nature of the linguistic descriptions which either withheld information completely or were sufficiently brief to allow possible shallow processing. Another key aspect of crime-solving is the consideration of suspects. Christie again relies on the cognitive limitations of readers to facilitate their deception, providing a challenging puzzle which can be misleadingly set up in order to focus readers' attention in the wrong direction.

From a psychological perspective, the manipulation in this case depends on the fact that when readers are concentrating on a specific task, they may fail to notice other possibilities. In a classic experiment, Simons and Chabris (1999) demonstrated this for visual attention by asking viewers of a basketball video to count the number of passes of the ball. Readers were so focused on this task that many failed to notice that a man in a gorilla suit walked right through the centre of the picture. Simons and Chabris refer to this as 'sustained inattentional blindness' (p. 1059). In crime-solving, the standard task is to consider a list of suspects and try to eliminate some of them by means of alibis, hence narrowing down the investigation to those without adequate alibis. However, this relies on having the right list in the first place. In one of Christie's novels, *Three Act Tragedy* (1957 [1934]), there is a comment by Hercule Poirot:

> 'A really clever criminal would have realised that *anyone whose name was on that list would necessarily be suspect,* and therefore he or she would arrange for it not to be there.' (p. 181, Christie's italics)

This is a remark within the text-world itself, but this comment about omitting people from the suspect list could also be made about a clever detective author, such as Christie. She can (and frequently does) use this strategy to draw the attention of readers away from suspecting particular characters during the puzzle stage. This means that certain characters are effectively 'invisible' both to the investigators and to the reader, just as the gorilla was 'invisible' to many of those watching Simon and Chablis' video.

In Christie's stories, often a 'suspect list' is created by the detective, the police or other characters – at its simplest, this may be simply a list of names (often quite literally presented in list form vertically down the page) of those who are suspected. Sometimes, the list includes additional information such as motives and alibis. Even when no formal list is created, the investigators and/or other characters often discuss who is suspected and who has been eliminated from suspicion at various points in the story (this may, of course, change, as alibis are established, new evidence is produced and further deaths occur).

There may be various reasons for not including certain characters on the list. If alibis have already been checked, then anyone with a supposedly unbreakable alibi might be excluded. However, a more subtle way to leave a person off the list is simply never to consider that person. Some who may be (largely) immune from active suspicion, but may sometimes be guilty are:

(i) Those who are perceived as being highly respected in the social hierarchy.
(ii) Those assisting the detective and/or apparently privy to his/her speculations.
(iii) The detective or police officer investigating the crime.
(iv) Those who have been apparently the victims of murder attempts.
(v) Those who are apparently dead.
(vi) Those who are apparently too minor to be main participants (e.g. script-based characters, such as servants and workmen).

Other characters may be actively eliminated because of an (apparent) lack of motive, opportunity or physical capability, but those factors would normally have to be established. By contrast, when characters are in one of the above categories,[4] they may be either 'above' or 'beneath' suspicion and are not even considered as possible suspects. Being 'above' suspicion might be because the character is heavily trusted, whereas being 'below' suspicion might be because they are so minor that they are not fully considered. In both cases, this can create significant surprise when the murderer is revealed. *Peril at End House*, discussed in Section 3.1, provides an example of a character who is 'above' suspicion and who is not included on the suspect list, but who is actually guilty. In Section 3.2, the character discussed in *Death on the Nile* is eliminated prior to the suspect list being created, but is nevertheless involved in the crime, although is not the main murderer. In Section 3.3, we see how Christie handles the suspect list in her well-known subversion of the crime-solving genre, *Murder on the Orient Express*.

3.1. *Peril at End House*: Making the murderer 'invisible'

In *Peril at End House* (1961 [1932]), we see a character, Nick Buckley, who is not actively considered as a suspect by the other characters since it is her life which appears to be threatened. At the start of the novel, she appears to have to be convinced by the detective, Hercule Poirot, that what she describes as accidents are, in his view, attempts to murder her. After his initial investigations, Poirot draws up a list of suspects labelled A. to J., with A. to I. being specific named characters and J. being a possible unnamed outsider (pp. 85–7). These designations even appear as a chapter title, 'A. to J.' so are heavily foregrounded. Poirot argues that among these possibilities must be the murderer (p. 85). This list is evaluated by his companion Hastings who says that 'it sets all the possibilities out most clearly' (p. 87). In fact, both Poirot and Hastings are mistaken here and hence unreliable at the puzzle stage.

At the solution stage, Poirot reveals that 'K.' was missing from the list, with 'K.' standing for

> 'a person who should have been included in the original list, but who was overlooked'. (p. 180, Christie's italics)

K is actually Nick Buckley herself, the supposed victim. Hence the original list appeared to offer an *inclusive* choice (i.e. someone included on the list), but actually the solution is based on an *exclusive* choice (i.e. someone not mentioned on the list). Poirot's initial difficulty (at the start of the book) in persuading Nick of her (apparent) danger may prompt cognitive commitment to this idea on the part of the reader, as the reader wills her to take note of Poirot's concern – the denouement shows that this idea was erroneous since she herself had staged these supposed attempts on her life. The reader's focus of attention has been misdirected away from the culprit and hence the reader has been trying to solve the wrong puzzle when considering the suspect list. The strategy for manipulation in *Peril at End House* relies on the reader not actively considering the victim as being possibly guilty. The guilty character may be central to the story overall, but if that person is already cast in the role of victim, then it may seem unlikely that they are also responsible for the crime. Psychology studies

(Sanford and Garrod 1981) show that readers create 'scenarios' for characters (e.g. the classic restaurant script (Schank and Abelson 1977)) and, in the process of inference-making, they allocate the characters to roles, so it may be that there is cognitive commitment to those roles following allocation. If the task is to find the murderer, then the person already in the role of victim may not be considered for that role.

3.2. *Death on the Nile:* Overlooking the accomplice

A different strategy for manipulation of the suspect list is to carefully consider possible suspects and then eliminate them conclusively (either before the main suspect list is even drawn up and/or after they have appeared on the suspect list). This is seen in *Death on the Nile* (2014 [1937]). Jacqueline de Bellefort has the most obvious motive for the crime, since she apparently hated the murdered woman, Linnet Doyle, for stealing her former fiancé, Simon Doyle and marrying him. Nevertheless, Jacqueline lacks the opportunity to do the crime since she has been under observation by several witnesses within the crucial time band that the murder must have occurred, so she has an extremely robust alibi. Characters discuss the unlikelihood of her actually shooting the murdered woman (pp. 174–5), then consideration of the lack of opportunity upgrades this to impossibility (since Jacqueline was under observation by 'three independent witnesses' (p. 185)):

> 'it is not only *unlikely* that the young Fräulein did the murder – it is also I think *impossible.*' (p. 175, Christie's italics)

Impossibility is foregrounded here by the contrast and the italics, and then repeatedly the idea of impossibility is reiterated to reinforce this interpretation and to counter any objections (e.g. 'physically impossible' (p. 177), 'definitely cleared of the crime' (p. 187), '*It wasn't Jacqueline de Bellefort*' (p. 188, Christie's italics)). Even Poirot stresses this point when addressing Jacqueline, saying:

> 'We know that you did not kill Madame Doyle. It is proved – yes, proved, *mon enfant*. It was not you.' (p. 189, Christie's italics)

In fact, it is true that Jacqueline could not have committed the main murder (in the sense of shooting the victim), but this does not disqualify her from the role of accomplice (she planned this murder and provides the alibi for the murderer). The suspect list generally not only acts as a means of focusing attention and eliminating characters but can also control the key cognitive task of puzzle-solving – it places the emphasis on finding the person who is directly responsible for the actual physical act of killing, but may sometimes be used to detract attention from the accomplice role. Hence, the task provided for the puzzle-solving reader is too narrow, providing a means of misdirecting the reader's cognitive efforts.

3.3. *Murder on the Orient Express*: Overlooking a fully maximally solution

In the above examples, the manipulation relies on criminals being either disregarded in the compilation of the list or explicitly excluded from it. At the other extreme is the unusual situation in *Murder on the Orient Express* (1959 [1934]). Here the list does include all the relevant possibilities, that is, twelve passengers (excluding Poirot and other officials) and the conductor (pp. 144–7). The well-known solution is that they were all[5] involved. The rhetorical interest here is in how the puzzle-solving switches from the attempt to make a standard inclusive choice between the suspects to a radical solution which encompasses the whole group acting together, thereby subverting the expectations of the genre by invalidating supposedly independent alibis.

Christie controls the reader by employing a standard crime-solving script and implying that the task is one of selection and elimination. After the examination of the passengers' luggage, the need to make a choice is emphasized, with a chapter heading 'Which of them'? (p. 141). Bouc is still asking 'Which of them?' (p. 144) at the point at which Poirot produces his list of suspects and the subsequent chapter ends with the question *'Which of them?'* highlighted in italics (p. 152). This foregrounded question directs attention from the real solution, which is maximally inclusive of those on the list.

Following the above-mentioned questions, Poirot contemplates the case further and claims to have found a solution 'that would explain everything' (p. 153). Although Poirot and Bouc continue to try to eliminate suspects, more and more passengers are found to have motives (being linked with the Armstrong family who have a strong reason to kill the murdered man). It is at this point that the observations of Bouc and Poirot begin preparing the way for the denouement. Within the text-world, there may be some genuine incredulity on the part of Bouc, but the statements below also provide a means of allowing the author, Christie, to start moving towards a group solution, as the possible common properties of 'everyone' and 'everybody' are discussed:

> (Bouc) 'But does everybody on this train tell lies?' (p. 174)
>
> (Bouc) 'Nothing would surprise me now [...] Nothing! Even if everybody in the train proved to have been in the Armstrong household I should not express surprise.' (p. 174)

(Poirot) 'Even if in the end everybody on the train proves to have a motive for killing Ratchett, we have to know. Once we know, we can settle once for all where the guilt lies.' (p. 176)

As more connections to the Armstrong house and hence more motives appear, the idea of all the characters not only having motives but all being involved is mentioned, although in negative form. Within the text-world, Bouc is still incredulous, but nevertheless, Christie as author may be employing a technique that Morley (2009: 170ff), in the rhetorical manual for barristers mentioned earlier, describes as 'bounce'. Morley argues that the aim of 'bounce' is 'bending perceptions' (p. 170), explaining this as follows. The lawyer presents his version of events piece by piece as a story with the witness required to answer yes or no after each element is presented. Even if the witness repeatedly denies the lawyer's version, the story may become planted in the mind of the audience. Likewise, in Christie's story, the characters' negatives begin to broach the idea of group involvement, even while Bouc and Hardman (who is in fact one of the guilty group) are still discussing which of the suspects did it:

(Hardman) 'They can't all be in it; but which one is the guilty party is beyond me.' (p. 178)

(Bouc) 'They cannot all be in it.' (p. 179)

(Hardman) 'Which of them was it?' (p. 179)

When Poirot starts to reveal the solution, he transforms the idea of group involvement from negative to positive:

'I said to myself, "This is extraordinary – they cannot *all* be in it!"'
'And then, Messieurs, I saw light. They were *all* in it.' (p. 186, Christie's italics)

This solution is bizarre, so acceptance on the part of the reader relies on persuasive rhetoric, with the detective's closing speech having a strong sense of conviction (Alexander 2009).[6] In addition to specific explanations of the evidence and revelations about the true identities of characters, the unorthodox group solution is reinforced by the analogy of 'a self-appointed jury of twelve people' (p. 186) and the positive metaphors of 'a perfect mosaic, each person playing his or her allotted part' (p. 186) and 'a very cleverly-planned jigsaw puzzle' (p. 186).

4. Conclusion

Agatha Christie is a manipulative author and she uses rhetorical strategies which withhold key information and exploit the cognitive limitations of her readers.

In this article, we have focused on two of her techniques. First, she carefully constructs descriptions of evidence about a crime. This may involve providing information at a broad descriptive level to avoid details which would reveal contradictions in the evidence or might be too suggestive about the nature of the crime. Alternatively, she can provide relevant information, but handle relevant details only briefly and without highlighting key semantic features. Readers may fail to notice the lack of specificity or brief mentions since people generally read with shallow processing, failing to notice every apparently minor point in a description. Secondly, readers can be cognitively misdirected by Christie focusing their attention on a specific task which occupies their attention but detracts from finding the key solution. The suspect list provides a recurrent device in her work, which draws on the script of providing a pool of possible guilty characters for consideration and elimination. This controls the focus of attention, detracting from anyone who is not on the list at all or fulfils an alternative role such as accomplice. In addition the script assumes that the reader's job is to eliminate suspects, assuming that those with alibis are unlikely to be guilty – this script fails when all suspects are involved in the crime and provide each other with false alibis. Christie uses these techniques alongside many other strategies in plots that are full of complexities and red herrings, so it is not surprising that her heavily manipulative strategies have been so successful in cognitively misdirecting readers.

Notes

1 This is Christie's comment in her Author's Foreword to *Death on the Nile*. The book was first published in 1937 – the date of the foreword is not specified and may have been added at a later stage.
2 These include the plots of classic works such as *Murder on the Orient Express*, *The Murder of Roger Ackroyd* and *And Then There were None*.
3 See Emmott and Alexander (2019) for a discussion of (un)reliability in this story.
4 These categories give an overview of some reasons for not including characters on suspect lists, but there may be other possibilities. Examples of these categories in Christie are (i) 'The incredible theft' (1964 [1937]), (ii) *The Murder of Roger Ackroyd* (1957 [1926]), (iii) *Curtain: Poirot's Last Case* (1976 [1975]), (iv) *Peril at End House* (1961 [1932], (v) *And Then There were None* (2003 [1939]), and (vi) 'Ingots of gold' (1977a [1932]).
5 Actually one of the passengers, Countess Andrenyi appears to be technically 'innocent' of the murder itself (p. 188), but is nevertheless complicit in the plot.

6   Alexander (2009) has used Rhetorical Structure Theory to show how rather tenuous or spurious conclusions in sections of this speech may be made persuasively convincing by the argument structure.

References

Alexander, M. (2009) 'Rhetorical structure and reader manipulation in Agatha Christie's *Murder on the Orient Express*', *Miscelánea: A Journal of English and American Studies* 39: 13–27.
Christie, A. (1957 [1926]) *The Murder of Roger Ackroyd*. Glasgow: Fontana.
Christie, A. (1957 [1934]) *Three Act Tragedy*. Glasgow: Fontana.
Christie, A. (1959 [1934]) *Murder on the Orient Express*. Glasgow: Fontana.
Christie, A. (1959 [1940]) *One, Two, Buckle My Shoe*. Glasgow: Fontana.
Christie, A. (1961 [1932]) *Peril at End House*. Glasgow: Fontana.
Christie, A. (1961 [1943]) *The Moving Finger*. Glasgow: Fontana.
Christie, A. (1962 [1936]) *The ABC Murders*. Glasgow: Fontana.
Christie, A. (1964 [1937]) 'The incredible theft', in *Murder in the Mews*, pp. 56–99. Glasgow: Fontana.
Christie, A. (1965 [1962]) *The Mirror Crack'd from Side to Side*. Glasgow: Fontana.
Christie, A. (1970 [1934]) 'Sing a song of sixpence', in *The Listerdale Mystery*, pp. 64–80. London: Pan.
Christie, A. (1976 [1975]) *Curtain: Poirot's Last Case*. London: Book Club Associates.
Christie, A. (1977a [1932]) 'Ingots of gold', in *The Thirteen Problems*, pp. 32–43. London: Pan.
Christie, A. (1977b [1932]) 'Motive v. opportunity', in *The Thirteen Problems*, pp. 53–64. London: Pan.
Christie, A. (1978 [1977]) *An Autobiography*. London: Fontana.
Christie, A. (2003 [1939]) *And Then There Were None*. London: HarperCollins Publishers.
Christie, A. (2014 [1937]) *Death on the Nile*. London: HarperCollins Publishers.
Curran, J. (2010) *Agatha Christie's Secret Notebooks*. London: Fontana.
Emmott, C. and Alexander, M. (2010) 'Detective fiction, plot construction and reader manipulation: Cognitive-rhetorical misdirection in Agatha Christie's *Sparkling Cyanide*', in McIntyre, D. and Busse, B. (eds) *Language and Style: In Honour of Mick Short*, pp. 328–46. Houndmills: Palgrave Macmillan.
Emmott, C. and Alexander, M. (2014) 'Foregrounding, burying, and plot construction', in Stockwell, P. and Whiteley, S. (eds) *The Handbook of Stylistics*, pp. 329–43. Cambridge: Cambridge University Press.
Emmott, C. and Alexander, M. (2019) 'Reliability, unreliability, reader manipulation and plot reversals: Strategies for constructing and challenging the credibility of

characters in Agatha Christie's detective fiction', in Page, R., Busse, B. and Nørgaard, N. (eds) *Rethinking Language, Text and Context: Interdisciplinary Research in Stylistics in Honour of Michael Toolan*, pp. 177–90. New York: Routledge.

Haining, P. (1990) *Agatha Christie: Murder in Four Acts*. London: Virgin Books.

Hobbs, J. R. (1985) 'Granularity', in Aravind, K. J. (ed.) *Proceedings of the Ninth International Joint Conference on Artificial Intelligence*, pp. 432–5. New York: Academic Press.

Morley, I. (2009) *The Devil's Advocate: A Short Polemic on How to be Seriously Good in Court*. London: Sweet & Maxwell.

Mukařovský, J. (1964) 'Standard language and poetic language', in Garvin, P. L. (ed.) *A Prague School Reader on Esthetics, Literary Structure and Style*, pp. 17–30. Georgetown, DC: Georgetown University Press. (First published in Czech in 1932.)

OED Online (2018) *Oxford English Dictionary*. Oxford: Oxford University Press. Available at: http://www.oed.com (accessed 26 February 2018).

Sanford, A. J. (2002) 'Context, attention and depth of processing during interpretation', *Mind and Language* 17(1–2): 188–206.

Sanford, A. J. and Emmott, C. (2012) *Mind, Brain and Narrative*. Cambridge: Cambridge University Press.

Sanford, A. J. and Garrod, S. C. (1981) *Understanding Written Language: Explorations in Comprehension beyond the Sentence*. Chichester: John Wiley & Sons.

Sanford, A. J. and Sturt, P. (2002) 'Depth of processing in language comprehension: Not noticing the evidence', *Trends in Cognitive Sciences* 6(9): 382–6.

Sanford, A. J. S., Sanford, A. J., Molle, J. and Emmott, C. (2006) 'Shallow processing and attention capture in written and spoken discourse', *Discourse Processes* 42(2): 109–30.

Schank, R. C. and Abelson, R. P. (1977) *Scripts, Plans, Goals and Understanding*. Hillsdale: Lawrence Erlbaum.

Simons, D. J. and Chabris, C. F. (1999) 'Gorillas in our midst: Sustained inattentional blindness for dynamic events', *Perception* 28: 1059–74.

Talmy, L. (1983) 'How language structures space', in Pick, H. L. and Acredolo, L. P. (eds) *Spatial Orientation: Theory, Research and Application*, pp. 225–82. New York: Plenum.

Talmy, L. (2000) *Toward a Cognitive Semantics, Volume 2: Typology and Process in Concept Structuring*. Cambridge, MA: The MIT Press.

Werth, P. (1999) *Text Worlds: Representing Conceptual Space in Discourse*. London: Longman.

10

Untranslatable clues: Reader manipulation and the challenge of crime fiction translation

Christiana Gregoriou

1. Introduction: On crime fiction's reader manipulation

This chapter approaches the literary 'reader manipulation' subject matter through the ever so popular 'crime fiction' genre, a genre which, though highly formulaic, 'in its sheer diversity, defies any simple classification' (Scaggs 2005: 1) and, indeed, definition. Nevertheless, given the need to define the genre, I, much like elsewhere (Gregoriou 2017: 1), here use 'crime fiction' to refer to contemporary fictional and suspenseful storylines featuring one or more victims of crimes such as, but not limited to, murder (see Gregoriou 2007: 39–48 for genre definitions, terms, rules, formulaic regularities and constraints).

A number of factors contribute to this genre having always been popular, including its constant reinvention and adaptation in response to various social and cultural changes and challenges; 'in its engagement with the urban social ground and the problems to be found there, crime fiction tackles head-on territory which other literary forms seem often to evade' (Messent 1997: 1). Along similar lines, Horsley (2013: 62) argues that (the similarly defined) genre of 'detective fiction has remained a resilient and versatile genre because of its capacity to raise difficult questions about corruption and moral failure. It represents the investigation of individual crimes but can also work to expose the defects, traumas, and brutalities of political and social life'. Others, like Platten (2013: 33), explore 'the possibility that the enduring appeal of crime literature may be attributed wholly or in part to the ways in which it has mined, and continues to mine, a realist aesthetic'. Despite this realism, crime fiction is a genre whose formula most often reassures readers that, however upsetting life can get, criminal wrongs can be remedied, problems solved, justice served and criminals captured and sufficiently punished. Besides, 'traditionally the detective story ends with the "dénouement" when the knots are untied, the clues explained and (importantly) order is restored to a society disturbed by the eruption of violent crime' (Platten 2013: 47).

To return to the collection's subject matter though, I here argue that what also contributes to this crime fiction genre's persistent readability directly and precisely relates to the author's intentional reader[1] manipulation which itself relates to the 'clues' Platten refers to. Emmott and Alexander (2010: 328) agree: 'Detective fiction provides cognitive stylisticians with a prime example of how an author can manipulate readers for plot purposes.' Even more so, this is a manipulation that readers themselves crave, and respond to with satisfaction rather than frustration. I focus on contemporary crime fiction narratives specifically designed to significantly 'manipulate' – as in 'misdirect' (Emmott and Alexander 2010) or 'mislead' – readers and which hence carry the element of surprise resolution, even if that desired surprise is, contradictorily perhaps for experienced crime fiction readers, expected. Put simply, such readers may well expect, and know, the surprise is coming; what they do not or are not expected to know is what precise form that surprise will take. Porter (1981: 99) likens crime fiction novels to the equally formulaic minor genre of jokes. Jokes similarly feature an expected yet startling plot twist: 'The final solution of a crime, like a punch line of a joke, is recognized as the predictable formal term whose actual content is appreciated most when it comes as a surprise.' It is because of this 'predictable formal term' that the crime fiction narratives I next focus on ultimately come to merit at least some storyline literal or metaphorical rereading – as in re-interpreting – on the reader's part; in short, they require at least some reader plot rethinking. Though not solely related to crime-solving, and in fact extending to surprises in general, essential to this narrative rethinking effect is what is known as the genre's 'fair play rule' (see Sayers 1947: 225), which Scaggs (2005: 27, 36) defines as the notion that the careful and observant reader should, at least in theory, be able to solve the crime at the heart of a story of detection, so should have access to the same information as the fictional detective. In other words, according to 'fair play', the reader should have the information necessary with which to supposedly 'solve' aspects of the story's crime at first read or, in the case of the first[2] of the novels next analysed, foresee the surprise to come, even if that surprise does not necessarily relate 'who' it was that actually 'did it'. The 'fair play rule' ensures the reader's 'retrospective repatterning' (Porter 1981) of the text, forcing the reader to, in retrospect, reconstruct a previous and erroneous reading of earlier text with a newer and corrected reading of this text, when newly appreciating what was unseen, and indeed how this came to be so. Emmott (1997: 225) uses the term 'frame repair' to refer to such instances. This is where 'a reader becomes aware that they have misread the text either through lack of attention or because the text itself is potentially ambiguous'. Repairs over a whole stretch of text, and those stretching across the whole of the text, are most typical of crime fiction, and these Emmott (1997) argues can be thought of as 'frame replacements' instead; contrary to mere repairs, and for the reader to fully appreciate the storyline in question, the reader might as well reread/reinterpret the whole of the text, and pretty much from scratch. Emmott and Alexander (2010) list several rhetorical techniques with which readers can be misdirected from the story's eventual solution. One is burying information, as in diminishing the importance of crucial plot-relevant details (also see Emmott and Alexander 2014). Such burying, they argue, encourages shallow processing (Sanford and Sturt 2002; Sanford et al. 2006), ensuring that certain character comments, for instance, are given low prominence until what is known as the novel's reversal stage. Other techniques Emmott and Alexander (2010) list are using supposedly reliable characters to vouch for the reliability of other characters, setting false trails as a distraction to readers and final authentication of the solution. Seago (2014a: 208) also lists some such examples: this is 'where the author attempts to lead the reader astray by providing partial information, foregrounding irrelevant clues and burying crucial evidence, giving facts out of context so that their relevance is not apparent or by suggesting associations and emphasising details which are later revealed to be misleading'. As these examples hint, these manipulative narrative techniques come down to language, which is why stylistics is ideally placed to uncover the means, and precise linguistic markers, through which manipulation takes form, a device which renders this unique and readable genre – somewhat contradictorily – also un-rereadable. The reader can engage in the process of rereading the text for the narrative puzzle pieces to fall into place, but they cannot be manipulated into misreading it in the subsequent, second time round (even though they might pretend to do so). What linguistic analysis can do is shed light on clues which were cleverly hidden at first read. Besides, the game to which the 'play' refers is not in actuality 'fair' but more of a case of 'fake play under the guise of fair play', or 'a game with loaded dice' (Mandel 1984: 48), and the reader is, again in actuality, never meant to outwit the author, and neither would they want to; the information or aspects needed to 'win' the game the author cleverly buried in the text, ensuring that these deliberately remained unseen. And if crime fiction is a 'game', its readers want to be 'losers'; a 'winning' reader would render the crime novel unsuccessful, in fact.

To stay with the same metaphor, I next investigate the game's 'winning moves', as in crime novels' embedded hidden clues. As noted, not all of these point to 'who did it', but all of these generate the generic element of surprise resolution.

2. On the translatability of crime fiction's reader manipulation

However necessary, this popular narrative crime fiction 'reader manipulation' device can prove challenging to the genre's literary translator.[3] To begin with, such a translator needs to be crime-fiction-aware. They also need to be a crime fiction writer of sorts,[4] for them to, in the target language this time, reinvent the stylistic markers with which – equally to the source-text writer – they too can skilfully bury clues which later generate the much desired narrative surprise the crime fiction reader craves.

> Crime fiction is a hugely creative genre making very great demands on authors and translators alike, demanding literary and aesthetic skills and the ability to deploy these within the constraints of genre norms. Genre does not make crime fiction writing or translation easier; like the formal constraints of poetry, genre constraints can produce greater creativity and ingenuity.
>
> Seago (2014b)

As Seago (2014b) also argues, 'genre-specific challenges of crime fiction translation remain an under-researched field'. What this chapter attempts to do is address the need for analysis of the un/translatability of those deliberately ambiguous linguistic expressions which, while keeping with the genre's supposedly fair play rule, intentionally mislead readers and later trigger a pleasurable surprise which itself comes to generate the previously described repatternings, repairs and replacements. How do crime fiction translators respond to this challenge, reinventing this author-reader 'game', yet in another language?

Given this collection's contemporary focus, I explore the 'reader manipulation'-specific stylistic devices embedded in post-2000 crime novels, and opt for two: one of which has been translated[5] from English to Greek, and one from Greek to English. Focusing on these two languages (which I am a bilingual native speaker of) allows me to investigate their respective limitations and/or flexibility with respect to literary translation more broadly, and the migration of (crime fiction) reader manipulation devices, more specifically. Given that the first section deals with a longer novel that is more reader-manipulative, and its translation proves more challenging, compared to the second, I here devote more space to the English-Greek translation than I do the Greek-English one.

The original English-language crime fiction novel I focus on is Lionel Shriver's *We Need to Talk About Kevin*, published in 2003. It is this novel's popularity and critical and commercial success that necessitated its translation into various languages, including Greek. Though I start Section 2.1 by revisiting the reader manipulation devices of this novel already discussed in Gregoriou (2017, see chapter 2.2.1), I this time investigate their translation into Greek, and Gogo Arvaniti's (2010) *Prepei na milisoume gia ton Kevin* (*Πρέπει να μιλήσουμε για τον Κέβιν* – Shriver's novel's translation) specifically. For analysis of the source-text clues' adaptation into film, see Gregoriou (2017, chapter 2.2.2). As Massey (2011: 50) puts it

> In Britain, [the first decade of the twenty-first century] has witnessed a boom in sales of crime fiction in translation, the appetite for which seems to defy the usual Anglo apathy towards translated literature. … While foreign literature as a whole does not, therefore, seem to find a receptive audience in Britain, crime fiction in translation has … carved out a successful niche for itself, spearheaded by independent publishers such as the Harvill Press.

The Greek crime novel I inspect in Section 2.2, *Zone Defence* [1998] (2010), was written by Petros Markaris. This is the second novel of his popular crime series featuring detective Costas Haritos, a series translator David Connolly, himself also a crime novel author, published for Harvill Press into English (2006). Here, I again uncover the source novel's embedded clues and investigate their translation from Greek to English (for analysis of the Greek-English translation of the series' first novel, i.e. Markaris [1995] 2009 into Connolly 2004, see Gregoriou 2017, chapter 3.1).

2.1. Translating misdirection in Shriver's *We Need to Talk About Kevin*

Shriver's (2003) *We Need to Talk About Kevin* is an epistolary English-language novel written in the form of a series of letters by protagonist Eva to her husband Franklin, a man she comes to reveal she first shares a son, Kevin, and then a daughter, Celia, with. These letters are meant to allow Eva to express her thoughts about childbearing and, most importantly, extreme frustration around the difficult upbringing of teenage Kevin, who, two years prior to the novel's present letter writing, is said to have gone on a premeditated school murder spree during which he killed seven of his school mates, a teacher and a cafeteria worker. Though readers are manipulated into believing that Kevin only killed these nine people, the end of the novel comes to reveal that he killed as many as eleven in fact. Even more so, the other two victims prove to be none other than his sister Celia and father Franklin, the latter hence ultimately revealed to be not just the person to whom Eva writes the letters, but also a person who the letters Eva knows will sadly never reach. The book hints at the letters remaining unsent, such as in reference to them being thought of as 'respondence' rather than 'correspondence' (Shriver 2003: 328), though Arvaniti (2010: 541) translates this into a correspondence that is 'μονόπλευρη', which literally translates to 'one-sided', and hence is, compared to the source text, more explicit about Franklin's non-responsiveness in fact. I start by revisiting (see Gregoriou 2017: chapter 2.2) the means with which the English language reader is first misled/misdirected into believing Franklin and Celia to be alive, before interrogating these buried clues' translation into Greek. As noted, crime authors exploit readers' 'shallow processing' to bury information which later becomes important, for the text to be ultimately repatterned via frame replacement accordingly. In the case of the novel at hand, this buried information does not regard 'whodunit', but instead concerns Franklin's absence from Eva's life during her letter writing. To explain this absence, readers are led to believe that Eva and Franklin are divorced or, at least, legally separated. As for Celia, she is implied to be alive and living with Franklin at the time.

As discussed in Gregoriou (2017: 50–1), 'miscuing' (Emmott 1997: 160) of the signals needed in order to understand the information offered takes place early on in the novel, such as in the reference to Franklin as a husband 'estranged' (Shriver 2003: 7, and back cover blurb), to her and Franklin having been 'separated' (p. 1), 'parted' (p. 20), her being 'stripped of [a] handsome husband' (p. 167) and her having come to 'lose the man that [she] most wanted to talk to' (p. 24). As I argue in the same source (Gregoriou 2017: 51), 'separation, parting and the notion of losing Franklin are deliberate, and meant to be misconstrued in terms of physical separation and most likely and inferentially activate a misleading "divorce" schema at the novel's start', schema being a bundle of knowledge regarding a given subject, which the text comes to activate (for an introduction to 'schema theory', see chapter 5.2 in Gregoriou 2009). Using the polysemous words 'estranged' and 'separated' proves key; these have both an 'everyday' sense relating to a couple no longer being together (in whatever way), and the more specialized legal sense of a married couple living apart and most probably heading for divorce. See, for instance, one of the *Oxford English*

Dictionary's definitions of 'separated' as 'withdrawn from a conjugal relationship without being divorced'. Whereas the reader is manipulated into a first text reading which activates such words' legal definition, the text's repaired/revised reading points towards a separation of the two in terms of life and death; Eva is merely 'separated' and 'estranged' from her husband as, unlike him, she is still alive. As noted, the book lets it be assumed that Celia is well and in residence with Franklin while Eva writes these letters to him, with such references as that of Eva having not 'been allowed to keep Celia' and Eva 'imagining the two of [them] together' (Shriver 2003: 224), suggesting that Franklin 'kept' her instead, the 'allowing' being ascribed to law via child custody perhaps (Gregoriou 2017: 51). Eva's letters recalling the two characters actually discussing child custody and a trial separation in the weeks leading up to Kevin's killing massacre help sustain the illusion of the marriage having merely broken down, as do references to their marriage having a certain 'duration' (Shriver 2003: 78). Similarly, references to Franklin's reactions to, and manner of reading, the letters she writes (i.e. references to him potentially managing to read her scribbles, or skim-reading certain letter sections), presuppose him being alive. The same presupposition is embedded in her letters' good wishes for him to have a '*Merry Christmas*' and a '*Happy New Year*' (Shriver 2003: 120, 143, author's italics).

It is only later that readers come to appreciate that it was Kevin who disallowed Eva from 'keeping' Celia, the previously discussed 'keeping' being reinterpreted along the lines of 'on earth' or 'alive' rather than purely 'in legal residence with Eva'. Finally, 'the overall passive voice choice ("we've been separated", "we're parted", and "been allowed to") also enables Eva to hide the agency of the force which would have featured in the ellipted "by x" (read here as perhaps "by law") prepositional phrase in all clauses, a force now keeping Celia and Franklin away from her' (Gregoriou 2017: 51). Grammar hence also proves useful is sustaining the illusion of a legal rather than life/death separation. It is not until the end of the book when readers eventually come to interpret this force as Kevin, and death, rather than the law.

Turning now to the Greek translation of the novel, this too alludes to the couple being apart, such as in Arvaniti's (2010: 12) reference 'τώρα που δεν είσαι εσύ εδώ', as in 'now you are no longer here', which is used to translate the source text's reference to Eva being 'without' (Shriver 2003: 1) Franklin, and Arvaniti's (2010: 376) reference to 'τον χωρισμό μας', a literal translation of the source text's physical 'separation' (Shriver 2003: 224). The same goes for various other expressions which, literal translations of the source text, refer to things Franklin left behind, him not being there with her, him having never been to her present home, her being alone, her having lost him, her being without/stripped of him, her wanting him back, her being his parents' former daughter-in-law and yet still a family member, the two of them literally living in different worlds and so on. Notice also, however, references such as in 'δεν είμαστε πια μαζί' (Arvaniti 2010: 11, 44) and 'δεν είμαστε μαζί' (Arvaniti 2010: 21), which literally translate into them 'no longer being together' and 'not being together' respectively, translations of the English text's previously discussed (respective) references to the two having 'been separated', having 'parted' and being 'estranged' (Shriver 2003: 1, 20, 7). Though the Greek wording is here ambiguous and similarly interpretable along the previously described senses (the legal separation and the life/death one), the Greek writer's word choices are not *as* misleading as the English-language ones. Greek wording that would have more clearly referred to a legal separation, that is, whereby a couple being separated is referred to as being 'σε διάσταση', gets avoided altogether as it is unambiguous and hence not usefully misleading. In other words, unlike the author Shriver, translator Arvaniti finds herself unable to employ words that can be clearly defined along the lines of, and hence explicitly trigger the schema of, a legal separation; she is restricted to only hinting at one such separation instead. And the translated text reader is not as exploited into drawing on the wrong inferences when bridging the textual gaps the source-text writer deliberately left open to interpretation. Besides, as Seago (2014b) argues,

> The translator has to work within the constraints of genre norms, but their task is further complicated by the shift to a different set of linguistic resources, a target cultural context which may not supply relevant real world knowledge to close inferential gaps, and a possibly very different set of social and cultural norms which define what is deviant or transgressive along different boundaries.

For Arvaniti, the Greek language's 'linguistic resources', and it not having words that are aligned with a legal and also a non-legal separation, proves somewhat problematic. Most interestingly still, the Greek translation's back cover reference to Franklin as 'χαμένος', which literally translates as 'lost, wasted, missed' (Stavropoulos 1988: 961) to Eva somewhat gives the 'game' away; it alludes to a disappearance of some kind, interpretable more along the lines of him having gone missing or being dead, and much less so to separation/divorce. Compared to the source-text blurb's reference to him being her 'estranged' husband, the Greek back blurb is arguably not interpretable along the lines of a legal separation, or reader-manipulative, at all. Much like some of the examples Seago (2014a) draws on, through the use of 'χαμένος', Arvaniti here closes down on the specific set of possibilities of interpretation that the polysemous word 'estranged' usefully had for the preferred meaning of a legal separation to be opted for on the basis of knowledge the reader brings to the text, with the help of the various co-textual clues previously noted.

Translating various importantly ambiguous comments that Eva makes throughout also proves challenging to the translator. When Eva describes visiting Franklin's parents after the massacre, she talks of a nominalized and hence agentless '*irretrievable breakdown*' (p. 138, author's italics) preventing Franklin from being able to accompany her, again leading the reader to think along the lines of a marriage breakdown, whereas the Greek translation here merely makes reference to '*ανωτέρας βία*' (Arvaniti 2010: 235, translator's italics), which literally translates into a 'higher power' stopping Franklin from joining her instead. The Greek 'higher power' is suggestive of a God-like power over and beyond Eva's control, but is certainly not interpretable along the lines of a legal separation/divorce. Equally, when offering condolences to one of Kevin's victim's parents, Eva accidentally says 'I'm so sorry for my loss' as opposed to 'your loss', her 'gaffe' reduced to a 'miscue' by Eva herself (Shriver 2003: 141). Though Eva's reference to 'loss' is ambiguous and can be (in retrospect) interpretable along the lines of her own losses (i.e. her losing her husband and daughter), the Greek translator opts for a reference to her passing on condolences 'για τον γιό μου' (Arvaniti 2010: 241), as in 'for my son' instead, which is unambiguous and does not bring any death- or 'legal separation'-like 'loss' into the equation at all. In other words, unlike the English text, the Greek translation does not bear any clues to Eva's husband and daughter passing here. Interestingly and contrastingly, Arvaniti (2010: 431) translates references Eva makes to her family's 'misfortune' (Shriver 2003: 258) to 'καταστροφή' which literally translates into 'destruction' and is hence arguably less ironic and a lot more explicit and clue-like than the source text's 'misfortune'.

As for the clues to Celia's passing, much like the English text's, the Greek text's reader also encounters Kevin's warnings that Eva will regret/be sorry to bring his sibling into the world, and various other rather literal translations of Shriver's references to Franklin being 'with', or being allowed to 'keep' Celia ('να την κρατήσω', as in to 'hold/keep' her), the two of them being together and the two of them getting to know each other better (Arvaniti 2010: 376). In contrast though, Arvaniti (2010: 573) elsewhere translates the reference to Franklin ultimately 'keeping Celia' (2003: 347) with 'κατέληγες με τη Σίλια', as in 'ended up with Celia' which is perhaps more interpretable along the lines of 'death' than the source text's corresponding reference is.

As discussed in Gregoriou (2017), Eva's recollection of the family's conversation on the morning of the attack takes new meaning at the end of that day's letter-narrative, and hence also manipulates the reader at first read. Arvaniti stays close to the source text when translating references to Kevin's encouragement for Eva to kiss Celia one more time and to Eva dwelling on her kiss with Franklin, both of which are differently interpretable later, when the reader appreciates these being Eva's last encounters with her daughter and husband. Arvaniti nonetheless steers further from the English text in places, too. Eva's reference to Kevin being a 'heartbreaker' (Shriver 2003: 362) in his outfit is ominous and is immediately pragmatically interpretable seeing that Kevin later that day, the reader knows, is to shoot arrows through people's hearts, both physically ('Struck perfectly through the heart, [Laura] was dead', Shriver 2003: 375) and, where surviving family members are concerned, metaphorically and emotionally. Though the Greek language does offer a near-literal translation of 'heartbreaker' as 'καρδιοκατακτητής' (as in 'heart conqueror'), Arvaniti (2010: 596) opts to translate this into Kevin 'κάνει θραύση', as in 'wreak[ing] havoc' (Stavropoulos 1988: 378) instead, which is still metaphorical but literalized differently later when compared to the source text; whereas 'heartbreaking' alludes to physical and emotional hurt, 'wreaking havoc' alludes to a large amount of harm or damage (see *Oxford English Dictionary*) instead. Contrastingly, though less manipulatively this time, Kevin saying he would later that day be 'tied up' (Shriver 2003: 365) Arvaniti (2010: 601) translates into 'κλεισμένος', as in 'booked/closed up', which is just as literal an expression as the source text's.

As discussed in Gregoriou (2017: 49–50),

> object-less references to Kevin having 'decided' something after overhearing his parents discuss a trial separation ('That moment ... is when he decided', p. 349) leave the ellipted object for readers to infer. It is in fact the murder of others as well as his father and sister that Kevin made a decision over that day, the readers come to realise later.

The text's Greek and literal translation 'τότε το αποφάσισε' (Arvaniti 2010: 575), as in 'that's when he decided (it)', is similarly open to interpretation; the expression's embedded indirect object pronoun 'το', as in 'it', is neutral and cataphorically[6] and suspensefully points forward, to what is yet to come. Later in the English text, when Kevin, now arrested, looks into his mother's eyes trying to assess whether she has yet gone home to discover her husband and daughter dead is also meaningfully object-less: 'He was searching. He was looking for something in my face' (Shriver 2003: 382) Eva says, the intransitive use of the transitive verb 'searching' later understandable as in: looking to establish if she, as yet, knew the whole of what he had done (Gregoriou 2017: 54). The Greek text similarly makes reference to Kevin looking for a non-specified 'something' ('κάτι') just the same, again generating suspense.

As for Eva's discovery of her daughter and husband's dead bodies, both the English (Shriver 2003: 388) and Greek (Arvaniti 2010: 639) texts first refer to Celia as if she were alive with references to her 'standing' ('ήταν όρθια'), 'being still' ('σε στάση προσοχής, ακίνητη'), 'trusting' ('ανυποψίαστη') and 'eager' ('πρόθυμη') to play 'William Tell', only to later reveal her body to be affixed to the family's garden target, drawing on the inference of her actually being dead. Having said that, where the English text refers to Celia being able to 'wait' for Eva, Arvaniti uses 'δεν θα έφευγε απο εκεί', as in 'she wouldn't leave from there', which animates Celia less compared to the source text. As for the discovery of Franklin's dead body, Shriver (2003: 388) refers to Eva having 'felt compelled to weave some thread of connection between the otherwise meaningless dishevelment of that backyard and the finest in the man I married', which Arvaniti (2010: 639) translates mostly closely, though uses 'θάνατο', as in 'death', instead of 'dishevelment', and 'στον υπέροχο άνθρωπο', as in 'the fine man', instead of 'the finest in the man'. As argued in Gregoriou (2017: 51–2), the English text reveals both family members' deaths indirectly, shockingly and with an air of inevitability on Eva's part. In translating the text into Greek, Arvaniti opts for wording that is also shocking, and still requires the previous text frame 'replacement'; in revising their understanding of Eva's predicament as a woman now all alone, the reader needs to rethink the whole of the novel's storytelling from scratch, as Eva's trauma stretches far beyond what the reader first conceived. Much like an example that Seago (2014a) draws on though, the Greek wordings for 'death' and 'the fine man' here close down on the reader's cognitive enjoyment and interaction with the text; rather than allowing the reader to deduce the death by spotting the inferential gap, that is, that the connection Eva tries to draw is one between her husband's alive and dead body, Arvaniti reveals it directly. Ultimately, Shriver's grammar triggers a literary and visual double take when inviting readers to take on Eva's position at the discovery of all of what Kevin has done (see Gregoriou 2017: 52), but Arvaniti's explicit word choices lower the intensity of the shock this reveal conveys. In short, Arvaniti's Greek translation of *We Need to Talk About Kevin* comes to 'rob' some of the English source text's manipulation away from the Greek language reader.

2.2. Translating misdirection in Markaris's *Amyna Zonis*

As noted, Petros Markaris's ([1998] (2010) Άμυνα Ζώνης (*Zone Defence*) is his second crime novel in the author's original Greek series featuring Homicide Division Inspector Costas Haritos. I start with a necessary plot outline, leaving aside the story's red herrings for now. While outlining the means with which certain 'whodunit' clues are hidden in the Greek language source text, I also inspect Connolly's (2006) translation of them into English.

While on an island vacation with relatives, Inspector Haritos gets called in to help solve the murder of an unidentified young man, the body of which an earthquake uncovers on a mountainside. On his return to Athens, he additionally gets invited to help solve yet another mysterious murder, but this time one of a very well-known nightclub owner, Konstantinos Koustas. Though the two cases initially appear to be entirely unrelated, they incidentally prove to be related, with the former victim, Christos Petroulias, proving to have served as a referee in football matches of a team the latter victim, Koustas, owned. Along with being an entrepreneur and owner of various businesses, Koustas is also revealed to be involved in organized crime in the form of money laundering and fraud, and to have had illegal dealings with Petroulias, dealings over which he had the latter murdered. When two more murders get added to Haritos's pile, this time of Kalia Kourtoglou, a singer who worked for Koustas, and Loukia Karamitris, Koustas's remarried first wife and mother of his now two adult children, the plot thickens. Petroulias's murder ultimately turns out not to have been purely motivated by illegal dealings gone bad, after all. Petroulias had formed a relationship with Koustas's daughter, Niki, much to her father's dismay, for which the entrepreneur ended up having the referee killed. As for Koustas, Haritos discovers he was murdered by his drug addict son, Makis, who despised his father's ill treatment of him. Even more so, the text lets it be implied that Makis was manipulated into killing his father by his sister Niki, who wanted to avenge her lover's murder, and was Makis's driver on the day of the shooting, and hence an accomplice to her father's murder. Makis is also revealed to be his mother's (Loukia's) killer, who he loathed for abandoning him when little, and Kalia's killer, who he murdered out of fear that she would disclose his involvement with his father's murder. Clearly, 'Markaris believes that crime fiction is a suitable vehicle for the investigation of social issues' (Muždeka 2018; 84). Throughout this novel, Markaris seems to be commenting not only on organized crime but also on social ills in the form of bribery and favouritism and, lastly, on the lasting impact that child abandonment can potentially have on children. I first briefly touch on references to Petroulias's killing before analysing Markaris's and Connolly's texts' description of Niki and Makis, and uncover and inspect hidden clues as to their involvement in the murder of their father specifically. How was information about the two siblings buried, encouraging shallow processing, and how was such information translated into English exactly?

As previously noted, using supposedly reliable characters to vouch for the reliability of other characters (see Emmott and Alexander 2010) is a technique many crime authors favour. Markaris proves no exception to this tendency. One such reliable character is Haritos, the first-person character-narrator through whom the novel is focalized. As mentioned, Haritos comes to discover that Petroulias was murdered by two killers hired by Koustas. When Haritos is contemplating who had killed Petroulias, Markaris [1998] (2010: 188) has him presume 'θα βρώ τον δολοφόνο', as in 'I would find the murderer'. Interestingly, in contrast, and less reader-manipulatively, Connolly (2006: 133) here uses 'I would find the murderer, or murderers', somewhat 'correcting' the source text here instead, given that two individuals prove to have collaboratively killed Petroulias.

When Haritos first meets Makis, he describes him as 'ένα παλικάρι κάτω από τα τριάντα, ψηλό και αξύριστο' (Markaris [1998] 2010: 62), which Connolly (2006: 40) translates literally into 'a young man of no more than thirty, tall and unshaven'. When later detailing an onlooker's account of Koustas's killing though, Markaris ([1998] 2010: 76) opts for the shooter being '[μ]έτριος προς το ψηλό', which literally means 'of medium height, somewhat tall', and thus conflicts with the author's previous description of Makis being actually tall. Perhaps to compensate, Connolly (2006: 50) opts for 'average build, pretty tall', which is less misleading than the source text's description of the killer, and is hence more consistent with the description of Makis as previously set, as in 'tall'. As for Makis's psyche, Connolly (2006: 40) closely and literally translates Markaris's ([1998] 2010: 62–3) references to the actual man's (possibly drugged) gaze being bleary and lifeless, only to liven and fix threateningly at others when angered, this suggestive of the violence that he proves capable of having inflicted upon others later on. The same goes for references Niki makes to contrast between the great dreams and ambitions that Koustas had for his son and the small dreams and ambitions that the young man had for himself, which prove to have caused great problems between the two. When admitting to having killed his father, Makis ironically draws attention to his own competence: 'I'm the one who killed him. If it wasn't for me, he'd still be alive. All my life he called me idle, worthless and incompetent. I had to kill the bastard for him to realise that I'm more than able to start something and finish it' (Connolly 2006: 330). The guilt admission is a close translation of the original (Markaris [1998] 2010: 464), though Connolly colours the admission with the swear word 'bastard' the original lacks, and hence strengthens the impression of Makis's shooting being driven by extreme anger at his own father.

In contrast to Makis, Niki is instead said to be educated and employed, and therefore more respectable and trustworthy than Makis. Her later reflecting over her mother's abandonment with unexpected detachment proves to be a premonition of the lack of feeling she proves to have towards her own father. As touched on, crime authors can suggest associations and emphasize details which are later revealed to be misleading (Seago 2014a: 208). Such 'detail' here concerns Niki's physical description throughout. What proves particularly misleading here are consistent and repetitive references, in both languages, to her being make-up free and simply dressed, and, most importantly, to her having an 'innocent, almost childlike smile' which makes her look younger than her twenty-five or so years (see Markaris [1998] 2010: 104, 105, 106, 109, 225, 256, 272–3, 374, 433, 453, 455 and correspondingly Connolly 2006: 71, 72, 73, 75, 159, 181, 192–3, 266, 308, 322, 323). The repetition is significant, this being an important strategy for misdirection which builds on the processing capacity of the reader and can be used to confuse or to aid recall (Seago 2014a). The childlike- and innocent smile-association and implication here is that she comes across as an innocent, noncriminal individual we should overlook, and hence leave unsuspected of any involvement in the murders. Noticeable also are references to this childlike smile of hers vanishing (Markaris [1998] 2010: 264, 275) when Haritos mentions her abandoning mother, references that Connolly (2006: 186, 194) translates, but without the 'childlike' descriptor of her smile this time, possibly as over-repeating the descriptor might well compromise the shallowness needed of its processing. Lastly, when Niki admits to her involvement with Petroulias, her innocent smile is said to, this time, be mixed with bitterness in both texts (Markaris [1998] 2010: 436, Connolly 2006: 310), this alluding to the smile having been particularly misleading all the way through the story thus far perhaps. When Connolly (2006: 323, 326) refers to her reaction when Haritos theorizes over her involvement in her father's murder, he opts *not* to correspondingly translate Markaris's descriptor of her smile as innocent ('αθώο' [1998] 2010: 455), or any description of her smile altogether elsewhere ([1998] 2010: 458), thus flagging her *lack* of innocence more so than the source text does perhaps.

What is equally interesting is the translation of onlookers' descriptions of Makis's accomplice/driver, who is later revealed to be Niki. Whereas the Greek language requires a gendered description of the role that this, as yet unknown, individual has in the murder, and Markaris ([1998] 2010: 53, 77) opts for this being someone, if generically, male ('έτρεξε στον συνεργό του', as in 'ran toward his (male) accomplice'; 'Πάμε στον συνεργό του', as in 'Let's turn to his (male) accomplice'; and 'ο συνεργός θα περίμενε νωρίτερα' as in 'the (male) accomplice would have been there earlier'), the English-language translation allows for a non-gendered description of this individual ('ran towards an accomplice', 'Let's turn to his accomplice' and 'the accomplice would have been there earlier' (Connolly 2006: 33, 50–1)) instead. Similarly, another eyewitness later offers a similar account of a male accomplice (Markaris [1998] 2010: 244) that Connolly (2006: 172), less misleadingly than Markaris, translates into 'an/the', hence non-gendered, 'accomplice' instead. In other words, Connolly's English-language translation of this role descriptor is less misleading than the source text's is; it does not manipulate the reader into believing the driver to be male, as the source text does. Besides, and as Seago (2014a) argues, English is a language that lends itself particularly to the masking of an unknown character's biological sex; unlike inflected languages, it does not have gendered endings or gendered definite articles. Elsewhere, when Haritos traces a witness to the pair responsible for Koustas's murder during that evening, we encounter references to Haritos asking after 'two men', 'two riders' and 'two people' in both Greek (Markaris [1998] 2010: 447, 450) and the close translations of these references into English (Connolly 2006: 318, 320). Though the onlooker responds with a non-gendered descriptor of 'δυο τύπους' (Markaris [1998] 2010: 450), which literally translates into 'two individuals', Connolly (2006: 320) problematically translates this into 'two men', which proves contradictory, given that the onlooker, having soon realized that one of the two was in fact female, subsequently reveals:

'And the other man?' I asked ...
'Not man, woman.'
'It was a woman?'

Connolly (2006: 321)

In other words, Connolly's attempt to mislead the reader here provides a contradiction in the man's account; the source-text writer's use of 'τύπους' is more in-keeping with the fair play rule the genre demands, in fact.

Even so, where Connolly (2006: 50–1) is forced to use a gendered pronoun in relation to this accomplice's actions, he, much like Markaris ([1998] 2010: 77), employs male pronouns instead, with literal translations of what this 'he' was doing, like 'him' waiting with the motor running, him not wanting to attract attention 'to himself', him wearing a helmet which turns out to have disguised their (female) gender and so on. Elsewhere, when Markaris ([1998] 2010: 86) details Haritos's contemplation of there being potentially three, rather than two, individuals involved in Koustas's killing, there is reference to a 'δολοφονία με τρεις δράστες' as in 'a murder with three (non-gendered) culprits'. Here, Connolly (2006: 58) is arguably more misleading than Markaris, as the translator opts for 'a murder with three men' instead, which hence diverts attention away from female suspects altogether.

3. Concluding remarks

'Solving' crimes is no easy feat. Neither is crime fiction writing, as reader engagement depends on it. As Seago (2014a: 208) notes, crime fiction 'reader engagement – and entertainment – largely relies on the cognitive involvement of the armchair detective attempting to solve the puzzle despite authorial misdirection, to match their wits against the genius of the detective, to avoid and recognise the traps laid for them'. The crime fiction writer needs to have the skills with which to cognitively misdirect their reader for this reader 'involvement' at 'solv[ing] the puzzle' to fail, for fail the reader must. Such skills are also required of the crime fiction translator though. Seeing that language plays a crucial role in the pleasure of crime fiction cognitive misdirection and, on many instances, this cognitive misdirection is language-specific, the crime fiction translator encounters an interesting challenge of their own, and a challenge that requires crime-fiction-specific creative skills all the same. 'Translating crime fiction is no easy feat' (Gregoriou 2017: 114), either. Several linguistic areas need tending to when one inspects the reader manipulation of the crime fiction genre and the challenges involved in translating these aspects into another language. Repetition, schema-oriented or gendered language, unclear, ambiguous and polysemous lexical choices and their associated inferences and associations (including early references to who turns out to be a killer), not to mention various language-specific grammatical restrictions are but a few aspects that the crime fiction translator needs to consider when trying to 'replay' the crime fiction game in a target language the rules of which are often different to the source text's. To replay the game is to 'translate' the crime story's reader manipulation capably and effectively. Stylistics is ideally placed when offering a set of tools with which to unpick these manipulative linguistic devices and shed light on the strategy of reader misdirection in relation to translation.

Notes

1   One can argue that there are such things as intended text readings, or readings implied by texts, though that is not to say that all readers 'read' texts the same way. 'Mock' (Booth, 1961) or 'implied' (Leech and Short 1981: 259) readers are ostensibly guided towards particular judgements of characters and events. It is perfectly possible to read literary texts specifically designed to manipulate readers *without* being manipulated, though such readings would be inconsistent with these texts' implied or intended 'readings'.
2   As I argue in Gregoriou (2017: 50), *We Need to Talk About Kevin*, the first of the two novels here analysed, is not a whodunit; it *turns out* to be more of a whoduniTO.
3   Not all crime novels prove challenging in translation, of course. In translating the reader misdirection in Haddon's (2003) *The Curious Incident of the Dog in the Night-Time* into Greek, Anna Papastavrou's (2004) *Poios skotose to skilo ta mesanichta* (*Ποιός σκότωσε το σκύλο τα μεσάνυχτα* – Haddon's novel's translation) stays close to the source. In this novel, an Asperger's syndrome teenage boy who lives with his father goes in search of a murdered dog's killer. Further to discovering that his own father killed the dog, he also comes to realize that his mother, who he is led to believe died, is in fact alive and well. It is for this reason that the various conversations the boy engages in throughout the novel are differently interpretable at second novel read (see discussion in Gregoriou 2017: 75–6). Papastavrou finds herself easily able to employ literal translations of these conversations, conversations the language of which allows her to retain the clues, and relevant reader misdirection, in Greek, intact.
4   My analysing the translated text in relation to the nature of the source text does not mean that the former cannot be treated as an independent, creative piece, regardless of the latter.
5   In the interest of ease of reference to multiple translated texts, and clarity in analysis, I here refer to translated texts by means of their translator rather than the source-text author. For instance, where 'Shriver (2003)' refers to the English-language source text *The Curious Incident of the Dog in the Night-Time*, 'Arvaniti (2010)' refers to its Greek translation, though copyright remains with the source-text author, regardless.
6   Cataphora refers to 'textual references pointing to subsequent information in the text' (Wulff 2009: 2).

References

Arvaniti, G. (2010) *Prepei na milisoume gia ton Kevin* (*Πρέπει να μιλήσουμε για τον Κέβιν, We Need to Talk About Kevin*). Athens: Metaixmio (in Greek).

Booth, W. (1961) *The Rhetoric of Fiction*. Chicago: University of Chicago Press.
Connolly, D. (2004) *The Late-Night News*. London: Harvill Press.
Connolly, D. (2006) *Zone Defence*. London: Harvill Press.
Emmott, C. (1997) *Narrative Comprehension: A Discourse Perspective*. Oxford: Oxford University Press.
Emmott, C. and Alexander, M. (2010) 'Detective fiction, plot construction, and reader manipulation: Rhetorical control and cognitive misdirection in Agatha Christie's *Sparkling Cyanide*', in McIntyre, D. and Busse, B. (eds) *Language and Style: In honour of Mick Short*, pp. 328–46. Basingstoke: Palgrave Macmillan.
Emmott, C. and Alexander, M. (2014) 'Foregrounding, burying, and plot construction', in Stockwell, P. and Whiteley, S. (eds) *The Handbook of Stylistics*, pp. 329–43. Cambridge: Cambridge University Press.
Gregoriou, C. (2007) *Deviance in Contemporary Crime Fiction*. Basingstoke: Palgrave Crime Files Series.
Gregoriou, C. (2009) *English Literary Stylistics*. Basingstoke: Palgrave Perspectives on the English Language.
Gregoriou, C. (2017) *Crime Fiction Migration: Crossing Languages, Cultures, Media*. London: Bloomsbury.
Haddon, M. (2003) *The Curious Incident of the Dog in the Night-Time*. London: Vintage.
Horsley, K. (2013) 'Interrogations of society in contemporary African crime writing', in White, M. and Evans, L. (eds) *Moving Worlds* 13(1): 62–76.
Leech, G. N. and Short, M. (1981) *Style in Fiction*. London: Longman.
Mandel, E. (1984) *Delightful Murder: A Social History of the Crime Story*. London: Pluto Press.
Markaris, P. (2009 [1995]) *Nichterino Deltio (Νυχτερινό Δελτίο, Late Night News)*. Athens: Gabrielides Publishing (in Greek).
Markaris, P. (2010 [1998]) *Amyna Zonis (Άμυνα Ζώνης, Zone Defence)*. Athens: Gabrielides Publishing (in Greek).
Massey, S. (2011) 'Inheriting the Mantle: Wallander and daughter', in Effron, M. (ed.) *The Millennial Detective: Essays on Trends in Crime Fiction, Film and Television, 1990–2010*, pp. 50–65. Jefferson, NC: McFarland.
Messent, P. (ed.) (1997) *Criminal Proceedings: The Contemporary American Crime Novel*, London: Pluto Press.
Muždeka, N. (2018) 'Inspector Costas Haritos', in Sandberg, E. (ed.) *100 Greatest Literary Detectives*, pp. 83–4. London: Rowman and Littlefield.
Oxford English Dictionary Online. Oxford University Press. Available at: http://www.oed.com (accessed 18 June 2018).
Papastavrou, A. (2004) *Poios skotose to skilo ta mesanixta (Ποιός σκότωσε το σκύλο τα μεσάνυχτα, Who Killed the Dog at Midnight)*. Athens: Psichogios (in Greek).
Platten, D. (2013) 'Mediatized realities: The modern crime narrative', in White, M. and Evans, L. (eds) *Moving Worlds* 13(1): 33–48.

Porter, D. (1981) *The Pursuit of Crime: Art and Ideology in Detective Fiction*. New Haven: Yale University Press.

Sanford, A. J. and Sturt, P. (2002) 'Depth of processing in language comprehension: Not noticing the evidence', *Trends in Cognitive Sciences* 6(9): 382–6.

Sanford, A. J. S., Sanford, A. J., Molle, J. and Emmott, C. (2006) 'Shallow processing and attention capture in written and spoken discourse', *Discourse Processes* 42(2): 109–30.

Sayers, D. L. (1947) *Unpopular Opinions*. New York: Harcourt, Brace.

Scaggs, J. (2005) *Crime Fiction*. London: Routledge.

Seago, K. (2014a) 'Red herrings and other misdirection in translation', in Cadera, S. and Pintarić, A. P. (eds) *The Voices of Suspense and their Translation in Thrillers*, pp. 207–20. Amsterdam: Rodopi.

Seago, K. (2014b) 'Introduction and overview: crime (fiction) in translation', *Journal of Specialised Translation* (special issue, July). Available at: http://www.jostrans.org/issue22/issue22_toc.php (accessed 18 June 2018).

Shriver, L. (2003) *We Need to Talk About Kevin*. London: Serpent's Tail.

Stavropoulos, D. N. (1988) *Oxford Greek-English Learner's Dictionary*. Oxford: Oxford University Press.

Wulff, H. J. (2009) 'Suspense and the influence of cataphora on viewers' expectations', in Vorderer, P., Wulff, H. J. and Friedrichsen, M. (eds) *Suspense: Conceptualisations, Theoretical Analyses and Empirical Explorations*, pp. 1–18. New York: Routledge.

Multimodal manipulation of the reader in Abrams and Dorst's *S*.

Nina Nørgaard

1. Introduction

At its very core, fiction may be perceived as manipulation in the sense that it beguiles readers into 'suspending their disbelief' (Coleridge 1967 [1817]) and thereby accept the fictional microcosm of characters, settings and actions as true to life and in some sense 'real'. This type of manipulation obviously differs from manipulation as it is explored in, for example, psychology, philosophy and sociology (see e.g. Coons and Weber 2014) and would, in principle, be better captured by Mill's (2014) concept of 'aesthetic manipulation', which focuses on manipulation in artistic forms of communication where 'the person being manipulated generally accepts the manipulative experience voluntarily' (2014: 139; see also Sorlin 2016: 193–228). However, while Mill directs her attention exclusively to manipulation in terms of emotional influence, I follow Thompson (2016: 363) in finding this approach somewhat restrictive. Instead, in this chapter, I am inspired by David Foster Wallace's view of literary realism being manipulative in its creation of the illusion of verisimilitude (Wallace in Thompson 2016: 360).

Different periods in literary history have seen different types of 'realism', realized by different textual strategies for the creation of verisimilitude and thereby also by different ways of positioning readers in relation to the literary text and the fictional universe it constructs. A case in point is the difference in that respect between nineteenth-century literary realism and early-twentieth-century modernism. While nineteenth-century realism was characterized by a general belief that reality could be described objectively through particularity of description, credibility of character, setting, plot and action and a relative transparency of style, modernist writers turned to the subjective reality of the individual consciousness and developed new techniques for representing that reality, most importantly perhaps, the stream-of-consciousness technique. Today, new affordances in publishing and printing allow authors to incorporate multimodal elements such as images, colour and special typography in their novels more easily than before. In some cases, these multimodal features appear to create a new kind of realism, as when photographs and handwritten pages in colour align the readers of Jonathan Safran Foer's novel, *Extremely Loud and Incredibly Close* (2005) with the protagonist, Oskar, so that they see what he sees and (almost) experience what he experiences (see Gibbons 2012 and Nørgaard 2019, on the multimodal positioning of the reader in Foer's novel). In this chapter, I will examine how the illusion of verisimilitude is constructed in J. J. Abrams and Doug Dorst's novel, *S.* (2013), which employs a wide range of multimodal strategies to position the reader as having picked up and reading an old library book. This aspect of the novel, in fact, caused one critic to describe the novel as 'deception', 'conceit' and as 'messing with' the reader (Berman), thus indirectly reflecting the relevance of this particular book as an object of analysis with regard to literary manipulation.

Methodologically, my chapter is situated within (social semiotic) multimodal stylistics (see Nørgaard 2014 and 2019), which is a relatively new subbranch of stylistics that extends the traditional stylistics toolkit with tools that can handle the meaning-making of semiotic resources other than language. The tools are applied (and further developed) from central work in social semiotic multimodal theory, focusing on individual modes such as images (Kress and van Leeuwen 1996, 2006), colour (Kress and van Leeuwen 2002; van Leeuwen 2011) and typography (van Leeuwen 2005b, 2006) as well as on the multimodal meaning-making involved in the interaction and integration of semiotic modes in communication (e.g. Kress and van Leeuwen 2001; van Leeuwen 2005a; Jewitt, Bezemer and O'Halloran 2016; Bateman, Wildfeuer and Hiippala 2017). The tools employed for analysis have been developed with the aim of enabling description which is – at least ideally – as detailed and systematic as the description of language in linguistics.

In addition to investigating the meaning-making of individual modes and their multimodal integration, Kress and van Leeuwen (2001) furthermore argue that meaning is created at four different levels: *discourse, design, production* and *distribution*. In relation to meaning-making in the novel, this claim is of particular significance, since authors typically design and produce the verbal narrative of their novel (by means of different discourses) yet typically have very little say when it comes to the choices involved in the design and production of the physical artefact of the book. Even so, choices in typography, layout, paper, binding, cover art and so on are also semiotic and consequently add extra meaning to that of the verbal narrative. In this respect, Abrams and Dorst's novel is special, since all aspects of the novel's design were carefully devised by the authors and the designers with whom they collaborated and were executed in close cooperation with the people involved at the level of production.

Doing a comprehensive multimodal stylistic analysis of Abrams and Dorst's novel would be an extensive enterprise, beyond the scope of a book chapter. Instead, after a brief survey of the variety of multimodal features involved in its semiosis to contextualize my analysis, I shall devote my attention to the novel's use of typography for its meaning-making. To this end, I will draw on the *distinctive features* and *semiotic principles* approaches to typography (see van Leeuwen 2005b, 2006; Nørgaard 2009, 2019) and also consider the significance of *modality* in relation to the typographic semiosis in the novel. The primary focus of my analysis will be on the ways in which different typographic choices position the reader in relation to the novel and its fictional universe, however, further related aspects of the novel's typographic semiosis will be considered where relevant.

2. The multimodal feast of Abrams and Dorst's S.

To readers and scholars interested in multimodality in the novel, Abrams and Dorst's novel is a virtual feast – reflected, for instance, by the fact that a quick YouTube search for 'Abrams and Dorst novel' results in numerous videos showing people opening the book while talking about what they see and feel in the process. The book comes in a cassette on which is printed conventional information such as title (*S.*), name of authors, publisher, book description, author biographies and bar code; however, when the cassette is removed, no further references are made to the real-world authors, and so on, apart from a small text unit in very small (almost unreadable) print on the inside of the back cover that conveys obligatory information about publisher, copyrights and so forth. Instead, readers are facing a book, titled *Ship of Theseus* authored by 'V. M. Straka', in a hardback format that looks and feels like a traditional cloth binding. On the spine is a white sticker with ciphers that some readers may recognize as those of a library classification system as well as the year 1949. On opening the novel, readers encounter a red library stamp ('BOOK FOR LOAN') and on the inside of the back cover is another library stamp requesting readers to 'KEEP THIS BOOK CLEAN' as well as stamps making up the check-out history of the book from 1957 to 2000. In addition to these signifiers of 'library book' and 'old library book', even the choice of paper plays a significant role in the creation of verisimilitude, since *Ship of Theseus* is printed on yellowed, stained paper, which makes the book look old. I shall examine the meaning of typography in detail below, but it should be mentioned here that the perhaps most striking feature of *Ship of Theseus* is the occurrence of handwritten notes in the margins throughout the book. The notes are comments exchanged by two students, Jen and Eric, about the narrative they read, about its enigmatic author, V. M. Straka, and about themselves and their own lives, thus developing into a narrative that turns out to be as important as the story in the margins of which it unfolds. That story, in turn, revolves around an amnesic man, S., who is shanghaied onto a mysterious ship with an unknown destination. Finally, the novel also consists of material that is inserted between its pages: letters, postcards, photocopied material, a page from a university newspaper and even a map, drawn on a napkin from a (fictional) coffee house. Like the notes in the margins, the inserted paraphernalia is material which is exchanged between Jen and Eric and which relates closely to the two narratives, thus functioning as an integrated part of the novel. All of the above has been devised, written and designed by Abrams, Dorst and the design firms, Melcher Media and Headcase Design. V. M. Straka is fictional, as are Jen and Eric. The paper is not old and the cloth binding not genuine. Altogether, large amounts of effort and care have been invested in the creation of verisimilitude by the multimodal features just listed in order to create the meaning of 'old library book' that is of central importance to the novel. While all the features and their interaction could be put up for detailed systematic multimodal stylistic analysis (see Nørgaard 2019), I shall here narrow my analytical focus to typographic semiosis in the novel.

3. Typography – a multimodal stylistics approach

In multimodal semiotics, typography is typically analysed in terms of distinctive features, semiotic principles and metafunctionality. While my analysis of typographic semiosis below is inspired by and builds on van Leeuwen's work on typography (especially 2005b, 2006), my categories differ in some respects from his as explained in Nørgaard (2019), where detailed discussions and qualifications of the approach are presented. My concept of typography is broad, extending from handwriting to printed typography (see Nørgaard 2009: 143). At the same time, I distinguish between typography and layout as separate modes which are, however, closely integrated in the semiosis of a given text. I thus distinguish between typography as the graphic appearance of writing in terms of the shape, size, colour, and so on of the letters and layout as the overall spatial page design of a given text, including margins, *leading* and *kerning*.

The distinctive features approach to typography centres on the features that set one typeface – and instance of typographic use – off from another. As proposed elsewhere (Nørgaard 2019) and illustrated by the system network in Figure 11.1, a given typeface may be described in terms of its *weight, expansion, slope, curvature, connectivity, orientation, endings, regularity, colour* and *size*. While one typeface may thus be characterized as bold, wide, upright, angular, disconnected, and so on, another typeface will display different characteristic traits with different signification as a result. Regarding typographic meaning, I concur with van Leeuwen's (2006: 147) claim that typographic distinctive features have semiotic potential in the sense that an angular typeface may signify qualities such as 'masculine' and 'technical', while roundness may signify for example, 'organic', 'natural' and 'female'. It is, of course, important to realize that typographic meaning is largely contextually determined and that no automatic one-to-one relationship exists between typographic form and meaning.

In the social semiotic analysis of typography, the distinctive features approach combines with considerations about typographic semiotic principles (see van Leeuwen 2005b; Nørgaard 2009, 2019). In my view, much typographic meaning can be described as indexical, iconic, symbolic (see Peirce, for example, in Merrel 2001) and discursive import (van Leeuwen 2005b: 139). Indexical typographic meaning is seen when a typographic signifier shows traces of its own coming into being. Iconic typographic meaning refers to instances where the typographic signifier resembles or imitates what it signifies (in a pictorial or a conceptual sense). Symbolic typographic meaning occurs when an arbitrary relation exists between the typographic signifier and that which is signified. And typographic discursive import is seen in cases where a typographic signifier and its connotations are imported from one context into another where they did not previously belong. It should be noted that a given typographic use in context may be characterized in terms of more than one semiotic principle, since a typographic signifier often reveals something about its own coming into being, for instance, while at the same time, displaying an iconic relation to that which is signified or expressing meaning that stems from it being imported along with its

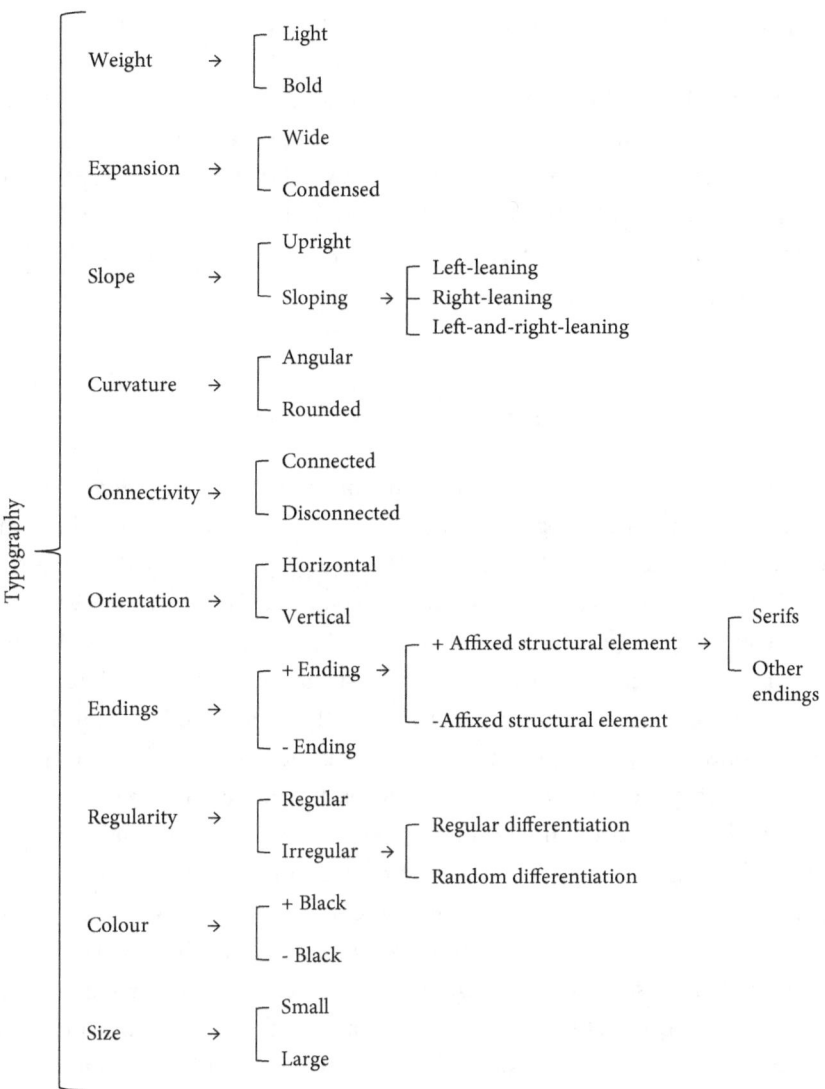

Figure 11.1 The distinctive features of typography (adapted from Nørgaard 2019).[1]

associated meanings into the novel from a different context. Even so, one type of meaning is usually more prominent than the others.

In his work on typography, van Leeuwen (2006: 142–3) furthermore claims that typography is metafunctional, meaning that – like for example, wording and images – it can express experiential, interpersonal and compositional meaning.[2] In this respect, I have found the concepts of *salience* and *modality* particularly useful in a literary context. Visual salience primarily refers to aspects of a text that stand out visually and are thereby given a certain prominence (see Kress and van Leeuwen 2006: 201), while visual modality concerns the truthfulness of a given representation, that is, the question of whether what the viewers see is 'what they would have seen if they had been there' or whether what they see has been manipulated in any perceptible way (e.g. van Leeuwen 2005a: 160–77). With regard to the positioning of the viewer by the typography of Abrams and Dorst's novel, the concept of modality turns out to be of particular relevance.

4. Typographic meaning in *S*.

The first typographic instance readers encounter on removing *Ship of Theseus* from its slipcase is the typography by means of which the title and author name are realized on the cover of the novel. The typography employed on the front cover is a version of Max Salzmann's art deco typeface Dolmen from 1922 and is hence a suitable choice for a novel allegedly published in 1949. For readers who recognize the style of the typeface and the historical period to which it belongs, these meanings are arguably imported into the context of *Ship of Theseus*, thereby contributing to the creation of verisimilitude as regards the meaning of 'old book'. The meaning thus created by means of typographic discursive import is specified further through wording on the 'library sticker' on the spine of the novel and on the title page encountered when opening the book where the year of publication is made explicit. As for the distinctive features of the typeface, its most salient feature is its weight. In combination with the angularity of the letters, their almost massive boldness may be perceived as having a certain masculine feel to it. While talking about 'masculine' and 'feminine' in relation to typefaces may seem to be taking the semiotic analysis of typography too far, scrutiny of the typographic choices made on products primarily targeted at men and women respectively reveals a certain cultural bias with the distinctive features of 'angular', 'bold' and 'upright' being repeatedly employed in male contexts (such as the packaging of protein powder for body builders), whereas the features of 'rounded', 'ordinary' (or 'light') and 'sloping' are often used in contexts for women (such as the covers of chick lit novels, cf., Montoro 2012). On the front cover of *Ship of Theseus*, the possible iconic signification of the typeface of something 'male' or 'masculine' is enforced by the graphic image of an old sailing ship, printed between title and author name, since sailing ships were decidedly a men's sphere in 1949.

The choice of typeface for the spine differs notably from that of the cover in being much slimmer. This choice is probably motivated by the more restricted affordances of the spine, where limited space would make the bold typeface of the front cover an unsuitable choice. As a result, the relationship between typographic form and meaning on the spine is best described as arbitrary and hence symbolic with there being no natural relationship between the look of the typeface and that which is signified.

On opening the book, readers are met by a different typeface employed for the title on the title page (see Figure 11.2). The typeface encountered here, Umbra, was designed by Robert Hunter Middleton in 1935 and is – like Dolmen – a suitable choice for constructing the illusion of a novel published in 1949. While some contemporary readers may not recognize the historical meaning thus created by typographic discursive import, they are probably likely to consider other aspects of meaning since the visual appearance of Umbra is rather unique for a typeface. Its most striking feature is the absence, or negation, of the letters it realizes. Building on Machin's (2007: 123) concept of visual 'non-representation', I agree that visuals – like language – may negate; however, for something to be a case of visual negation (or non-representation), there must in my view be *something* in the image which indicates that something else is missing (see Nørgaard 2019). To judge from the typeface examined here, similar meaning can be created typographically. The Umbra letters are characterized by their own absence, however this absence does not (and cannot) exist in itself, but is established by edges that create a shadow effect of the letters and make them look three-dimensional in spite of their absence.

Describing Umbra in terms of its distinctive features challenges the system presented in Figure 11.1. In spite of their 'absence', the letters can still be described as for example, 'upright' and 'disconnected'; however, the system does not capture their most characteristic features, which are those of absence and edges. Since the negative space that characterizes the letters is defined by the presence and shape of the edges, adding 'edges' to the system network would, in fact, enable analysts to handle both features in their description. This is an illustrative example of one of the core pillars of stylistics: that analysts must be

SHIP OF THESEUS

Figure 11.2 Typographic realization of *Ship of Theseus* on the title page.

willing to adjust their analytical tools when encountering data which suggests a need for such adjustment.

As for the meaning created by Umbra on the title page of *Ship of Theseus*, an iconic connection appears to exist between the look of the typeface and the narrative contents of the novel. When looking at the letters, readers get the impression that what they see are the sides, or shadows, of the letters while the letters themselves are intangible and elusive, just as the identity of the protagonist, S., is unknown even to himself. As a matter of fact, the only tangible clues to his identity are his (initially wet) clothes, 'a tiny black orb that might be a pebble, or perhaps a piece of ancient and petrified fruit' in his trouser pocket and a piece of paper with 'an ornate S-shaped symbol' on it in his coat pocket (Abrams and Dorst 2013: 6). In addition to this, the elusive nature of the letters may also be perceived as relating iconically to V. M. Straka, the (fictive) author of *Ship of Theseus*, whose identity is unknown and at the centre of a heated scholarly debate in which Eric and his former supervisor are intricately involved. That such a connection may exist is supported by the very first words of the (fictive) translator's note and foreword that follow the title page:

> Who was V. M. Straka? The world knows his name, his reputation as the prolific author of provocative fictions, novels that toppled governments, shamed ruthless industrialists, and foresaw the horrifying sweep of totalitarianism that has been a particular plague in these last few decades. It knows him as the most nimble of writers, one whose mastery of diverse literary idioms and approaches was on display from book to book, even chapter to chapter. But the world never knew Straka's face, never knew with certainty a single fact of the man's life.
>
> Predictably, though disappointingly, the mystery of Straka's identity has become more intensely studied than his body of work. (Abrams and Dorst 2013: v–vi)

In contrast to the typefaces used for the front cover and title page of the novel, the typeface employed for the verbal narrative of *Ship of Theseus* is a relatively plain black old-style typeface (Caledonia, digitalized as Transitional 551) with an arbitrary relation to the contents of the narrative as is typical of most conventional novels. Even so, the typeface may signal something about the time of production of the novel to those who recognize the typographic style and the time to which it belongs, as was the case with the typographies selected for the front cover and title page. While old typefaces may, of course, still be used today and can therefore not be used for unambiguously determining the time of production of a particular novel, it clearly participates in the creation of verisimilitude of *Ship of Theseus* as a novel published in 1949 in a way that would be absent had a distinctively more contemporary typeface been employed.

Altogether, the typefaces selected for the front cover, the title page and the verbal narrative position the readers as having picked up and reading an old book. In the cause of the printed verbal narrative, they furthermore encounter an ornate 'S' in gothic type. The letter is salient because of its size (large) and weight (bold) and, at a very basic level, by its iconic contrast to the plain black typography of the rest of the text, signifying 'different text'. The typographic meaning of the letter appears to be best described as discursive import, with the gothic type bringing something old and gothic or mysterious with it into the (allegedly likewise old, yet still younger) narrative in which it occurs. This is meaning that is created in close integration with wording. The readers first see the letter in the (fictional) translator's note and foreword to the novel, where it is drawn in black ink in the margin. The symbol is accompanied by the following handwritten exchange between Eric and Jen, which foreshadows the mystery in which the symbol is shrouded in the rest of the novel: [Eric] 'I've always been impressed that you could draw this so well.' [Jen] 'Wait – I've always thought *you* drew it. Tell me you're joking ... .' In the narrative of *Ship of Theseus*, the reader next encounters a description of the letter as the only readable letter on an ink-stained scrap of paper in the pocket of the protagonist's wet coat, and shortly after, the letter occurs in gothic type among the printed narrative in plain black type when the protagonist sees it painted on the brick wall of a tavern. In the rest of the narrative, the ornate S reoccurs in unexpected places and is surrounded by a sense of mystery that also resonates with the protagonist being told that his name is 'S_' by an unknown sailor who holds him captive on a ship with an unknown destination (Abrams and Dorst 2013: 32).

Including the letter in gothic type in the verbal narrative of *Ship of Theseus* rather than just describing it creates typographic verisimilitude and has the effect of positioning the reader with the protagonist, S., seeing what he sees. Following Herman's (1994) work on 'doubly deictic you' in verbal literary narratives, Gibbons (2012: 77–81) finds such positioning – or doubly deictic alignment – of the reader with a character characteristic of multimodal novels. A similar alignment arguably also occurs when the readers encounter the drawn gothic 'S' in the margins which Eric and Jen communicate about in the handwritten notes. In this example, the readers may even be surprised (and slightly spooked) along with Eric and Jen by the symbol being drawn by a third character, unknown to the two protagonists as well as to the reader. In Gibbon's words, such and similar examples of multimodally triggered doubly deictic alignment of the reader with one or more characters has the effect of 'the reader [being] at once both an observer of the fiction and powerfully involved in that fiction' (2012: 77). In the example just mentioned, the manipulation of the reader thus arguably extends beyond the creation of multimodal mimesis to a more active involvement of the reader in the fictional universe.

The probably most salient typographic feature in Abrams and Dorst's novel is the occurrence of handwritten notes in the margins throughout the book, realizing Jen and Eric's exchange about *Ship of Theseus* and its mysterious author as well as about their own lives. In the novel and in other contexts, the meaning of 'handwritten' can be constructed in different ways, of which the following are the most typical: (1) handwriting, (2) italics, (3) printed typography that has been constructed to look handwritten, and (4) wording stating that something is written by hand (see Nørgaard 2019 for a detailed treatment of the phenomenon). Where the last example displays an arbitrary, symbolic relationship between the typographic signifiers and the signification of 'written by hand', italics and (most) typographies that have been constructed to look handwritten are better described in terms of the iconic similarity to handwriting of, for example, their sloping. Notes that are actually written by hand, in turn, like those encountered in Abrams and Dorst's novel, are likely to be perceived as material traces of the people who wrote the notes and of the tools with which they were produced and are consequently examples of indexical typographic meaning. Since Jen and Eric never existed, the handwritten notes are *fictional* indices, created by the designers of the book as a means of manipulating readers into suspending their disbelief in this respect.

From a social semiotic multimodal perspective, typographic verisimilitude can be described in terms of modality. Producing Jen and Eric's notes by hand to ensure that they look handwritten obviously results in a high degree of truthfulness of the representation, that is, high modality, meaning that readers can easily imagine that 'what they see is what they would have seen if they had been there' with Jen and Eric (see van Leeuwen 2005a: 160–77). Although the multimodal stylistics approach to analysis that I advocate in my work focuses primarily on the semiotic object of the text while paying less attention to the intentions behind a given semiotic artefact and the processes by means of which it came into being, I nevertheless believe that insight into the design and production of *S.* will throw some light on the concept of modality. According to Lauren Nathan from Melcher Media and Paul Kepple from Headcase Design (both quoted in Berman), the process of designing and producing the pages with handwritten notes was rather complex. First, Abrams and Dorst submitted the manuscript as a Word file with all the handwritten notes as 'Track Changes' comments. Subsequently, two people wrote all the comments by hand on tracing paper, which was then scanned, transferred to InDesign and combined with the main text. According to Kepple (in Berman),

> That all took layers of adjusting in Photoshop to do it in the various pen colors and in pencil. But with the process of doing it on tracing paper and scanning it, when we placed it in InDesign, the colours all changed. The purple ink looked too blue, the orange got too red at times, and the pencil just didn't look like pencil anymore. So we'd have to do layer adjustment to adjust the colors to look like they were supposed to look.

As revealed by Kepple's comment, the high typographic modality of the handwritten notes is, in fact, not a matter of the *truth* (of handwriting, written on tracing paper, scanned into a computer programme and printed in a book) but of the *truthfulness of the representation* since in order to make the different colours of the ink a truthful *representation* of ink they had to be adjusted before print. Kepple's comment thus reveals something about the manipulation of materials that went into the creation of the novel's multimodal verisimilitude. Furthermore, Nathan's comments (in Berman) expose yet another means of manipulating readers with regard to the credibility of the typographic realism of the novel since letting the notes be written by two people automatically increases the typographic verisimilitude as it results in two different styles of writing.

Where the use of actual handwriting for the realization of Jen and Eric's comments in the margins of *Ship of Theseus* may thus be perceived as high modality in one respect, signifying what the readers would have seen if they had been there with the two characters may, in fact, be seen as low modality in another respect, as it radically breaks the genre conventions of the novel, known to consist of layout units of text realized by printed typography surrounded by empty margins. This is an illustrative example of the claim made by White (2005) that the multimodal features of explicitly multimodal novels may have mimetic and defamiliarizing functions at the same time. The look of the handwritten notes in the margins plays a significant role as regards the manipulation of readers into accepting the reality claims of the novel in this respect, while, simultaneously, this feature also defamiliarizes conventions and draws the readers' attention to the textuality and fictionality of the novel. This double function appears to apply not only to the handwritten notes but also to the other unconventional multimodal features by which the novel is characterized such as it being a contemporary novel whose pages are nevertheless yellowed, stained and marked with what looks like old library stamps.

As for the more specific typographic meaning of the handwritten notes, differences in meaning are created by means of differences in typographic form which can be captured by the distinctive features approach to typography. As mentioned above, the notes in the margins are written in two distinctively different styles. This is the natural result of the notes being produced by two (real-life) people, but it also results in different meaning. At the most basic level, it is of great importance to the reader's ability to decode Jen and Eric's narrative in the margins of the novel that their comments are realized by different styles. More specifically, the handwriting of Jen's notes is characterized by being irregular, rounded, sloping and connected. In contrast, the style of Eric's writing, in block capitals, is more regular (however less so than printed type), more angular and disconnected. Where Eric's hand is mostly sloping to the left, Jen's tends to slope (more irregularly) to both sides. Even if these typographic choices – of selecting one style for Jen and another for Eric and not vice versa – may be random and the resulting meaning unintended, it is interesting to note that the features of Jen's handwriting are those often associated with female contexts while the style of Eric's writing may be seen to construct the iconic conceptual meaning of 'male'. Alternatively, it may have been exactly those culturally founded typographic meanings that motivated the designers of the book to choose the specific styles for the two characters, whether consciously or not.

Another significant distinctive feature that helps readers keep track of who is communicating in the margins of the book is that of colour. In the first part of the novel, Jen's notes are primarily blue and Eric's black, however at intervals Jen also uses an orange and a purple pen, while some of Eric's comments are green and red. Later in the narrative, the use of orange, purple, green and red becomes increasingly prominent. Added to this, notes in pencil grey occur throughout the novel in Eric's style of writing. The pencilled text turns out to be Eric's original academic notes about *Ship of Theseus*, while the text in coloured ink makes up Jen and Eric's exchange. Since there is nothing 'blue', 'orange' and 'purple' about Jen or the topics she writes about, and since there is nothing 'black', 'green', 'red' and 'pencil grey' about Eric and the contents of his writing, there is an arbitrary, symbolic relation between the typographic signifiers and that which is signified as regards colour. Instead, colour is employed locally (i.e. in this particular novel) for signifying time of writing. As it turns out, Jen and Eric go back through their notes, adding new comments and commenting on old ones. Had this been explained through wording, it would probably have undermined the verisimilitude of Jen and Eric communicating without the mediation of a narrator. Instead, the difference in meaning of the different colours is revealed by the multimodal integration of typography and wording. An example of this occurs already on the back of the half title (i.e. the very first page of the book). Here Jen and Eric are discussing an aspect of *Ship of Theseus* in blue and black ink, followed by the following comment made by Eric in red, of which the deictic marker 'still' indicates that the note has been made at a later point in time: 'Do you still think so?' In other cases, past tense combined with pronominal reference to the comments in blue and black interact multimodally with ink in different colour to create that meaning the way it is seen on page 7: 'Can't believe how flippant I *was* about *this*' (my emphasis).

In addition to juggling the two narratives of *Ship of Theseus* and Jen and Eric's notes in the margins respectively, readers are thus also faced by notes in the margins that have been made at different points in time. This complicates the narrative structure of the novel considerably and forces readers to make active decisions about how to read the novel. Should they read the entire narrative of *Ship of Theseus* first and then embark on Jen and Eric's notes? And, if so, would it then make sense to read the blue and black strand of notes before the orange and green strand and the purple and yellow strand? Or are all the narrative strands best taken in page by page, although this choice makes the reading of *Ship of Theseus* a very fragmented experience? In itself, the occurrence of notes in the margins of the novel positions the readers as facing a complex narrative. The distinctive feature of colour by which the notes are realized enhances this complexity considerably. Apart from the colours of the typography indicating how the notes belong together temporally, the book provides no clues or guidelines that would offer practical reading strategies. The absence of such clues arguably adds to the realism of the novel by giving the reader a feeling that the notes are not intended for readers other than Jen and Eric.

5. Concluding remarks

In this chapter, I have presented a first tentative step into investigating from a stylistic perspective how readers may not just be manipulated by verbal means in the process of reading a work of fiction but also by other semiotic modes and their interaction. By focusing on typography, I have shown how different types of reality claims are created in Abrams and Dorst's novel by this semiotic mode as a means of manipulating readers into believing that they are reading an old library book with handwritten notes in the margins. I have thus demonstrated how one type of verisimilitude is created by means of discursive import through the selection of typefaces that belong to a particular historical context for the realization of what is, in actual fact, a contemporary novel, that is, the printed typefaces selected for the title on the front cover and title page of *Ship of Theseus* and for its main text. At the same time, the typographic choices made for the front cover and title page also turned out to create meaning that related iconically to the contents of 'Straka's' narrative, while the typeface chosen for the main text displayed an arbitrary, symbolic relationship to the contents of the narrative as is conventional in most prose fiction. I have also shown how another type of verisimilitude is created by handwriting in different styles and colours in the margins of *Ship of Theseus*, functioning as (fictional) indexical markers of the two characters, Jen and Eric, possibly combined with culturally founded iconic signification of gender. Finally, my analysis also revealed how in the case of the gothic type chosen for the mysterious 'S', the typeface, imported into the plain black typography of the main text of *Ship of Theseus* and into Jen and Eric's handwritten exchange, has the effect of aligning the readers with the characters of the respective scenes, seeing what they see and to some extent almost experiencing what they experience. Throughout my analysis, I have demonstrated how typographic semiosis can be captured and described in a systematic way by means of (social semiotic) multimodal stylistic methodology. As indicated in my introductory contextualization of the typographic analysis above, the typographic claims to reality combine with other multimodal reality markers such as the yellowed, stained paper, the library sticker on the spine of the novel, the textured cover and the library stamps which could all be put up for more detailed systematic multimodal stylistic analysis.

But how successful is the multimodal manipulation of Abrams and Dorst's novel really? Where some of the reality markers such as the period typefaces selected for *Ship of Theseus*, the high modality of most of the handwritten notes, the inserted postcards, the photocopied material and the napkin with the map are very true to life, other features are slightly less convincing. Attentive readers may note, for example, that the margins of *Ship of Theseus* are considerably more spacious than those of comparable novels (to fit in all the handwritten notes), that the notes in grey have not actually been pencilled onto the pages that the readers are leafing through but are representations of 'pencil grey', and that the 'cloth binding' is not genuine in spite of its textured surface. Furthermore, the communicative context of the novel arguably undermines the positioning of the reader as someone who might be persuaded by the novel's aesthetic manipulation. The readers' awareness that *S.* is actually a contemporary novel through which contemporary writers communicate with contemporary readers will thus keep them from truly believing that the novel is an old library book with handwritten notes made by two other readers in its margins. Instead, the multimodal reality markers of the novel arguably position the reader as someone who is likely to recognize the various signifiers involved in constructing the meaning of 'old library book' and the fact that this meaning is a construct. The deliberate and thoroughly executed attempt to make the novel look as '1949-library-book-real' as possible appears to play with the readers' expectations and bring them to offer a specific type of response which – to judge from the many YouTube videos of the book – in its essence boils down to the exclamation 'wow!'

Notes

1 The original network is slightly more complex, including four levels at which the distinctive features may be realized. However, for my analyses in the present chapter this further level of complexity is not necessary.
2 Alternative terms being ideational, interpersonal and textual meaning (see Halliday 1994; Kress and van Leeuwen 1996).

References

Abrams, J. J. and Dorst, D. (2013) *S.* New York: Mulholland Books.
Bateman, J., Wildfeuer, J. and Hiippala, T. (2017) *Multimodality: Foundations, Research and Analysis. A Problem-Oriented Introduction.* Berlin: Mouton de Gruyter.
Berman, A. 'The most complex project of 2013?' Available at: https://www.paperspecs.com/caught-our-eye/s-by-jjabrams-complex-project/ (accessed 13 April 2018).
Coleridge, S. T. (1967 [1817]) *Biographia Literaria.* London: Oxford University Press.
Coons, C. and Weber, M. (eds) (2014) *Manipulation: Theory and Practice.* Oxford: Oxford University Press.
Foer, J. S. (2005) *Extremely Loud and Incredibly Close.* London: Hamish Hamilton.
Gibbons, A. (2012) *Multimodality, Cognition, and Experimental Literature.* London and New York: Routledge.
Halliday, M. A. K. (1994) *An Introduction to Functional Grammar.* 2nd edition. London: Arnold.
Herman, D. (1994) 'Textual "you" and double deixis in Edna O'Brien's *A Pagan Place*', *Style* 28(3): 378–410.

Jewitt, C., Bezemer, J. and O'Halloran, K. (2016) *Introducing Multimodality*. London and New York: Routledge.

Kress, G. and van Leeuwen, T. (1996) *Reading Images: The Grammar of Visual Design*. 1st edition. London and New York: Routledge.

Kress, G. and van Leeuwen, T. (2001) *Multimodal Discourse: The Modes and Media of Contemporary Communication*. London: Arnold.

Kress, G. and van Leeuwen, T. (2002) 'Colour as a semiotic mode: Notes for a grammar of colour', *Visual Communication* 1(3): 343–68.

Kress, G. and van Leeuwen, T. (2006) *Reading Images: The Grammar of Visual Design*. 2nd edition. London and New York: Routledge.

Machin, D. (2007) *Introduction to Multimodal Analysis*. London: Hodder Education.

Merrel, F. (2001) 'Charles Sanders Peirce's concept of the sign', in Cobley, P. (ed.) *The Routledge Companion to Semiotics and Linguistics*, pp. 28–39. London and New York: Routledge.

Mills, C. (2014) 'Manipulation as an aesthetic flaw', in Coons, C. and Weber, M. (eds) *Manipulation: Theory and Practice*, pp. 135–50. Oxford: Oxford University Press.

Montoro, R. (2012) *Chick Lit: The Stylistics of Cappuccino Fiction*. London: Bloomsbury.

Nørgaard, N. (2009) 'The semiotics of typography in literary texts: A multimodal approach', *Orbis Litterarum* 64(2): 141–60.

Nørgaard, N. (2014) 'Multimodality and stylistics', in Burke, M. (ed.) *The Routledge Handbook of Stylistics*, pp. 471–84. London and New York: Routledge.

Nørgaard, N. (2019) *Multimodal Stylistics of the Novel: More than Words*. London and New York: Routledge.

Sorlin, S. (2016) *Language and Manipulation in* House of Cards: *A Pragma-Stylistic Perspective*. Basingstoke: Palgrave/Macmillan.

Thompson, L. (2016) '"Sincerity with a motive": Literary manipulation in David Foster Wallace's *Infinite Jest*', *Critique: Studies in Contemporary Fiction* 57(4): 359–73.

van Leeuwen, T. (2005a) *Introducing Social Semiotics*. London and New York: Routledge.

van Leeuwen, T. (2005b) 'Typographic meaning', *Visual Communication* 4(2): 137–43.

van Leeuwen, T. (2006) 'Towards a semiotics of typography', *Information Design Journal + Document Design* 14(2): 139–55.

van Leeuwen, T. (2011) *The Language of Colour: An Introduction*. London and New York: Routledge.

White, G. (2005) *Reading the Graphic Surface: The Presence of the Book in Prose Fiction*. Manchester and New York: Manchester University Press.

Index

Abrams, J. J.   5, 21, 234–48
anticipation   31, 41, 146–7, 152, 155, 168–9
Armitage, Simon   18, 172–3, 178, 190
attention   6–8, 11–13, 16, 20–1, 38, 45–6, 50–1, 54, 61, 71, 86, 102–3, 110, 147, 149, 150–1, 153–4, 188, 196–7, 201–2, 206–8, 209–10, 212, 217, 227, 230, 234, 244, 245
author's manipulation   46, 70–1, 73, *see also* manipulation

Batuman, Elif   17, 117–18, 122–3, 125, 134, 141

characterization   8, 9, 35, 42, 74, 82
Christie, Agatha   11, 19–20, 149, 195–212
clues   9, 11, 18, 20, 147, 152–5, 158–61, 163, 168, 176, 202, 206, 215–20, 223, 226–7, 242, 247
cognitive   4, 5, 7–8, 10–14, 16, 19, 20–1, 39, 93, 98, 132, 146, 148–9, 172, 175, 195–7, 206, 208–12, 216, 225, 230
cognitive stylistics   vi, viii, 172, *see also* stylistic(s)
communication   2–4, 6–9, 15, 17, 51, 53, 61, 63, 65, 75, 77–8, 80–1, 87, 119, 121, 141, 160–1, 164, 166, 234–5
conceptual(ly)   15, 19, 51–2, 61, 93–4, 99, 175–6, 180–2, 184–5, 187–9, 238, 246
conceptualization   19, 172, 189
conceptualize   35, 39, 52, 58–9, 62, 181–2, 187, 189
control   2, 3, 5, 6, 8–12, 19, 38, 45, 66, 70, 72, 93, 149, 195–6, 198, 206, 209–10, 212, 223
corpus pragmatics   16, 83, *see also* pragmatic(s)
corpus stylistics   71, 83, *see also* stylistic(s)

counterfactual storytelling   15, 31, 34, 39, 43, 46
creative writing   6, 16, 92, 127, 177–8, 189
crime   1, 11–12, 14, 19, 20–1, 195–9, 202, 204–10, 212, 215–20, 226, 228, 230
crime fiction   12, 14, 20–1, 215–19, 226, 230
Cusk, Rachel   17, 117–19, 121–3, 127–8, 130, 133–6, 141

deception   3, 4, 206, 235
deictic   8, 15, 50–3, 55–7, 59–1, 63–5, 105–6, 108, 173–5, 243, 247
deixis   8, 14–15, 50–7, 106, 173, 175, *see also* social deixis; socio-relational
detective   196, 198, 207–8, 211, 216, 219, 230
detective fiction   12, 146, 148–9, 153, 195, 215–16
detective stories   195, 196, 216
diegesis   16, 34, 35, 38–9, 45, 94–6, 98, 100, 103–5, 110, 112
discourse architecture   15, 50, 53, 61–3, 65–7
discourse presentation   16, 93–4, 96–9, 101, 105, 107, 109–10, 112
disnarrated   8, 15, 42–3, 46
disnarration   8, 15, 42–3, 46
Dorst, Dough   5, 21, 234–48

emotion   3–5, 7–8, 13, 18, 38, 53, 55, 63, 101, 149, 151–2, 156, 161
emotional(ly)   4, 7–8, 18, 38, 53, 54, 57, 59, 87, 146–7, 155, 161, 167–8, 224, 234
evidence   11, 19, 196–201, 204, 206–7, 211–12, 217
experiential deixis   15, 59, 60, 67, *see also* deixis
experimental study   147

forked path   31, 34, 39, 41, 42, 46
Fowles, John   6, 14, 32, 36–8, 42, 44–6

genre 2, 11, 14, 19–20, 31–3, 37–8, 44, 146, 149–50, 153, 162, 168, 176, 195, 208, 210, 215–18, 222, 229–30, 245
global inference 117, 121–2, 126, 135–7, see also inference; local inference
Greek 12, 16, 20, 218–26, 228–9
Green, Henry 6, 16, 70–81, 84–9
Gricean 3, 71, 75–8, 83

homodiegetic 6, 16–17, 34, 93–4, 98–9, 101–5, 109–11

immersion 14, 17, 37, 94, 103, 118, 131–2
inattentional 20, 206, see also attention
inference 17, 93, 117, 119–22, 124, 126, 130–1, 133–40, 179, 185, 204, 209, 222, 225, 230
inferential 17, 117–18, 122, 124, 131–4, 137–8, 140–2, 220, 222, 225
influence 4, 5, 7, 9, 35, 39, 61, 70, 73, 88, 96, 103, 167, 172, 195, 234
Ishiguro, Kazuo 17, 105–7, 109–10

layout 21, 236, 238, 245
local inference 117, 130, 136, see also global inference; inference

McBride, Eimear 17, 117–18, 123, 130–4, 137–8, 141
manipulate 5, 7–8, 10, 12, 16, 17–21, 32, 38–9, 46, 51, 52, 64, 79, 96, 102, 105, 172, 176, 179, 185, 189, 195, 216–17, 220–1, 224, 226, 229, 234, 240, 247
manipulation 1–6, 8, 10–20, 37, 46, 50–1, 53, 61–2, 70–3, 79–80, 88, 92, 146–53, 155–6, 159–63, 167–8, 172–3, 177, 188–9, 195–6, 206, 208–10, 215–19, 225, 230, 234–5, 244–5, 248–9
Markaris, Petros 20, 219, 226–30
metalepsis 14, 31–2, 34–8, 45–6
metaphor 5, 17, 19, 39, 93, 103, 147, 152, 156, 165–6, 172–3, 175–6, 179–85, 187–9, 197, 218
metaphorical(ly) 18–19, 52, 55, 57, 64–5, 162, 164–5, 168, 173, 175–6, 178–80, 182, 187–9, 216, 224
mimesis 16, 94–6, 103–5, 110–11, 244
misdirect 17, 20, 149, 195–6, 219, 226, 228, 230

misdirection 17, 20, 149, 196, 208, 210, 212, 216, 217, 220, 230
misleading(ly) 3, 10–11, 20, 153, 206, 217, 220, 222, 227–30
modality 16, 21, 44, 50, 56–7, 59, 92, 107–8, 236, 239–40, 244–5, 248
multimodal 14, 19, 21, 235–6, 243–5, 247–9
multimodal stylistics 235, 237, 244, see also stylistics
multimodal verisimilitude 245

narratological(ly) 5, 8, 95, 108–9
narratology 14, 92

paranarratable 8, 14, 31, 37, 44
perception 9, 14, 94, 104, 150, 176, 211
persuasion 3, 8, 13, 73
plot 7–9, 12–15, 19, 31–3, 35–45, 125–6, 151, 153, 158, 187, 195–7, 200–1, 204, 212, 216–17, 226, 234
point of view 6, 9, 13, 34, 40, 56–7, 92, 173–4
positioning 5, 8, 10, 14–15, 21, 50, 53, 63, 66, 67, 234–5, 240, 243, 248
pragmatics 2–5, 9, 11–12, 14–16, 17, 21, 50–1, 58, 60, 66–7, 70, 71, 77, 78, 79, 83, 84, 87, 117–21, 131, 133–5, 140, 142, 224, see also corpus pragmatics
propaganda 1, 4

reader response 2, 148, 157, 172
reading group 5–6, 14, 18–19, 172–3, 175–9, 184–5, 187–9
realism 131–2, 215, 234–5, 245, 247
realistic 17, 36, 40, 111, 118, 131–2, 134, 137, 140, 142
relevance theory 14, 21, 140

Salinger, J. D. 7, 18, 146–7, 154, 164
short story 7, 19, 41, 146–54, 155–8, 160–3, 165, 168, 198, 201
social deixis 15, 50–4, 56–67, see also deictic; deixis
socio-relational deixis 15, 59, 60, 63–4, 66–7, see also deictic; deixis
stance 8–10, 13–14, 34, 40, 50, 70, 132, 155
story ending 18, 146–7, 155–6, 158–60, 162, 164, 166, 168

strategies   1–2, 4–5, 9–10, 14, 16, 17, 21, 31–2, 93, 96, 103, 107, 146–50, 152, 156, 168, 172, 196, 211–12, 234–5, 247
stylistic(s)   34, 56, 71, 73, 83, 92–4, 96, 98–9, 101–6, 108–11, 117, 119–21, 131, 146, 148–9, 172–3, 175, 177, 179, 189, 217–18, 230, 235–7, 241, 244, 247–8, *see also* corpus stylistics; multimodal stylistics
suspects   19–20, 196, 206–12, 230

techniques   12–14, 16, 19–21, 32, 34, 36, 39, 45, 72–3, 76, 83, 88, 92, 94, 96, 104–5, 110, 127, 131, 132, 146–7, 149–53, 156, 159–60, 162, 168, 195, 197, 200, 211–12, 217, 227, 235
Text World Theory   8, 16, 17, 35, 39, 93–4, 98, 105, 107, 118, 131, 142
Thomas, Dylan   15, 50, 62–7
translation   12, 19, 20, 126–7, 215, 218–26, 228–30
typographic(al)   5, 21, 236–8, 240–6, 248
typographic distinctive features   238
typographic semiotic principles   238
typography   19, 21, 235–40, 243–8

Victorian   15, 31–3, 37–8, 44, 46

www.ingramcontent.com/pod-product-compliance
Lightning Source LLC
Chambersburg PA
CBHW070029010526
44117CB00011B/1753